ESTATE AND GIFT TAXES

ESTATE AND GIFT TAXES

CLAY B. APPERTON
EDITOR

Nova Science Publishers, Inc.
New York

For permission to use material from this book please contact us:
Telephone 631-231-7269; Fax 631-231-8175
Web Site: http://www.novapublishers.com

LIBRARY OF CONGRESS CATALOGING-IN-PUBLICATION DATA
Available upon request
ISBN: 978-1-60692-129-6

Published by Nova Science Publishers, Inc. ✝ New York

CONTENTS

PREFACE

Estate and gift taxes are used to tax large transfers of wealth between individuals. Gift taxes are imposed on transfers made during an individual's lifetime, and estate taxes are imposed on transfers made at the time of death. Although gift taxes and estate taxes are paid separately, they are a unified tax in the sense that a single graduated rate schedule applies to the cumulative total of taxable transfers made through gifts and estates. The 2001 tax cut legislation enacted by Congress and President Bush gradually phases out the estate tax over ten years but revives it after sunsetting at the end of 2010. Since the law does not treat the gift tax entirely the same (the gift tax is never fully repealed, for example) the two taxes are no longer fully unified. The effective marginal tax rates decrease gradually from 2001 through 2010 but generally range from around 38% to 44%, after accounting for the credit for state estate taxes. (The 2001 law replaces the credit with a deduction in 2006). This new book gathers important new information on issues directly concerned with estate and gift taxes.

Chapter 1 - Supporters of the estate and gift tax argue that it provides progressivity in the federal tax system, provides a backstop to the individual income tax and appropriately targets assets that are bestowed on heirs rather than assets earned through their hard work and effort. However, progressivity can be obtained through the income tax and the estate and gift tax is an imperfect backstop to the income tax. Critics argue that the tax discourages savings, harms small businesses and farms, taxes resources already subject to income taxes, and adds to the complexity of the tax system. Critics also suggest death is an inappropriate time to impose a tax. However, the effect on savings is uncertain, most farms and small businesses do not pay the tax, and complexity could be reduced through reform of the tax.

Chapter 2 - Data on both past revenues and revenue projections regarding the estate tax should be interpreted with awareness of the year-to-year changes in estate tax law from 1997 to 2011. Large increases in the prevailing estate tax exemption — from $675,000 in 2001 and 2002, to $1 million in 2003 and 2004, and to $1.5 million in 2005 and 2006 — led the number of taxable estate tax returns to fall by half, from about 45,000 in 2002 to about 22,500 in 2005 and 2006. Taxable estates fell from 2.15% percent of prior-year deaths in 2001, to 1.36% in 2003, and to 0.93%, or 9.3 per thousand deaths, in 2005 and 2006. Notwithstanding the steep decline in the number of taxable returns, estate taxes paid remained above $20 billion per year.

Gift tax revenues fell by roughly half after the enactment of the Economic Growth and Tax Relief Reconciliation Act of 2001 (EGTRRA, P.L. 107-16). Possibly, many wealthy people chose to forgo the certainty of taxes on lifetime gifts, hoping that the estate tax would later be repealed permanently as of 2010 and they would then be able to pass their assets along tax-free upon their death. Gift taxes accounted for 14% to 17% of estate and gift tax revenues in FY1999-FY2001, but only 6% to 9% in FY2002-FY2007. Gift tax revenues of $3.9 billion to $4.7 billion per year in FY1 999-FY200 1, fell to $1.4 billion to $2.4 billion in FY2002-FY2007.

The standard 10-year forecasts of both revenue from the estate tax and revenue losses from permanent repeal of the estate tax should be interpreted with caution. The forecasts should not be used to approximate revenues for a different 10-year period. This is because of the changes scheduled to occur in the estate tax exemption and top tax rate from 2008 through 2011. The exemption is $2 million for decedents dying in 2008, but $3.5 million for 2009. Under current law, there will be no estate tax in 2010. If EGTRRA is permitted to sunset at the end of 2010, the estate tax will apply again in 2011, but with an exemption of $1 million. The top tax rate will revert from 45% in 2007-2009 to 55% (with a 5% surtax in a certain range) in 2011 and beyond.

Revenues from estate and gift taxes were $26 billion in FY2007, contributing 1.0% of total federal revenue. The Congressional Budget Office projects that, if the estate tax is reinstated in 2011 as currently scheduled, revenue from the estate and gift taxes would climb steadily by about $7 billion per year, from $55 billion in FY2012, contributing 1.6% of total federal revenue, to $97 billion in FY2018, contributing 2.1% of total revenue.

President Bush's budget for FY2009 has proposed to make permanent the tax cuts enacted in 2001 and 2003, including those dealing with estates and gifts. The proposal to permanently repeal the estate tax after 2010 accounts for approximately one-quarter of the projected cost of this set of proposals over the 10-year forecast period, FY2009-FY20 18 — $522 billion out of $2,185 billion according to Treasury and $670 billion out of $2,414 billion according to the Joint Committee on Taxation.

Chapter 3 –The author has appended two articles to this testimony. The first presents a philosophical argument for wealth transfer taxation in the form of an accessions tax, which would turn the current U.S. wealth transfer tax system on its head by applying to the cumulative amount of gifts and inheritances received by individuals over the course of their lifetimes rather than aggregate amounts given by donors over the course of their lifetimes. The second article reviews the abolition of wealth transfer taxes in Canada, Australia and New Zealand, and attempts to derive lessons from this experience for the future of these taxes. The testimony is based on both articles and addresses the rationale for an accessions tax and lessons to be derived from the abolition of wealth transfer taxes in Canada, Australia and New Zealand.

Chapter 4 – The authors testimony makes three main points:

- First, inheritances tend to exacerbate existing economic disparities and may be the most important barrier to intergenerational economic mobility. These tendencies are most pronounced at the top of the income distribution. Inheritances are a significant component of household income. They are also the source of about 40 percent of all household wealth. While inherited income is distributed fairly evenly across most of the population, it rises sharply at the very top. Among households receiving a bequest in a given year, the average inheritance of those in the top 1 percent of the inheritance distribution is 34 times larger than the average inherited income of everyone else.
- Second, the estate tax system is the most important mechanism by which the current fiscal system mitigates the effect of inheritances on economic disparities and intergenerational mobility. The burden of the estate and gift taxes falls largely on heirs, not donors. On average, it also rises rapidly with the amount the heir inherits and his economic income [2]. Nevertheless, the relationship between the heir's financial circumstances and his or her estate tax burden is relatively imprecise. Some individuals who receive extraordinarily large inheritances bear little or no tax burden, while a small number who inherit relatively small amounts bear substantial tax burdens.
- Finally, the scheduled repeal of the estate tax in 2010 and reinstatement at higher levels in 2011 create an opportunity to better focus the estate tax system on unearned income that inheritances represent. We should use that opportunity to reform, not repeal, the estate tax system so that we

continue to tax inherited income, but in a more equitable manner. I will discuss two potential reform options.

- o The first would replace the estate tax system with a comprehensive inheritance tax, under which an individual inheriting an extraordinary amount over his lifetime would pay income tax and a flat 15 percent tax on a portion of his inheritance. Relative to the 2009 law, this reform could be implemented on a revenue-neutral basis if approximately the first $2 million in lifetime inheritances were tax-exempt. In effect, extraordinary amounts of inherited income would be taxed at about the same rate that families pay on earned income under the income and payroll taxes. This reform would substantially alter tax burdens, and improve the fairness of the current system by more accurately targeting the unfair advantages that exceptionally large inheritances create.
- o If this reform is considered too ambitious, a second alternative would be to retain and improve the estate tax system by better focusing it on the amount transferred as a proxy for the amount inherited. Specifically, I will discuss a package of simplification reforms that would limit the extent to which the tax burden on heirs depends on their access to sophisticated tax advice.

Chapter 5 – Invidivual income tax rate reduction

Chapter 6 - The estate tax has been an important source of federal revenue for nearly a century. It also encourages billions of dollars in charitable donations each year (http://www.cbpp.org/6-7- 06tax.htm), since donations substantially reduce the tax on large estates. Despite these benefits, a number of misconceptions continue to surround the tax.

Chapter 7 - There are five possible alternatives to the current estate, gift, and generation- skipping system:

(1) classic inheritance tax
(2) accessions tax
(3) income-inclusion approach
(4) deemed-realization-at-gift-or-bequest approach, and
(5) carryover-basis approach.

What these approaches have in common is the imposition of tax (sooner or later) by reason of a gratuitous transfer. The first two (inheritance tax and accessions tax) are transfer taxes. A transfer tax is a separate tax from the income tax, and a transfer tax can operate as a "second" tax on previously-taxed income of the transferor. The last two (deemed-realization and carryover-basis approaches) are designed to overturn the current rule, found in § 1014, that eliminates unrealized gains of a decedent permanently from the income tax. The motivation of either proposal is to eliminate an existing hole in the income tax. Since transfer taxes can exist simultaneously with an income tax, it is possible to combine either (1) or (2) above (or an estate tax) with either of (4) or (5).

In: Estate and Gift Taxes
Editor: Clay B. Apperton
ISBN 978-1-60692-129-6

Chapter 1

ECONOMIC ISSUES SURROUNDING THE ESTATE AND GIFT TAX: A BRIEF SUMMARY*

Jane G. Gravelle

ABSTRACT

Supporters of the estate and gift tax argue that it provides progressivity in the federal tax system, provides a backstop to the individual income tax and appropriately targets assets that are bestowed on heirs rather than assets earned through their hard work and effort. However, progressivity can be obtained through the income tax and the estate and gift tax is an imperfect backstop to the income tax. Critics argue that the tax discourages savings, harms small businesses and farms, taxes resources already subject to income taxes, and adds to the complexity of the tax system. Critics also suggest death is an inappropriate time to impose a tax. However, the effect on savings is uncertain, most farms and small businesses do not pay the tax, and complexity could be reduced through reform of the tax.

The estate and gift tax has been the subject of legislative interest for several years, with increases in the exemption enacted in 1997. Proposals to reduce or eliminate the tax were adopted in the 106th Congress, but were vetoed by the President. President Bush had also proposed eliminating the tax and the Ways and Means Committee reported out a bill, H.R. 6, that would phase out the tax. Similar provisions were included in the Senate bill and the final tax cut bill, H.R.

* Excerpted from CRS Report RS20609, dated April 24, 2007.

1836, was signed by the President on June 7, 2001, although this legislation retained a gift tax with a large exemption [1]. The entire bill is to sunset after 2010, but there are proposals to make the change permanent, including H.R. 8 which passed the House on April 13, 2005. Further consideration to making the tax change permanent was originally scheduled for the fall of 2005, but was delayed because Congress was considering legislation relating to Hurricane Katrina. There were also proposals to shift to a permanent estate tax with a larger exemption and lower rates and these proposals were considered in 2006. H.R. 5970 in the 109th Congress, passed by the House, would have increased the exemption to $3.5 million and taxed gains at the capital gains tax rate (currently 15%, but scheduled to return to 20% after 2010).

The estate and gift tax is a comparatively small source of federal tax revenue, accounting for 1.2% of federal receipts, an amount which has declined following the reduction in rates and the increase in exemptions enacted in 2001. Estates and gifts to spouses are exempt from tax as are gifts to charity. The first $2 million of the net estate value is exempt from tax. Gift taxes have a $1 million effective exclusion in addition to an annual gift exclusion of $11,000 per donee. Taxable estates are subject to a 45% rate. The exemption from tax is scheduled to rise and the tax rate to fall with the estate tax (but not the gift tax) permanently eliminated in 2010, when a tax on capital gains in excess of an exempt amount will be imposed. The 2001 tax cuts, absent legislation, will sunset after 2010 and the rates and exemptions return to the values prior to the 2001 tax changes. The House recently passed legislation to make the repeal permanent.

ARGUMENTS FOR THE ESTATE AND GIFT TAX

Perhaps the principal argument in support of an estate and gift tax is its contribution to progressivity in the income tax system. The estate tax is the most progressive of any of the federal taxes. According to the latest data from the Internal Revenue Service (2004), out of the approximately 2.4 million deaths per year, only 1.3 % of estates paid the estate tax; based on the distribution of gross estate, that share is probably close to 0.5% for 2006 and will drop to about 0.2% in 2009. These numbers can be contrasted with the income tax where about 70% of families and single individuals owe tax. Because the exclusion has been rising, the share of decedents' estates paying estate taxes has been falling. Even prior to the 2001 tax cuts, however, only 2% of decedents paid an estate tax. Progressivity in the tax system, however, could also be altered through changes in the income tax.

Another argument made by proponents of the estate and gift tax is that, to the extent that inherited wealth is seen as windfall to the recipient, such a tax source may be seen by some as fairer than taxing earnings that are the result of work and effort.

Finally, many economists suggest that an important rationale for maintaining an estate tax is the escape of unrealized capital gains from any taxation, since heirs receive a stepped-up basis of assets. Families that accrue large gains through the appreciation of their wealth in assets can, in the absence of an estate tax, largely escape any taxes on these gains by passing on the assets to their heirs. The base of the estate tax is, however, quite different from the base of the capital gains tax, and the rates are higher. The 2001 tax revisions proposed to tax capital gains after allowing a significant exemption.

Arguments Against the Estate and Gift Tax

theory nor empirical evidence clearly indicate that the estate tax reduces savings. For example, while the estate tax may discourage saving for bequests because the cost of making a net bequest (in terms of forgone consumption) increases, the tax also requires a greater amount of saving to achieve a net target. Estate and gift taxes are unlikely to have much effect on assets accumulated for precautionary purposes. Bequests can also reduce saving by heirs because they increase resources for consumption [2].

A second major argument against the estate and gift tax is that it burdens family businesses and farms and makes it more difficult to pass on these assets to the next generation who can continue the business. However, only a small portion (less than 5%) of businesses and farms are likely to be affected; many of those have sufficient liquid assets to pay the tax. In addition, extensions of time to pay the tax are allowed [3].

Critics also argue that death is not an appropriate occasion to impose a tax; indeed, the tax is sometimes referred to as a "death tax." Another argument is that wealth has already been taxed through income taxes, though this is not the case for unrealized capital gains. Finally, critics assert that the complexity of the tax not only imposes administration and compliance burdens but undermines the progressivity of the tax [4]. Of course, this latter argument could also be a justification for reforming rather than reducing or abolishing the tax.

Other Issues

Two other economic effects of the tax that might be considered in evaluating changes are the possible negative effect on charitable contributions (because charitable contributions are deducted from the estate and gift tax base) and the effect on state and local estate taxes. A credit has been allowed against estate and gift taxes for state estate taxes in the past, although this credit has now been eliminated; these changes may create pressure on states to reduce these taxes which will now become a more visible burden on their residents.

References

[1] For a more extensive discussion of estate and gift tax issues, see CRS Report RL30600, *Estate and Gift Taxes: Economic Issues,* by Jane Gravelle and Steven Maguire. See CRS Report RL32818, *Estate Tax Legislation in the 109th Congress*, by Nonna A. Noto for further information on proposals. See also CRS Report 95-416, *Federal Estate, Gift, and Generation- Skipping Taxes: A Description of Current Law*, by John R. Luckey.

[2] For an analysis of these savings effects and indications of a limited and uncertain effect from empirical data, see William G. Gale and Maria G. Perozek, "Do Estate Taxes Reduce Savings?" and Woj ciech Kopczuk and Joel Slemrod, "The Impact of the Estate Tax on Wealth Accumulation and the Avoidance Behavior of Donors," both in *Rethinking Estate and Gift Taxation*, eds. William G. Gale, James R. Hines, Jr. and Joel Slemrod, Washington, D.C., The Brookings Institution, 2001.

[3] For analyses of the estate tax data, see CRS Report RL30600, *Estate and Gift Taxes: Economic Issues* by Jane G. Gravelle and Steven Maguire; CRS Report RS20593, *Asset Distribution of Taxable Estates: An Analysis*, by Steven Maguire; and Estate Taxes, Life Insurance, and Small Business by Douglas Holtz-Eakin, John W. Phillips, and Harvey S. Rosen, National Bureau of Economic Research working Paper 7360.

[4] For a discussion of avoidance methods and an estimate that indicates reasonable compliance and administrative costs, see Charles Davenport and Jay Soled, "Enlivening the Death-Tax Death-Talk." *Tax Notes*, July 26, 1999, pp. 59 1-629.

In: Estate and Gift Taxes
Editor: Clay B. Apperton

ISBN 978-1-60692-129-6

Chapter 2

ESTATE AND GIFT TAX REVENUES: PAST AND PROJECTED IN 2008*

Nonna A. Noto

ABSTRACT

Data on both past revenues and revenue projections regarding the estate tax should be interpreted with awareness of the year-to-year changes in estate tax law from 1997 to 2011. Large increases in the prevailing estate tax exemption — from $675,000 in 2001 and 2002, to $1 million in 2003 and 2004, and to $1.5 million in 2005 and 2006 — led the number of taxable estate tax returns to fall by half, from about 45,000 in 2002 to about 22,500 in 2005 and 2006. Taxable estates fell from 2.15% percent of prior-year deaths in 2001, to 1.36% in 2003, and to 0.93%, or 9.3 per thousand deaths, in 2005 and 2006. Notwithstanding the steep decline in the number of taxable returns, estate taxes paid remained above $20 billion per year.

Gift tax revenues fell by roughly half after the enactment of the Economic Growth and Tax Relief Reconciliation Act of 2001 (EGTRRA, P.L. 107-16). Possibly, many wealthy people chose to forgo the certainty of taxes on lifetime gifts, hoping that the estate tax would later be repealed permanently as of 2010 and they would then be able to pass their assets along tax-free upon their death. Gift taxes accounted for 14% to 17% of estate and gift tax revenues in FY1999-FY2001, but only 6% to 9% in FY2002-FY2007. Gift tax revenues of $3.9 billion to $4.7 billion per year in FY1 999-FY200 1, fell to $1.4 billion to $2.4 billion in FY2002-FY2007.

---

* Excerpted from CRS Report RL34418, dated March 19, 2008.

The standard 10-year forecasts of both revenue from the estate tax and revenue losses from permanent repeal of the estate tax should be interpreted with caution. The forecasts should not be used to approximate revenues for a different 10-year period. This is because of the changes scheduled to occur in the estate tax exemption and top tax rate from 2008 through 2011. The exemption is $2 million for decedents dying in 2008, but $3.5 million for 2009. Under current law, there will be no estate tax in 2010. If EGTRRA is permitted to sunset at the end of 2010, the estate tax will apply again in 2011, but with an exemption of $1 million. The top tax rate will revert from 45% in 2007-2009 to 55% (with a 5% surtax in a certain range) in 2011 and beyond. Revenues from estate and gift taxes were $26 billion in FY2007, contributing 1.0% of total federal revenue. The Congressional Budget Office projects that, if the estate tax is reinstated in 2011 as currently scheduled, revenue from the estate and gift taxes would climb steadily by about $7 billion per year, from $55 billion in FY2012, contributing 1.6% of total federal revenue, to $97 billion in FY2018, contributing 2.1% of total revenue.

President Bush's budget for FY2009 has proposed to make permanent the tax cuts enacted in 2001 and 2003, including those dealing with estates and gifts. The proposal to permanently repeal the estate tax after 2010 accounts for approximately one-quarter of the projected cost of this set of proposals over the 10-year forecast period, FY2009-FY20 18 — $522 billion out of $2,185 billion according to Treasury and $670 billion out of $2,414 billion according to the Joint Committee on Taxation.

CHANGES IN ESTATE TAX LAW

Data on both past revenues and revenue projections regarding the estate tax should be interpreted with awareness of the year-to-year changes in estate tax law from 1997 to 2011. The modest changes brought about by the Taxpayer Relief Act of 1997 (TRA, P.L. 105-34) were followed by big changes made by the Economic Growth and Tax Relief Reconciliation Act of 2001 (EGTRRA, P.L. 107-16). Both laws provided for increases in the applicable exclusion amount, commonly called the estate tax exemption, as shown in the first column of Table 1. EGTRRA also gradually lowered the maximum marginal estate tax rate, from 55% (plus a 5% surtax in a certain range) in 2001, to 46% in 2006, and 45% in 2007-2009, as shown in the second column of Table 1.

Table 1. Estate Tax Exemption and Maximum Tax Rate, 1988-2011

Calendar Year of Death	Exemption	Maximum Tax Rate for Taxable Estate Values Over (in $ millions)
1988-1997	$600,000a	55% over $3.0, plus 5% surtax from over $10.0 to $21.040d
1998	$625,000b	55% over $3.0, plus 5% surtax from over $10.0 to $17.184e
1999	$650,000b	"
2000	$675,000b	"
2001	$675,000b	"
2002	$1,000,000c	50% over $2.5c
2003	$1,000,000c	49% over $2.0c
2004	$1,500,000c	48% over $2.0c
2005	$1,500,000c	47% over $2.0c
2006	$2,000,000c	46% over $2.0c
2007-2008	$2,000,000c	45% over $1.5c
2009	$3,500,000c	"
2010	Estate tax repealed for 2010 onlyc	
2011 and thereafter	$1,000,000b	55% over $3.0, plus 5% surtax from over $10.0 to $17.184e

Notes:

Provision of the Economic Recovery Tax Act of 1981 (ERTA, P.L. 97-34). The exemption was $600,000 in 1987 as well.

Provisions of the Taxpayer Relief Act of 1997 (TRA, P.L. 105-34). TRA had also provided for the exemption to increase to $700,000 for 2002 and 2003, $850,000 for 2004, $950,000 for 2005, and $1 million for 2006 and beyond.

Provisions of the Economic Growth and Tax Relief Reconciliation Act of 2001 (EGTRRA, P.L. 107-16). The Revenue Act of 1987 (P.L. 100-203) provided for a 5% surtax to offset the benefits of both the graduated tax rates on taxable estate values below $3 million and the unified credit (exemption), such that the effective rate of tax on the entire estate was 55%.

As the result of a clerical error in the final text of TRA of 1997, later adopted by Congress, the surtax was intended to offset the benefits of only the graduated tax rates, and not the unified credit (exemption) as well.

For detailed schedules of the marginal estate tax rates by year, see CRS Report RL33718, Calculating Estate Tax Liability: 2001 to 2011 and Beyond, by Nonna A. Noto.

EXEMPTION

The estate tax exemption plays two important roles. First, it serves as the filing threshold for the estate tax. A federal estate tax return must be filed if a U.S. decedent's gross estate [1] (before deductions) equals or exceeds the exemption for the year of the decedent's death. Second, the transfer of an amount of assets up to the exemption is free from federal tax for every estate [2].

The value of the exemption is not indexed for inflation. Nor is it set in relation to any specific definition of wealth. Instead, Congress has intermittently raised the dollar amount.

From 1987 through 1997 the exemption remained at $600,000, under provisions of the Economic Recovery Tax of 1981 (ERTA, P.L. 97-34). TRA of 1997 provided for a gradual increase in the exemption over nine years. Under TRA, the exemption rose to $625,000 for 1998, $650,000 for 1999, and $675,000 for 2000 and 2001. It was scheduled to reach $1 million in 2006.

Before the provisions of TRA were fully phased in, however, they were superseded for tax years 2002-20 10 by much larger changes made by EGTRRA of 2001. EGTRRA raised the exemption to $1 million beginning immediately in 2002 and 2003. It further increased the exemption in large increments, to $1.5 million for 2004 and 2005, $2 million for 2006 through 2008, and $3.5 million for 2009. It repealed the estate and generation-skipping transfer taxes entirely for the estates of decedents dying in 2010 only.

The estate tax provisions of EGTRRA are scheduled to sunset on December 31, 2010, along with the act's other provisions. Unless new legislation governing the estate tax is enacted beforehand, in 2011 the law will revert to the law in effect prior to June 7, 2001. The estate tax will be reinstated with an exemption of $1 million — the amount that TRA had provided for 2006 and beyond — and the family-owned business deduction will be reinstated [3].

MAXIMUM TAX RATE

From 1988 through 1997, the maximum marginal tax rate was 55% on taxable estate values over $3 million [4]. In addition, there was a surtax of 5% on taxable values over $10 million up to $21.040 million. From 1998 through 2001, the maximum rate remained at 55% on taxable estate values over $3 million. But, under TRA of 1997, the 5% surtax applied from over $10 million only up to $17.184 million [5].

In addition to raising the exemption in large increments, EGTRRA significantly reduced the top marginal estate tax rate over a period of six years (column 2 of Table 1). At the outset, EGTRRA eliminated the 5% surtax and reduced the maximum tax rate from 55% to 50%, effective in 2002. It subsequently reduced the top tax rate by one percentage point per year, from 49% in 2003, down to 46% in 2006, and finally to 45% for 2007 through 2009 [6]. For decedents dying in 2010, there is no estate tax. For 2011 and beyond, if EGTRRA sunsets, the maximum tax rate will revert to 55%, the 49% and 53% marginal rate brackets will be restored, and the 5% surtax on taxable estate values from $10 million up to $ 17.184 million will be reinstated.

WHICH LAW IS REFLECTED IN REVENUE FOR A PARTICULAR YEAR?

The tax law that applies to an estate is the law in effect in the year of the person's death. However, the estate tax return is not due until nine months after the person's death, and an extension of six months is not uncommon. Complex returns may be granted a longer extension.

It follows that estate tax returns filed in any given calendar year will include a few returns of people who died in that year, mostly the returns of people who died in the previous year, and some returns from deaths in prior years that are filing under an extension. Of estate tax returns filed in calendar years 2001 through 2005, roughly 10% were filed in the year of death, 72% in the year after death, 14% two years after death, and 3% three or more years after death [7].

Consequently, for a given filing year (a calendar year), this report refers to the exemption that was in effect for a death in the prior calendar year as the "prevailing exemption" for that filing year. For example, the prevailing exemption for most estate tax returns filed in 2006 would be the $1.5 million exemption in effect for deaths in 2005.

Revenue in a particular fiscal year is most likely to reflect the estate tax law in effect in the previous-numbered calendar year. Recall that the estate tax return is not due until nine months after the date of death and that the fiscal year runs from October 1 of the previous calendar year until September 30 of the same-numbered calendar year. So, for example, deaths in calendar 2006 would be reflected in estate tax returns filed on time in the last three months of 2006 and the first nine months of 2007, which comprise FY2007.

Unexpected Patterns

An increase in the estate tax exemption would be expected to reduce the number of estate tax returns filed, the number of taxable returns, and the total amount of estate tax paid with those returns. But this is not always the case. In particular, from 1998 until 2000, the number of taxable returns continued to increase even though the prevailing exemption was gradually rising. Total estate taxes paid remained nearly the same between 2002 and 2003, even though the number of taxable returns fell by 26%, and between 2004 and 2005, when taxable returns fell by 29%.

Whether the number of taxable returns and the amount of tax revenues decline depends upon whether the increase in the exemption outpaces the increase in the value of wealthy decedents' estates. Broad market fluctuations in the value of widely held assets such as stocks or real estate can override the relationship that would otherwise be expected between an increase in the estate tax exemption and the number of taxable estate tax returns filed the next year. Estate valuations are likely to be unusually high in years of market peaks and unusually low in years of market crashes. This is likely to cause the number of taxable estate tax returns filed in the next calendar year to be higher and lower, respectively, than would otherwise be expected.

The standardized measurement of taxable estate tax returns expressed as a percentage of deaths has been tracked over time as an indicator of how deeply the estate tax reaches into the population. When this percentage has risen above a politically unacceptable level, the Congress has, at some point, raised the estate tax exemption in order to bring the percentage back down to the typical historical level. During the previous two decades, for years of death from 1982 through 2003, taxable estate tax returns measured as a percentage of adult deaths fluctuated within the range of just under 1% (0.88%) to 2.30% [8].

Increase in Exemption and Number of Taxable Returns

The relationship between the increase in the prevailing exemption amount and the number of taxable estate tax returns filed each year from 1998 through 2006 is illustrated by the juxtaposition of Figures 1 and 2. The data underlying these two graphs are presented in columns 1 and 2, respectively, of Table 2. To help highlight the relationships between these two measures, columns 1 and 2 of Table 3 show the percentage change from the previous year for the prevailing exemption and the number of taxable returns.

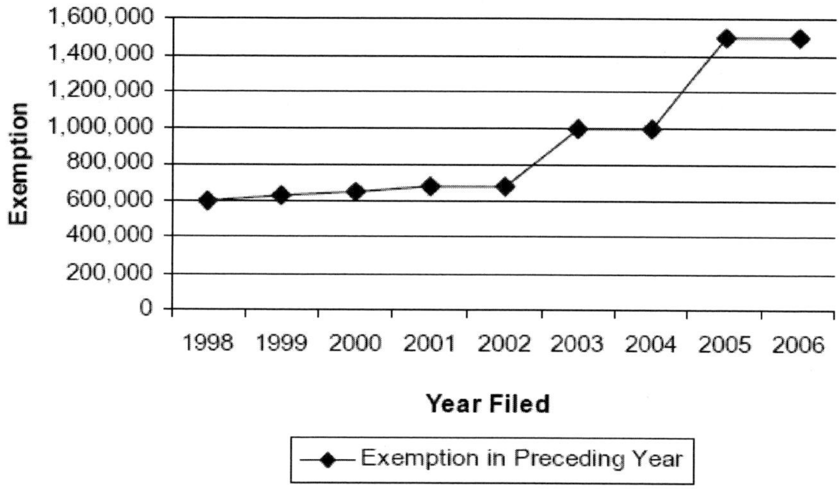

Source: See columns 1 and 2 of Table 2.

Figure 1. Dollar Amount of Prevailing Exemption, 1998-2006.

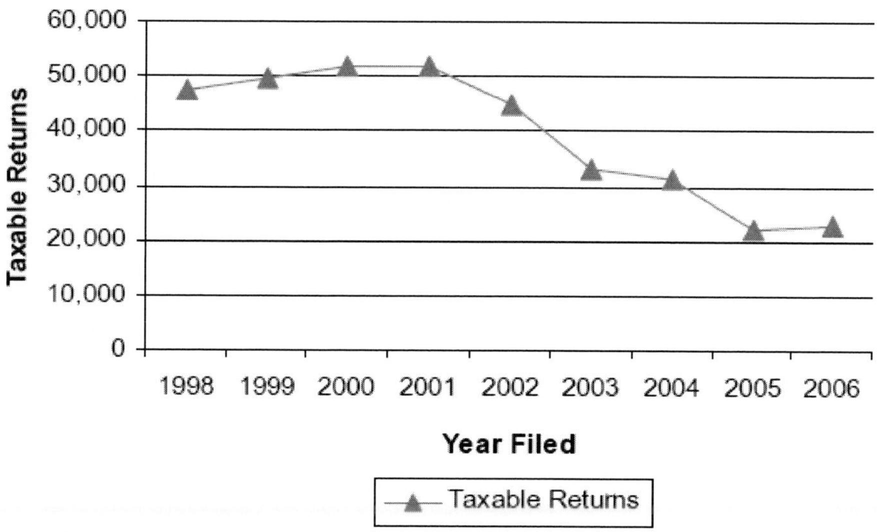

Source: See columns 1 and 2 of Table 2.

Figure 2. Number of Taxable Estate Tax Returns Filed, 1998-2006.

Table 2. Exemption, Taxable Returns in Number and as a Percent of Deaths, and Estate Tax Paid, for Returns Filed in 1998-2006

Year Filed	(1) Exemption in Preceding Year ($)	(2) Taxable Returns	(3) Taxable Returns as Percent of Deaths in Preceding Year[a]	(4) Estate Tax Paid[b] (in $ billions)
1998	$600,000	47,475	2.05%	$20.3
1999	625,000	49,863	2.13	22.9
2000	650,000	52,000	2.17	24.4
2001	675,000	51,736	2.15	23.5
2002	675,000	45,018	1.86	21.4
2003	1,000,000	33,302	1.36	20.8
2004	1,000,000	31,329	1.28	21.6
2005	1,500,000	22,250	0.93	21.7
2006	1,500,000	22,798	0.93	24.7

Sources: Exemption in preceding year (column 1) taken from Table 1. Data on number of taxable returns (column 2) and net estate tax paid (column 4) are from Internal Revenue Service, Table 1. Estate Tax Returns Filed in [year]: Gross Estate by Type of Property, Deductions, Taxable Estate, Estate Tax and Tax Credits, by Size of Gross Estate. Unpublished data from the Statistics of Income (SOI) for the years 1998 to 2006. Available on the IRS website [http://www.irs.gov/] visited February 6, 2008. See the source note to Table 4 for an explanation of the search sequence.

Table 3. Percentage Change from Previous Year in Prevailing Exemption, Number of Taxable Returns, and Estate Tax Paid

Year Filed	(1)Prevailing Exemption	(2)Taxable Returns	(3)Estate Tax Paid
1999	4.2%	5.0%	12.6%
2000	4.0	4.3	6.5
2001	3.8	-0.5	-3.6
2002	0	-13.0	-9.1
2003	48.1	-26.0	-2.8
2004	0	-5.9	3.9
2005	50.0	-29.0	0.3
2006	0	2.5	13.8

Source: Calculated by CRS from data presented in columns 1, 2, and 4 of Table 2.

In March 2007, IRS revised the tables for estate tax returns filed in 2001 through 2005 to include "late" returns for which the gross estate was below the prevailing exemption for the filing year. These are typically returns filed under an extension, for earlier years of death when the tax filing threshold was lower. In the revised tables, the categories for size of gross estate below $5 million were made consistent with the size categories of interest after EGTRRA. Taxable returns as a percent of deaths in preceding year (column 3) were calculated by CRS based on the mortality numbers shown in note a below.

Deaths in 1997-2001 from U.S. Department of Commerce, Economics and Statistics Administration, U.S. Census Bureau, Statistical Abstract of the United States, annual editions from 2000 to 2003. Deaths in 2002 from National Vital Statistics Reports, Deaths: Final Data for 2002, vol. 53, no. 5, Oct. 12, 2004, p. 1. Deaths in 2003 and 2004 from U.S. Department of Health and Human Services, Centers for Disease Control and Prevention, National Center for Health Statistics, Deaths: Final Data for 2004, posted Nov. 24, 2006, Table 1, available at [http://www.cdc.gov/nchs/ products/pubs/pubd/hestats/finaldeaths04_tables.pdf]. Preliminary estimate of deaths in 2005 from U.S. Department of Health and Human Services, Centers for Disease Control and Prevention, National Center for Health Statistics: H.C. Kung, D.L. Hoyert, J. Xu, and S.L. Murphy, Deaths: Preliminary data for 2005, Health E-Stats, Sept. 2007, available at [http://www.cdc.gov/nchs/products/pubs/pubd/hestats/prelimdeaths05/prelimdeaths05.htm], visited Feb. 6, 2008.

a) The total number of deaths in the United States rose slightly from year to year from 1997 through 2003, fell in 2004, but rose back to nearly its 2003 level in 2005 as follows:

1997	2,314,245	2002	2,443,387
1998	2,337,256	2003	2,448,288
1999	2,391,399	2004	2,397,615
2000	2,403,351	2005	2,447,903 preliminary
2001	2,416,425		

b) More precisely, this is the net estate tax paid. This is the estate tax due after claiming permitted tax credits.

Initially, from 1998 through 2000, when the prevailing exemption was rising in annual increments of $25,000 or about 4% — from $600,000 in 1998 to $625,000 in 1999, and $650,000 in 2000 — the number of taxable returns nonetheless continued to rise modestly. The rising pattern holds whether measured as the absolute number of returns (column 2 of Table 2) or standardized as tax returns as a percent of deaths (column 3 of Table 2). The number of taxable estate tax returns rose from 47,475 or 2.05% of deaths in 1998, to 52,000 or 2.17% of deaths in 2000. This suggests that value of assets broadly held by wealthy decedents was generally rising more rapidly than the exemption from 1997 to 1999. The stock market, for example, was generally rising over this period.

The number of taxable returns declined very slightly, by half a percent, in 2001, when the effect of the higher $675,000 exemption first registered. This suggests that at $675,000, the level of the exemption had caught up with the value of assets held by wealthy decedents in 2000. Between 2001 and 2002 the number of taxable estate tax returns dropped by 13%, even though the prevailing exemption remained at $675,000. This suggests that the value of assets widely held by wealthy decedents fell between 2000 and 2001. The stock market, for example, peaked in March 2000, and stock prices continued to fall until October 2002. It was not until 2002, the second year that the $675,000 exemption prevailed, that the number of taxable returns (45,018) and taxable returns measured as a percent of deaths (1.86%) fell below their levels in 1998, when the prevailing exemption was $600,000.

In 2003, the number of taxable returns dropped by 26% (from 45,018 in 2002 to 33,302 in 2003), when the prevailing exemption rose by 48% (from $675,000 for deaths in 2001 to $1 million in 2002). Taxable returns as a percent of deaths fell from 1.86% in 2002 to 1.36% in 2003. This suggests that at the $1 million level the exemption amount had outpaced the growth between 2001 and 2002 in the value of assets held by wealthy decedents. In 2004, the number of taxable returns dropped further, by a modest 6% (from 33,302 in 2003 to 31,329 in 2004), as the $1 million exemption continued to prevail. This suggest that there was a small decline between 2002 and 2003 in the value of assets held by wealthy decedents.

In 2005, the number of taxable returns again dropped significantly, by 29% (from 31,329 in 2004 to 22,250 in 2005), after the exemption rose by $500,000, or 50%, to $1.5 million for people dying in 2004. Finally, in 2006, the number of taxable returns increased slightly, by 2.5% (from 22,250 in 2005 to 22,798 in 2006), as the $1.5 million exemption continued to prevail. This suggests that there was a small increase in the value of assets held by wealthy decedents between 2004 and 2005. This was in contrast to the experience in 2004, when the number of taxable returns fell while the exemption remained unchanged. Taxable returns measured as a percentage of deaths in the prior year fell below 1%, to 0.93% or

9.3 per thousand deaths, in both 2005 and 2006, when the prevailing exemption rose to $1.5 million.

It can be expected that both the number of taxable returns and taxable returns measured as a percentage of deaths will drop substantially for returns filed in 2007, when the prevailing exemption rises to $2 million, and again for returns filed in 2010, when the prevailing exemption will rise to $3.5 million. The number of taxable estate tax returns is projected to drop far below the typical historical range of 1% to 2% of adult deaths [9].

Number of Taxable Returns and Total Taxes Paid

As shown in the last columns of Tables 2 and 3, total estate taxes paid moved in the same direction as the number of taxable returns filed from 1998 through 2003. Both measures rose from 1998 to 2000 and fell from 2000 to 2003. Then, somewhat surprisingly, estate tax payments rose slightly (by 4%), from $20.8 billion in 2003 to $21.6 billion in 2004, despite a decline of nearly 2,000 (or 6%) in the number of taxable returns. Even more surprising, estate taxes paid rose very slightly (by 0.3%) to $21.7 billion in 2005, even though the number of taxable returns dropped by 29%.

Although the number of taxable estate tax returns filed in 2005 was less than half that in 1998, essentially the same (nominal, not inflation-adjusted) amount of estate tax was paid for both years ($21.7 billion in 2005 compared with $20.3 billion in 1998).

What explains the persistence of revenues despite a dramatic drop in the number of taxable estates? While large in number, the smallest estates as a group contributed relatively little in estate taxes. Although the two lowest gross estate size classes accounted for 33,179 or 64% of the 51,736 taxable returns filed in 2001, they contributed only $2.7 billion or 11% of the $23.5 billion in estate taxes paid. The large decrease in the total number of taxable returns between 2001 and 2005 can be explained by the elimination from taxability of the large number of estates in the two lowest gross estate size categories (under $1 million and $1 million up to $1.5 million) after the prevailing exemption rose to $1 million in filing year 2003. There was a further large decrease in the number of taxable returns in the $1 million to $1.5 million category and a smaller decrease in the $1.5 million to $2 million category in filing year 2005, when the prevailing exemption rose to $1.5 million.

Between 2004 and 2005, the $1.4 billion loss in estate taxes paid by these two smallest size classes, plus a $0.7 billion loss in the $2 million to $3.5 million gross estate size class, was more than offset by the $2.1 billion increase in taxes collected from the largest size class, with gross estates of $20 million or more.

Table 4. Number of Taxable Returns Filed in 2001-2006, by Size of Gross Estate

Size of Gross Estate (In $ Millions)	2001	2002	2003	2004	2005	2006
All Taxable Returns	51,736	45,018	33,302	31,329	20,250	22,798
< 1.0	18,093	13,638	2,676	1,053	—	—
1.0 < 1.5	15,086	14,131	11,457	10,269	1,820[a]	819[a]
1.5 < 2.0	6,024	5,780	6,764	7,057	5,237	5,704
2.0 < 3.5	6,884	5,961	6,716	7,290	7,311	9,043
3.5 < 5.0	2,148	2,170	2,202	2,165	2,282	2,951
5.0 < 10.0	2,165	2,100	2,157	2,166	2,280	2,664
10.0 < 20.0	868	755	824	808	822	1,004
20.0 or more	469	484	504	520	498	614

Table 5. Estate Taxes Paid with Taxable Returns Filed in 2001-2006, by Size of Gross Estate in $ billions

Size of Gross Estate (in $ millions)	2001	2002	2003	2004	2005	2006
All Taxable Returns	23.5	21.4	20.8	21.6	21.7	24.7
< 1.0	0.7	0.5	0.1	0.1	—	—
1.0 < 1.5	2.0	1.9	0.9	0.7	0.2[a]	0.1[a]
1.5 < 2.0	1.8	1.6	1.5	1.5	0.6	0.5
2.0 < 3.5	4.0	3.3	3.5	3.7	3.0	3.4
3.5 < 5.0	2.7	2.4	2.4	2.4	2.3	2.7
5.0 < 10.0	4.3	3.9	4.2	4.4	4.5	5.2
10.0 < 20.0	3.1	2.8	2.9	3.2	3.3	4.0
20.0 or more	4.9	4.9	5.2	5.6	7.8	8.5

Sources for Tables 4 and 5: Internal Revenue Service, Statistics of Income, Estate Tax Returns Filed in [year]. Unpublished data available at [http://www.irs.gov/]. Use the following search sequence: Tax Stats, Individual Tax Statistics, Estate & Gift Tax, Estate Tax, Filing Year Data Tables, By Tax Status and Size of Gross Estate, and, finally, the filing year of interest.

Note for Tables 4 and 5: a. For returns filed in 2005 and 2006, the lowest category is under $1.5 million. In effect, this combines the first two rows of the table.

Between 2005 and 2006, estate taxes paid increased by 13.8% to $24.7 billion, even though the number of taxable returns increased by only 2.5%. There was an increase in the number of taxable returns in each of the six size classes of over $1.5 million in gross estate. This was accompanied by an increase in the amount of estate taxes paid by each of the five size classes of over $2.0 million in gross estate, totaling an additional $2.9 billion.

GIFT TAX REVENUES FELL AFTER 2001 TAX ACT

Gift Tax Law

The gift tax is levied on the taxable transfer of assets during a donor's lifetime [10]. Under the law prior to EGTRRA, the estate and gift tax exemption was "unified." That is, the exemption could be used to protect any combination of lifetime gifts and/or bequests at death that added up to the dollar amount of the exemption for the year of death. Under the Taxpayer Relief Act of 1997 (TRA), the "unified" applicable exclusion amount or exemption — for lifetime taxable gifts together with bequests — rose gradually from $600,000 in 1997, to $675,000 in 2001. The same graduated tax rate structure that applied to estates applied to cumulative taxable lifetime gifts in excess of the exemption amount. In contrast, under EGTRRA, the exemption for cumulative lifetime gifts was capped separately at $1 million, effective from 2002 onward, even as the combined exemption for gifts and bequests rose from $1 million for decedents dying in 2002 and 2003 up to $3.5 million for decedents dying in 2009 (refer back to Table 1). Furthermore, under EGTRRA, the gift tax is to remain in place in 2010 with a cumulative lifetime exemption of $1 million, even when the estate tax is repealed.

The EGTRRA law means that, beginning in 2002, once an individual has given away $1 million cumulatively over their lifetime, they will owe gift taxes on any further gifts, payable in the year following the gift. Any amount of the gift tax exemption (up to $1 million) used by a person during their lifetime is to be subtracted from the combined exemption applying in their year of death to determine the amount of the exemption remaining to protect the estate from taxation. So, for example, if an individual who has already given away $1 million in lifetime taxable gifts died in either 2006, 2007, or 2008, when the combined exemption is $2 million per decedent, there would be $1 million in exemption remaining for the estate. In 2010, under EGTRRA, the maximum gift tax rate will be capped at 35% (equal to the maximum individual income tax rate under EGTRRA) on cumulative lifetime taxable transfers over $500,000. This is lower than the maximum rate of 45% scheduled to apply to estates and gifts in 2007 through 2009. Under the bills that would permanently repeal the estate tax by simply repealing the sunset provision of EGTRRA, this gift tax would remain in place after 2010 [11].

Gift Tax Revenues

Through FY200 1, gift taxes accounted for a significant percentage of combined estate and gift tax revenues [12]. Ever since the adoption of EGTRRA in 2001, with its announcement of estate tax repeal in 2010, there has been a substantial decline in the revenue collected from the gift tax. The last column of Table 6 shows that gift taxes accounted for 14% to 17% of combined estate and gift tax revenues from FY1999 through FY2001. In contrast, from FY2002 to FY2007, gift taxes accounted for only 6% to 9%. Gift tax revenue fell by more than half, from the range of $3.9 billion to $4.7 billion per year in FY1999-FY2001, down to the range of $1.4 billion to $2.4 billion in FY2002-FY2007 (second column of Table 6). This is illustrated in Figure 3.

Table 6. Net Collections of Estate Taxes and Gift Taxes and Their Percentage Breakdown, Fiscal Years 1999-2007

Fiscal Year	Estate Taxes	Gift Taxes	Estate and Gift Taxes	Percent Estate Taxes	Percent Gift Taxes
	(in $ billions)				
1999	23.0	4.7	27.7	83	17
2000	24.9	4.0	28.9	86	14
2001	24.4	3.9	28.3	86	14
2002	24.8	1.6	26.4	94	6
2003	20.0	1.9	21.9	91	9
2004	23.4	1.4	24.8	94	6
2005	22.7	2.0	24.7	92	8
2006	25.9	1.9	27.8	93	7
2007	23.6	2.4	26.0	91	9

Sources: Internal Revenue Service Data Book for the fiscal years 1999-2007, Table 1: Internal Revenue Collections and Refunds, by Type of Tax. Available on the IRS website [http://www.irs.gov] under SOI Tax Stats. Net collections are equal to gross collections minus refunds. Percentage calculations by CRS.

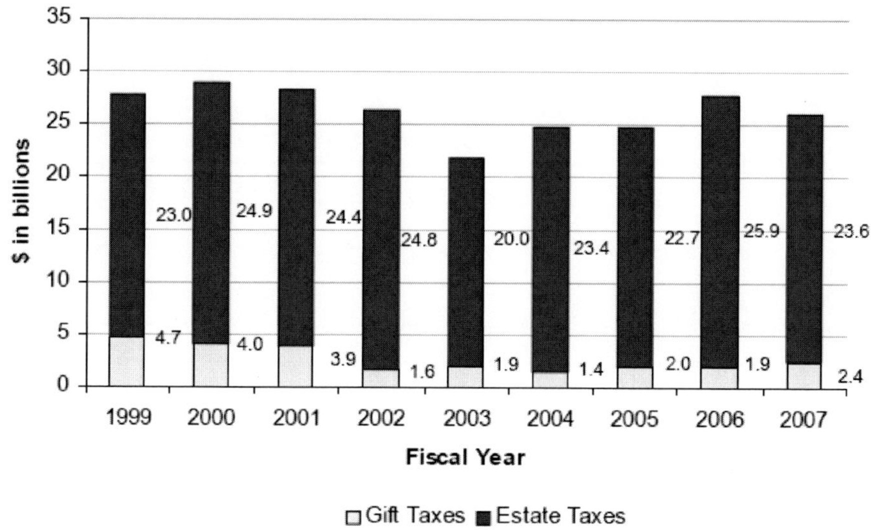

Source: Columns 1 and 2 of Table 6.

Figure 3. Net Collections of Estate Taxes and Gift Taxes and Their Percentage Breakdown, Fiscal Years 1999-2007.

A possible explanation for the decline in gift taxes is that many wealthy people chose to forgo the certainty of gift taxes if they transferred assets while they were alive, in the hope that the estate tax would be repealed permanently and they would then be able to pass the assets along to beneficiaries tax-free upon their death [13]. Forecasters at the U.S. Treasury Department predict that revenue from the gift tax will remain low in the years remaining prior to FY20 11 but will be higher in FY20 11, reflecting gifts made in 2010 before the scheduled return of the estate tax in 2011.

Estate and Gift Taxes Contribute Less Than 2% of Federal Revenue

As shown in Table 7, revenues from estate and gift taxes combined accounted for $27.8 billion or 1.5% of total federal revenue in FY1999 [14]. Their contribution remained at 1.4% for FY2000, FY2001, and FY2002, even though their absolute dollar amount fluctuated first above and then below their FY1999 level. Ever since the effects of EGGTRA began to register in FY2003, the share of revenue contributed by estate and gift taxes has remained below 1.4%.

Table 7. Estate and Gift Tax Revenues Combined, Dollar Amount and as a Percent of Total Federal Revenue, FY1999-FY2007

Fiscal Year	Estate and Gift Tax Revenues	
	In $ Billions	As a Percent of Total Federal Revenue
1999	$27.8	1.5%
2000	29.0	1.4
2001	28.4	1.4
2002	26.5	1.4
2003	22.0	1.2
2004	24.8	1.3
2005	24.8	1.1
2006	27.9	1.2
2007	26.0	1.0

Sources: Revenue data from U.S. Executive Office of the President, Office of Management and Budget, Historical Tables, Budget of the United States Government, Fiscal Year 2009 (Washington: GPO, 2008), Table 2.1, p. 31 (total receipts), Table 2.5, p. 46 (estate and gift taxes). Percentage calculations by CRS.

From FY2003 through FY2006 it fluctuated within the range of 1.1% to 1.3% of total revenue, even though the dollar amount rebounded from $22.0 billion in FY2003 to $27.9 billion in FY2006. In FY2007 estate and gift taxes fell back to $26.0 billion, accounting for 1.0% of total federal revenue. The percentage share of estate and gift taxes is influenced by fluctuations in other revenue sources as well.

CBO Projections Show Rebound in Estate Tax Revenues after FY2011 if EGTTRA Sunsets

In January 2008, the Congressional Budget Office (CBO) released its projections, under current law, of estate and gift tax revenues through FY20 18, as shown in Table 8. CBO assumes growth in the value of assets over time, reflecting both real economic growth and inflation. CBO noted that individuals' wealth has been growing slightly faster than GDP, on average, in recent years [15].

Table 8. CBO Projections of Combined Estate and Gift Tax Revenues Each Year from FY2008 through FY2018 under Current Law: Dollar Amount, Percent of Total Revenue, and Percent of GDP

Fiscal Year	Revenue in $ Billions	As a Percent of Total Revenue	As a Percent of GDP
Actual 2007	26	1.0	0.2
2008	27	1.0	0.2
2009	27	1.0	0.2
2010	22	0.8	0.1
2011	21	0.7	0.1
2012	55	1.6	0.3
2013	63	1.8	0.3
2014	70	1.9	0.4
2015	76	1.9	0.4
2016	83	2.0	0.4
2017	90	2.1	0.4
2018	97	2.1	0.4
First 5-year subtotal 2009-2013	188	1.2	0.2
Second 5-year subtotal 2014-2018[a]	416	2.0	0.4
10-year total 2009-20 18	604	1.6	0.3

Source: U.S. Congress, Congressional Budget Office, The Budget and Economic Outlook: Fiscal Years 2008 to 2018, Washington, Jan. 2008, Table 4-1: CBO' s Projections of Revenues, p. 83. Percent of total revenue calculated by CRS.

[a.] The second five-year subtotal for FY2014-FY2018 was added by CRS.

Starting from actual revenues of $26 billion in FY2007, CBO projected that revenues would rise slightly to $27 billion in both FY2008 and FY2009. In all three of these years, estate and gift taxes were estimated to account for 1.0% of total federal revenue and 0.2% of gross domestic product (GDP). This is based upon an estate tax exemption of $2 million for decedents dying in calendar years 2006-2008 Reflecting the large increase in the exemption to $3.5 million for 2009 and the repeal of the estate tax for decedents dying in calendar year 2010, CBO projected that estate and gift tax revenues would fall to $22 billion in FY20 10 and $21 billion in FY201 1. This corresponds to 0.8% of total federal revenue in FY2010 and 0.7% in FY201 1, and to 0.1% of GDP in both years.

Reflecting the reinstatement of the estate tax in 2011 with an exemption of $1 million, CBO projected that estate and gift tax revenues would rise markedly to $55 billion in FY20 12. That represents 1.6% of projected federal revenue (higher than the 1.5% share they contributed in FY1999) and 0.3% of GDP. CBO projected that estate and gift tax revenues would continue to rise steadily in nominal dollars by roughly $7 billion each year, to $63 billion in FY2013, and up to $97 billion in FY2018. That represents 1.8% of projected total revenue for FY2013 and 2.1% for FY20 18. Because the $1 million exemption amount is not indexed for inflation after 2011, and because the wealth of individuals is assumed to grow faster than inflation, CBO projected that estate and gift tax revenues would rise to 0.4% of GDP starting in FY20 14.

CBO's cumulative revenue projection for the standard 10-year forecast period, FY2009-FY2018, is $604 billion. There is a big difference, however, in the revenue expected for the first half of the 10-year period versus the second half. This is because of the large changes in the estate tax exemption each calendar year from 2008 through 2011 (refer back to Table 1, column 1). CBO's revenue forecast for the first five-year period, FY2009-FY2013, is $188 billion. This reflects one calendar year when the exemption is $2 million, one when it is $3.5 million, one when there is no estate tax, and two when the exemption is $1 million. The revenue projection for the second five-year period, FY2014-FY2018, is $416 billion. This projection is based on the assumption that the estate tax will be in effect for all of those years with an exemption of $1 million and that the top tax rate will be restored (from 45% in 2007-2009) to 55% for decedents dying in 2011 and after, as provided under pre-EGTRRA law.

Treasury Department and JCT Estimates of Revenue Loss from Permanent Repeal

In its FY2009 budget, the Bush Administration again proposed making the repeal of the estate tax permanent. The Administration's proposal to remove the sunset provision of EGTRRA would make permanent both the repeal of the estate tax and the generation-skipping transfer tax, as well as the modifications to the gift tax currently scheduled to be in effect for 2010 only Table 9 presents estimates of the changes in federal receipts expected each year, through FY20 18, if legislation to repeal the sunset provision of EGTRRA with respect to the estate and gift taxes were enacted in 2008, to take effect in 2010. These estimates were issued by the U.S. Treasury Department in February 2008 and by the Joint Committee on Taxation (JCT) in March 2008. The Treasury's estimates of revenue loss begin in FY2008. The JCT's estimates begin in FY2009. These estimates do not include the reduction in revenue expected as a result of impending changes made by EGTTRA, namely the increase in the estate tax exemption to $3.5 million for 2009.

Table 9. Treasury Department and JCT Estimates of Revenue Losses from Permanent Repeal of the Estate Tax, Each Year from FY2008 to FY2018

Fiscal Year	Treasury Department	Joint Committee on Taxation
	(millions of dollars)	
2008	-422	—
2009	-2,502	-1,401
2010	-3,453	-2,288
2011	-26,409	-30,521
2012	-57,639	-69,388
2013	-59,670	-76,957
2014	-64,670	-84,174
2015	-69,371	-90,728
2016	-74,379	-97,431
2017	-79,285	-104,890
2018	-84,604	-112,038
2009-2013	-149,673	-180,555
2014-2018	-372,309	-489,261
2009-2018	-521,982	-669,816

Sources: U.S. Department of the Treasury, General Explanations of the Administration's Fiscal Year 2009 Revenue Proposals (referred to as the Bluebook), Washington, Feb. 2008, p. 129. Column 2: U.S. Congress, Joint Committee on Taxation, Description of Revenue Provisions Contained in the President's Fiscal Year 2009 Budget Proposal, 1 10th Cong., 2nd sess., JCS-1-08 (Washington: GPO, Mar. 2008), p. 311. The second five-year subtotal for FY2014-FY2018 was added by CRS.

Notes: These estimates are based on the assumption that Congress acts in 2008 to permanently repeal the estate tax and generation-skipping transfer tax effective in 2010. The estimates include the projected accompanying loss of individual income tax revenue, in addition to estate and gift tax revenue, as explained in the text.

Reduced Gift Taxes and Income Taxes Also Expected

According to Treasury Department analysts, the revenue losses estimated for FY2008 through FY2010 stem primarily from a projected decline in gift tax revenues. As explained previously, the estimates are based on the assumption that taxpayers would immediately begin to reduce taxable gifts during their lifetimes if they knew that the estate tax would be permanently repealed in 2010.

In addition, it is expected that enactment in 2008 of permanent repeal of the estate tax (effective in 2010) would modestly affect revenues from the individual income tax, in two opposing ways. First, lifetime charitable donations and accompanying tax deductions would fall, thereby increasing income tax revenues. Second, and larger in effect, capital gains realizations by the elderly would fall as they wait to pass on their assets tax-free after death, thereby decreasing current income tax revenue. Treasury projected that, for FY2008 through FY2010, net reductions in income taxes would add to the decrease in revenue from gift taxes. For FY20 11 and beyond, the loss in income taxes would add to the decrease in revenue from estate taxes as well as gift taxes [16].

According to Treasury Department analysts, Treasury's estimates of revenue loss are lower than JCT's (for fiscal years 2011 and beyond) primarily because Treasury starts from a lower baseline (the projection of what revenues from the estate tax would otherwise be) than the Congressional Budget Office baseline used by JCT.

Ten-Year Forecast May Be Misleading Because of Changing Law

The U.S. Treasury Department and the Joint Committee on Taxation typically prepare a revenue-change forecast for 10 fiscal years forward whenever they evaluate a tax proposal. Similarly, in its budget outlook publications, CBO makes projections of specific revenue sources for the next 10 fiscal years. Because of the big changes in estate tax law scheduled over the next three calendar years, from 2009 through 2011, the standard 10-year forecast starting in FY2009 gives a misleading measure of the revenue — or revenue loss — that would be expected if the same tax law were in effect for each of the 10 years.

For the hypothetical case of legislation in 2008 to make estate tax repeal permanent for 2010 and beyond, the expected five-year revenue losses are far lower for the first five years, FY2009-FY2013, than they are for the second five years, FY20 14-FY20 18, when repeal of the estate tax would be fully in effect. The revenue loss estimate for the second five-year period better reflects the long-run cost of the permanent repeal proposal: $372 billion according to Treasury and $489 billion according to the JCT. For individual years reflecting full repeal of the estate tax, Treasury estimated a revenue loss of $60 billion for FY20 13, rising by about $5 billion each year to $85 billion in FY20 18. The JCT estimated a revenue loss of $77 billion in FY20 13, rising by about $7 billion each year to $112 billion in FY20 18.

Table 10. Treasury and JCT Estimates of Revenue Loss from Making Permanent Certain Tax Cuts Enacted in 2001 and 2003, Cumulatively for FY2009-FY2018

Tax Proposal	Treasury	JCT	Treasury	JCT
	In $ Billions		Percent of Total	
Lower marginal individual income tax rates	-1,008	-1,041	46.1	43.1
Estate tax repeal	-522	-670	23.9	27.8
Increase child tax credit[a]	-252	-261	11.5	10.8
15% dividend rate	-196	-217	9.0	9.0
15% capital gains rate	-105	-102	4.8	4.2
Marriage penalty relief[a]	-60	-81	2.7	3.3
Increase small business expensing	-27	-23	1.2	0.9
Education incentives	-12	-15	0.5	0.6
Other incentives for families and children	-5	-5	0.2	0.2
Total	-2,185	-2,414	100.0	100.0

Sources: U.S. Department of the Treasury, General Explanations of the Administration's Fiscal Year 2009 Revenue Proposals (referred to as the Bluebook), Washington, Feb. 2008, p. 129. U.S. Congress, Joint Committee on Taxation, Description of Revenue Provisions Contained in the President's Fiscal Year 2009 Budget Proposal, 1 10th Cong., 2nd sess., JCS-1-08 (Washington: GPO, Mar. 2008), p. 311. Percentage calculations by CRS.

Note: a. The estimates for the child tax credit and marriage penalty relief also include outlays for refundable tax credits associated with these proposals.

Estate Tax Repeal Accounts for One-Quarter of the Estimated Cost of Making the 2001 and 2003 Tax Cuts Permanent

Among the revenue proposals in its FY2009 budget, the Bush Administration has again proposed to "make permanent certain tax relief provisions enacted in 2001 and 2003." Table 10 lists the proposals within that category in decreasing order of their projected revenue loss over the 10-year forecast period, FY2009-FY2018.

According to the Treasury Department's estimates, repeal of the estate tax accounts for nearly one-quarter (23.9%) of the revenue losses associated with making permanent this group of tax cuts enacted in 2001 and 2003: $522 billion out of $2,185 billion for the group. The Treasury estimates that the revenue loss from permanent repeal of the estate tax is just over half the size of the most costly component of the package, extending the reductions in marginal individual income tax rates: $522 billion compared with $1,008 billion, or 52%.

According to the Joint Committee on Taxation, the estate tax accounts for just over one-quarter (27.8%) of the projected revenue cost of making the set of 2001 and 2003 tax cuts permanent: $670 billion out of $2,414 billion for the 10-year period, FY2009-FY2018. JCT estimates that permanent estate tax repeal would cost nearly two-thirds as much as making the individual income tax rate cuts permanent: $670 billion compared to $1,401 billion, or 64%.

The big role of estate taxes may seem surprising given that estate and gift taxes account for 2% or less of past and projected federal revenue (refer back to Tables 7 and 8)

REFERENCES

[1] Technically, the gross estate plus adjusted taxable gifts.

[2] In practice, each estate tax return receives a unified credit against the estate tax equal to the tax that would be due on the amount of the exemption. The unified credit is applied against both estate and gift tax obligations

[3] The Taxpayer Relief Act created a new exclusion from the estate tax for qualified family- owned business interests (QFOBI) that was in effect from 1998 through 2003. The exclusion was (up to) $675,000, but was limited to a total of $1.3 million in combination with the applicable exclusion amount, which was scheduled to rise. The family-owned business exclusion was converted to a deduction by the Internal Revenue Service Restructuring and Reform Act of 1998 (P.L. 105-206). Under EGTRRA, the family-owned

business deduction was repealed in 2004, when the applicable exclusion amount for all estates was increased to $1,500,000. For more information, see CRS Report 95-444, A History of Federal Estate, Gift, and Generation-Skipping Taxes, by John R. Luckey.

[4] Under ERTA of 1981, the top marginal estate tax rate was scheduled to fall to 50% in 1985. The Deficit Reduction Act of 1984 (P.L. 98-369) froze the top tax rate at the 1984 level of 55% until 1988. The Omnibus Budget Reconciliation Act of 1987 (P.L. 100-203) extended the maximum rate of 55% through 1992. The Omnibus Reconciliation Act of 1993 (P.L. 103-66) extended the maximum rate of 55% retroactively, from December 31, 1992, onward. See CRS Report 95-444, *A History of Federal Estate, Gift, and Generation Skipping Taxes*, by John R. Luckey.

[5] For an explanation of the surtaxes, see notes d and e of Table 1.

[6] For additional information on these changes in federal estate tax law, see CRS Report RL3 1061, *Estate and Gift Tax Law: Changes Under the Economic Growth and Tax Relief Reconciliation Act of 2001*, by Nonna A. Noto, Jan. 29, 2002, and CRS Report 95-444, *A History of Federal Estate, Gift, and Generation-Skipping Taxes*, by John R. Luckey.

[7] The five-year averages were calculated by CRS from annual statistics reported in Brian G.Raub, "Recent Changes in the Estate Tax Exemption Level and Filing Population," Internal Revenue Service, Statistics of Income (SOI) Bulletin, vol. 27, no. 1 (Summer 2007), Figure B, p. 114.

[8] Internal Revenue Service, *Statistics of Income Bulletin*, Spring 2007, Selected Historical and Other Data, Table 17, p. 279.

[9] For estimates made in July 2005 by the Urban-Brookings Tax Policy Center of the number of taxable estate tax returns, and calculations by CRS of taxable returns as a percent of adult deaths, under the higher exemptions scheduled under current law through 2009, see CRS Report RL33501, *Indexing the Estate Tax Exemption for Inflation*, by Nonna A. Noto, July 7, 2006, Table 2; for the historical series from 1934 through 2002, see Table 1 of that report.

[10] Under the gift tax, there is an annual exclusion per donor for each donee. This exclusion amount is indexed for inflation and rounded down to the nearest $1,000. The exclusion is $12,000 in 2008, the same as in 2006 and 2007. Gifts up to this limit are not counted as taxable gifts. A married couple may give up to twice that amount, $24,000, to an individual in a single year without having it count against their lifetime exclusion. In addition, there is an unlimited exclusion for gifts to pay for tuition or medical expenses or for transfers to a political organization for the use of

the organization. There is also an unlimited marital deduction for most gifts between spouses. Only gift amounts in excess of the annual exclusion need to be reported on a gift tax return. A gift tax return is due by April 15 of the year after a potentially taxable gift is made, even if no tax is currently due. No gift tax is due until cumulative taxable gifts over the donor's lifetime exceed the lifetime gift exclusion amount. For more information, see CRS Report 95-444, *A History of Federal Estate, Gift, and Generation-Skipping Taxes,* by John R. Luckey, and CRS Report 95-416, *Federal Estate, Gift, and Generation-Skipping Taxes: A Description of Current Law*, by John R. Luckey

[11] For further explanation, see CRS Report RL34374, *Estate Tax Legislation in the 110th Congress*, by Nonna A. Noto.

[12] The revenue numbers cited in the remainder of this report differ from those presented in the last column of Table 2 in at least three ways: 1) they include gift taxes in addition to estate taxes; 2) they are on a fiscal year rather than calendar year basis; and 3) they are based on revenue collections data, rather than on a sampling of estate tax returns.

[13] There is another tax advantage to delaying the transfer of assets until after death that was present in prior law and remains in practical effect for small estates under EGTRRA. Recipients are likely to owe less in capital gains taxes when they sell a capital asset received from a bequest after death, rather than from a lifetime gift, because of the difference in treatment of basis. Under both EGTRRA and prior law, assets transferred by gift receive a carryover basis (the donor's purchase price), in contrast to a step-up in basis (the value at the time of the transfer). Under the law in effect through 2009, while the estate tax remains in effect, recipients of assets transferred at death receive a step-up in basis. This cancels potential capital gains tax liability on the increase in the value of the asset during the decedent's period of ownership. Under EGTRRA, assets transferred at death during years when the estate tax is repealed (2010 and possibly subsequent years if extended) will receive a modified carryover basis. There is a step-up allowance of $1.3 million per decedent plus $3 million for a surviving spouse, both indexed for inflation after 2010. These step-up allowances are likely to shelter most capital gains in small estates from income tax when the heirs sell the assets.

[14] For information on state revenues from these types of taxes, see CRS Report RS20853, *State Estate and Gift Tax Revenue*, by Steven Maguire.

[15] These conclusions are based on a comparison of two sets of revenue change estimates for FY2008-FY2013, for the proposal to repeal the estate tax,

published in the U.S. budget for FY2009. See U.S. Executive Office of the President, Office of Management and Budget, *Analytical Perspectives, Budget of the United States Government, Fiscal Year 2009* (Washington: GPO, 2008), Table 17-3, p. 265, and Table 17-4, p. 269. According to conversations with Treasury Department analysts, the estimates in Table 17-3, Effect of Proposals on Receipts — for making permanent the repeal of estate and generation-skipping transfer taxes and modification of gift taxes — include the projected negative effects on income tax revenue, in addition to the effect on estate and gift tax revenue. These estimates (presented out to FY20 13) are the same as those shown in Table 7 of this report for the Treasury Department. In contrast, the estimates in Table 17-4, Receipts by Source — of the effects of proposed legislation on receipts, under the heading for estate and gift taxes — include only the effects on estate and gift tax receipts. The difference between the two series represents the estimated associated loss of income tax revenue.

In: Estate and Gift Taxes
Editor: Clay B. Apperton

ISBN 978-1-60692-129-6

Chapter 3

ALTERNATIVES TO THE CURRENT FEDERAL ESTATE TAX SYSTEM TESTIMONY TO THE SENATE COMMITTEE ON FINANCE*

David G. Duff

INTRODUCTION

I would like to begin by thanking the Chairman and the Committee for giving me the opportunity to speak with you today.

My name is David Duff, and I'm a professor of tax law and policy at the University of Toronto Faculty of Law, where I've taught since 1996. Before that, I worked for a tax commission in the Province of Ontario, and as a tax associate in a Toronto law firm. I received by law degree from the University of Toronto in 1989, and have Masters degrees in economics, politics, and law, the last of which I received from Harvard in 1991.

I have appended two articles to this testimony. The first presents a philosophical argument for wealth transfer taxation in the form of an accessions tax, which would turn the current U.S. wealth transfer tax system on its head by applying to the cumulative amount of gifts and inheritances received by individuals over the course of their lifetimes rather than aggregate amounts given by donors over the course of their lifetimes. The second article reviews the

---

* Report dated March 12, 2008.

abolition of wealth transfer taxes in Canada, Australia and New Zealand, and attempts to derive lessons from this experience for the future of these taxes. My testimony is based on both articles and addresses the rationale for an accessions tax and lessons to be derived from the abolition of wealth transfer taxes in Canada, Australia and New Zealand.

Why an Accessions Tax?

Beginning with the rationale for an accessions tax, let me explain briefly why I think that that a society should tax transfers of wealth, and why an accessions tax is a better tax for this purpose than the current federal wealth transfer tax system in the United States.

As a philosophical matter, I believe that it is both legitimate and desirable for a society to moderate extreme inequalities in the distribution of wealth and in the opportunities that wealth provides, by taxing substantial gifts and inheritances above a generous exemption. While I believe that a society should value and encourage the family bonds that can be associated with the transfer of assets from one generation to another, I also believe that this value needs to be balanced against the negative social and political consequences for a democratic society that can result from the transfer of large dynastic fortunes from one generation to the next. In addition, to the extent that recipients have not earned the gifts and inheritances that they receive largely by the luck of their birth, I do not think that they cannot legitimately complain about a tax that would require them to share some of their good fortune with others who have not been so lucky.

From this perspective, it is clear why an accessions tax would be better than the current federal wealth transfer tax system in the United States. While the current gift and estate tax applies to aggregate amounts transferred by donors over the course of their lifetimes and at death, regardless of how this wealth is distributed among recipients, an accessions tax would apply to the cumulative value of gifts and inheritances that are received by beneficiaries over the course of their lifetimes – which are the amounts that actually contribute toward inequalities in wealth and opportunities. As well, the gift and estate tax sends exactly the wrong message about a wealth transfer tax by taxing successful, hardworking and generous donors who have accumulated wealth out of income on which they have often paid tax already. In contrast, an accessions tax sends a very different and justifiable message by taxing the beneficiaries of substantial gifts and inheritances on amounts that they have not themselves earned and on which they have not themselves paid any tax.

WHY DID CANADA, AUSTRALIA, AND NEW ZEALAND ABOLISH THEIR WEALTH TRANSFER TAXES?

This brings me to the abolition of wealth transfer taxes in Canada, Australia and New Zealand, and the lessons that may be derived from this experience. Although the story in each country is necessarily unique, I think that three factors are common.

First, in each country legislative action or inaction led to increased burdens on small- and medium-sized estates – either because the rates on these estates were increased, because the value of exemptions eroded with inflation, or because of other tax changes like the introduction of capital gains taxation in Canada which applies to transfers of property by gift or bequest. With much higher exemptions, the U.S. wealth transfer tax system does not face the same pressure. Canadian experience, however, suggests that attention should be paid to the combined effect of a wealth transfer tax and capital gains taxes applied to gifts and bequests.

Second, in each country competition between jurisdictions hastened the demise of these taxes. In Canada and Australia, this occurred at the sub-national level when the federal governments in each country repealed their estate and gift taxes in 1972 and 1979. In New Zealand, concern about wealthy retirees moving to Australia contributed to the government's decision to eliminate its estate tax in 1992. Although these kinds of competitive pressures are not as great in a large country like the U.S., they point to a further deficiency of donor-based gift and estate taxes – that they are easier to avoid through emigration by affluent retirees than accessions taxes that apply to younger and less geographically-mobile recipients.

Third, and perhaps most importantly, the wealth transfer taxes in each of these countries took the form of donor-based estate taxes, either on their own or integrated with donor-based gift taxes. To the extent that these kinds of taxes send the wrong message about the taxation of wealth transfers, it is not surprising that they failed to generate many defenders when they were under attack. In contrast, it is worth noting that recipient-based inheritance taxes appear to have been far more resilient over the last 30 years, accounting for a larger share of total tax revenue and GDP in some countries today than they did in the early 1970s.

CONCLUSION

As a citizen and resident of Canada, I am obviously not directly affected by the decisions that the United States makes with respect to its wealth transfer tax system.

As you know, however, many countries around the world pay close attention to the United States when they formulate their own tax policies. This is particularly true of Canada, which shares with the United States not only the world's longest border between two countries, but also similar political values and an extremely close trading relationship.

As a result, the decisions that the United States makes for its own wealth transfer tax system can have a huge effect on the tax systems of other countries, including Canada. I hope that the United States will set a positive example for other countries of the world by replacing the current federal wealth transfer tax system with an accessions tax that would be a model for wealth transfer taxation in the 21st century.

In: Estate and Gift Taxes
Editor: Clay B. Apperton

ISBN 978-1-60692-129-6

Chapter 4

Reform Options for the Estate Tax System: Targeting Unearned Income

Lily L. Batchelder[1]

Testimony before the United States Senate Committee on Finance March 12, 2008

Good morning, Mr. Chairman, Ranking Member Grassley, and Members of the Committee. My name is Lily Batchelder and I am an associate professor at NYU School of Law. Thank you for the opportunity to testify before you today on alternatives to the current federal estate tax system. My testimony makes three main points:

---

[1] The views expressed in this testimony are those of the author alone and do not necessarily represent those of NYU School of Law. Portions of this testimony draw upon Lily L. Batchelder, Taxing Privilege More Effectively: Replacing the Estate Tax with an Inheritance Tax, in THE PATH TO PROSPERITY: HAMILTON PROJECT IDEAS ON INCOME SECURITY, EDUCATION AND TAXES (Jason Furman and Jason Bordoff, eds.) (Brookings Institution Press, forthcoming), Lily L. Batchelder and Surachai Khitatrakun, Dead or Alive: An Investigation of the Incidence of Estate Taxes versus Inheritance Taxes (work-in-progress), and Lily L. Batchelder, Taxing Privilege More Effectively: Replacing the Estate Tax with an Inheritance Tax, BROOKINGS INST. HAMILTON PROJECT DISCUSSION PAPER 2007-07 (June, 2007). My co-author also should not be held responsible for the views expressed in this testimony.

- First, inheritances tend to exacerbate existing economic disparities and may be the most important barrier to intergenerational economic mobility. These tendencies are most pronounced at the top of the income distribution. Inheritances are a significant component of household income. They are also the source of about 40 percent of all household wealth. While inherited income is distributed fairly evenly across most of the population, it rises sharply at the very top. Among households receiving a bequest in a given year, the average inheritance of those in the top 1 percent of the inheritance distribution is 34 times larger than the average inherited income of everyone else.
- Second, the estate tax system is the most important mechanism by which the current fiscal system mitigates the effect of inheritances on economic disparities and intergenerational mobility. The burden of the estate and gift taxes falls largely on heirs, not donors. On average, it also rises rapidly with the amount the heir inherits and his economic income [2]. Nevertheless, the relationship between the heir's financial circumstances and his or her estate tax burden is relatively imprecise. Some individuals who receive extraordinarily large inheritances bear little or no tax burden, while a small number who inherit relatively small amounts bear substantial tax burdens.
- Finally, the scheduled repeal of the estate tax in 2010 and reinstatement at higher levels in 2011 create an opportunity to better focus the estate tax system on unearned income that inheritances represent. We should use that opportunity to reform, not repeal, the estate tax system so that we continue to tax inherited income, but in a more equitable manner. I will discuss two potential reform options.

    - The first would replace the estate tax system with a comprehensive inheritance tax, under which an individual inheriting an extraordinary amount over his lifetime would pay income tax and a flat 15 percent tax on a portion of his inheritance. Relative to the 2009 law, this reform could be implemented on a revenue-neutral basis if approximately the first $2 million in lifetime inheritances were tax-exempt. In effect, extraordinary amounts of inherited income would be taxed at about the same rate that families pay on earned income under the income and payroll taxes. This reform would substantially alter tax burdens, and improve the fairness of the current system by more accurately targeting the unfair advantages that exceptionally large inheritances create.

- If this reform is considered too ambitious, a second alternative would be to retain and improve the estate tax system by better focusing it on the amount transferred as a proxy for the amount inherited. Specifically, I will discuss a package of simplification reforms that would limit the extent to which the tax burden on heirs depends on their access to sophisticated tax advice.

I. Background on Wealth Transfers

Gifts and bequests affect economic opportunities and outcomes in important ways. They tend to magnify income and wealth disparities. They also create barriers to intergenerational economic mobility.

In 2009, annual bequest flows in the U.S. will total about $400 billion, excluding transfers to spouses and charitable organizations [3]. Bequests will represent about 4 percent of all household income and, among households receiving a bequest that year, about half of their receipts from labor, saving and bequests. In addition, gifts and bequests (which I will refer to as inheritances or wealth transfers) are a tremendously important determinant of household wealth. According to the best estimates, between 35 and 45 percent of all household wealth is inherited [4].

Inheritances are distributed fairly evenly across most of the income distribution, but rise sharply at the very top. As illustrated in Figure 1, tax units in roughly the top 1 percent of the earned income distribution (earning more than $500,000) receive about four times as much income from bequests as other households do on average. Moreover, some individuals—whether highly-compensated workers or not—inherit extraordinarily large amounts. For example, Figure 2 shows that among tax units receiving a bequest in a given year, the average inherited income of those in the top 1 percent of the inheritance distribution is 34 times larger than the averaged inherited income of everyone else. Inheritances thus tend to magnify economic inequality.

In addition, inheritances are perhaps the most important barrier to intergenerational economic mobility, or the ability of a child to achieve a different standard of living than that of his parents. The income that a child earns over his lifetime continues to be heavily influenced by the income of his parents, and this correlation is even higher at the ends of the income distribution [5]. For example, on average, children born to the top decile of the income distribution are 53 times more likely to end up in the top decile than children born to the bottom [6].

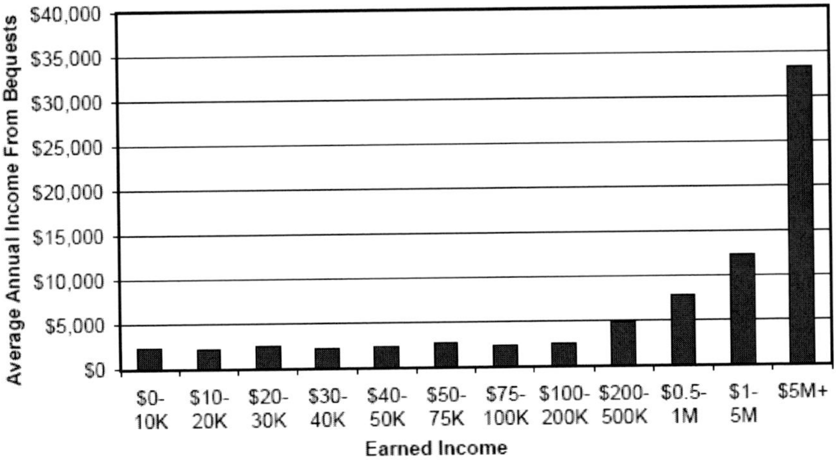

Figure 1. Estimated Average Annual Income from Bequests by Earned Income of All Tax Units in 2009.

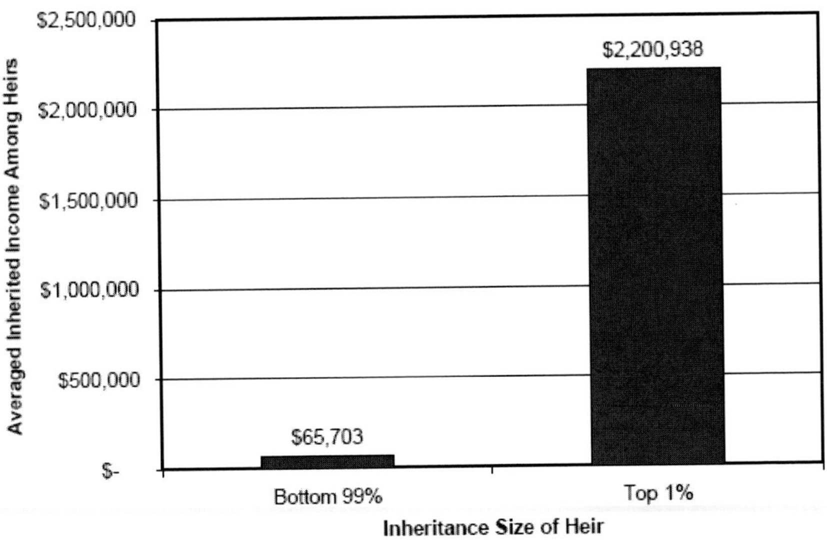

Figure 2. Average Annual Income from Bequests by Inheritance Size among Tax Units Receiving a Bequest in 2009.

There are many sources of these barriers to economic mobility. Most are factors society would find difficult to mitigate. For example, existing evidence suggests that about 18 percent of the intergenerational correlation of income is explained by the correlation between parent and child IQ, personality and schooling [7]. However, inheritances can be adjusted in a relatively straightforward manner through fiscal policy. Moreover, disparities in inheritances appear to be the most significant barrier to mobility—accounting for about 30 percent of the correlation between parent and child economic outcomes [8].

II. Magnitude and Distribution of Estate Tax Burdens

Currently the estate tax system adjusts the amount individuals inherit through three interconnected taxes: the estate tax, the gift tax, and the generation-skipping transfer (GST) tax. This estate tax system is effective at narrowing the distribution of inheritances by imposing higher tax burdens on those who inherit more over their lifetime. But it does so in a relatively rough manner.

Background on the Estate Tax System

In 2008, the estate tax system operates as follows. An individual can transfer $2 million in gifts and bequests ($4 million in the case of a couple) tax-free. Any portion of a bequest above this threshold is taxed at a 45 percent rate under the estate tax.

In order to prevent donors from avoiding the estate tax by making transfers during their life, the estate tax is coupled with a gift tax. Under the gift tax, gifts transferred prior to death that exceed $1 million over the donor's lifetime ($2 million in the case of a couple) are taxed at a 41 to 45 percent rate. A third tax, the GST tax, prevents donors from achieving lower tax rates by transferring wealth directly to their grandchildren instead of through their children.

In addition to the lifetime exemptions of the estate tax system, a number of other wealth transfers are tax-free. Each year a donor can completely disregard $12,000 of gifts to each of his or her beneficiaries ($24,000 in the case of a couple). All transfers to spouses and charities are disregarded. And all payments for education and health care are also tax-exempt.

The estate tax system only applies to the amount of gifts and bequests that a donor transfers. There is no separate tax on the amount of gifts and bequests that an heir receives. Importantly, under the income tax, gifts and bequests are not considered income of the heir, and are thus tax-free.

The estate tax system has been a small but stable source of revenue ever since the estate tax was enacted in 1916, generally raising between 1 and 2.5 percent of federal revenues as illustrated in Figure 3. Most revenue comes from the estate tax itself [10]. In 2007, the estate tax system raised about $26 billion [11]. Repeal of the estate tax would likely lose significantly more revenue [12]

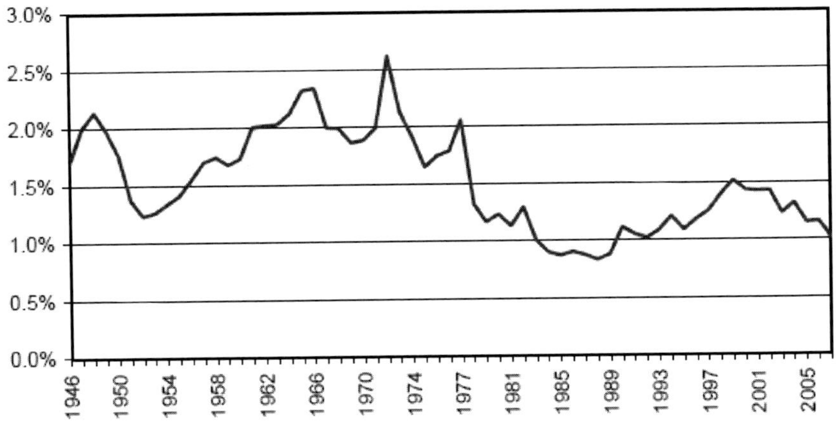

Figure 3. Estate and Gift Taxes as a Share of Federal Revenues, 1946-2007 [9].

The Distribution of Estate Tax Burdens

On average, the estate tax system is effective at mitigating the effect of inheritances on economic disparities and intergenerational mobility. This is the result of two factors. First, the economic burden of the estate tax system falls predominantly on heirs, not donors. Second, the tax burden rises steeply with the amount the heir inherits and his or her economic income.

The reason the burdens of the estate tax fall predominantly on heirs is that the tax typically reduces the amount that an heir receives. For example, suppose a mother would like to bequeath $10 million to her only son. If an estate tax is enacted that would tax such a transfer at 33 percent, she has three options. She can transfer $10 million as planned, leaving her son with $6.7 million after-tax. She can consume more and save less, leaving her son with an after-tax inheritance of less than $6.7 million. Or she can consume less and save more; for example, she could increase her saving to $15 million, leaving her son with $10 million after-tax. So long as she does not save more in response to the tax, her son will bear the tax burden in the form of a smaller inheritance [13]. In practice, wealthy donors appear to transfer the same amount or slightly less in response to the estate tax system (implying that it has a small effect or no effect on private savings) [14]. As a result, heirs generally bear most of the tax burden.

Most analyses of the distribution of estate tax burdens historically have assumed that it burdens donors, not heirs. This has been due to limited data on the financial circumstances of heirs inheriting from large estates, not to a belief among economists that donors truly bear the tax burden. Indeed, the President's former chairman of the Council of Economic Advisors, Gregory Mankiw, has stated that he believes that the burden of the estate tax system falls on heirs and not donors and decedents [15].

The fact that heirs appear to bear most of the burden of taxes on gifts and bequests has important implications for how such taxes should be conceptualized and designed. To the extent that the burden of wealth transfer taxes is borne by heirs, they are not double "death" taxes on the decedent, who may have worked hard to accumulate his or her wealth. They are taxes on the unearned windfalls that children who are fortunate enough to be born into wealthy households receive. As such, we may wish to tax inheritances in the same way that we tax other unearned windfalls, like lottery winnings or sunken treasure—by including them in taxable income. Moreover, because wealth transfer taxes tend to be borne largely by heirs, we may want the tax rate to depend on, and rise with, the financial circumstances of the heir, not the donor.

Under the current estate tax system, the tax rate does not directly turn on, or rise with, the amount the heir receives, but rather with the amount the donor transfers. In practice, estate tax burdens do, on average, rise steeply with the amount the heir inherits and his economic income, as illustrated in Figures 4 and 5 [16]. Overall, 98 percent of estate tax revenue comes from heirs with economic income above $200,000, while 96 percent of estate tax revenue comes from taxes on inheritances of more than $1 million. This is the case because, on average, the size of an inheritance rises with the wealth transfers of the donor and, on average, children born into high-income households are higher-income. But the relationship between the tax rate and the heir's financial circumstances is necessarily imprecise because the two are only linked indirectly.

Indeed, under the current estate tax system, some heirs inheriting extraordinarily large amounts bear little or no tax burden, while others inheriting relatively small amounts bear large tax burdens.

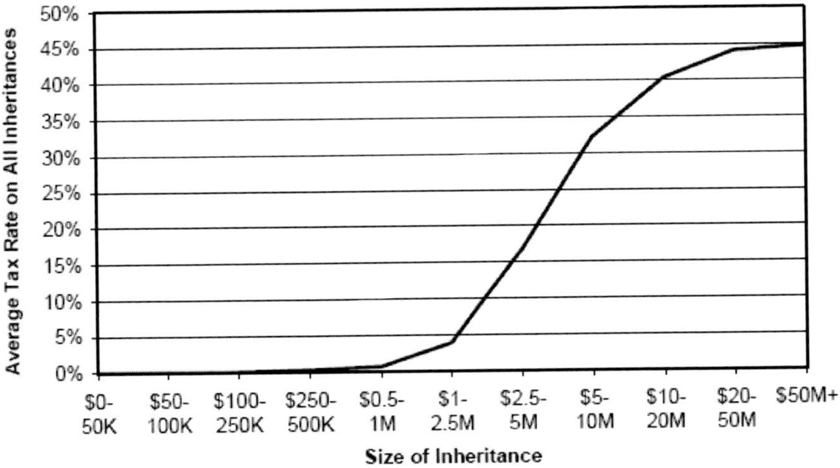

Figure 4. Estimated Average 2009 Estate Tax Burden on All Inheritances, by Inheritance Size.

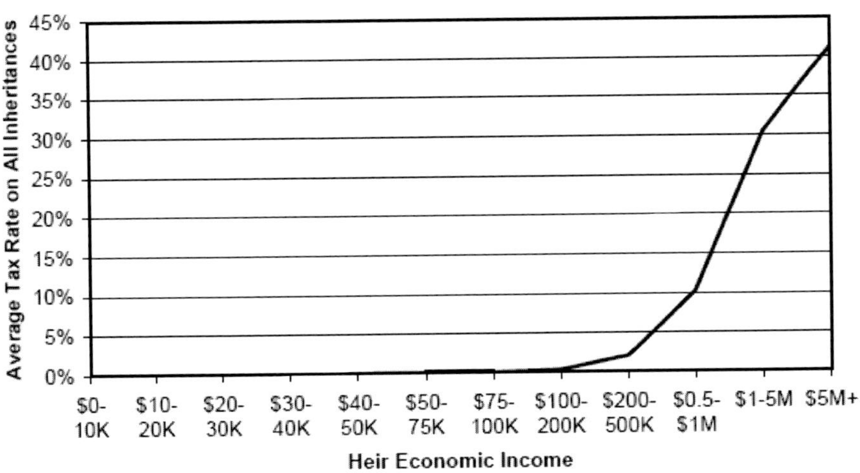

Figure 5. Estimated Average 2009 Estate Tax Burden on All Inheritances, by Heir Economic Income.

As Table 1 shows, in 2009 only about 5 in 1,000 people who receive an inheritance will bear any estate tax burden. In part, this is because more than 30 percent of heirs inheriting between $2.5 and $5 million are not burdened by the estate tax at all.

Table 1. Estimated Number of Heirs Burdened by 2009 Estate Tax in 2009

Size of Inheritance	Number of Heirs	Subject to Estate Tax Under 2009 Law	Percentage
$0+-100K	3,898,970	422	0%
$100-250K	532,391	961	0%
$250-500K	179,450	3,408	2%
$0.5-1M	90,693	3,246	4%
$1-2.5M	39,328	7,578	19%
$2.5-5M	5,049	3,495	69%
$5M+	2,410	2,410	100%

Generally these heirs have inherited all or part of an estate just below the exemption threshold. Meanwhile about 4 percent of those inheriting between $500,000 and $1 million are burdened by the estate tax, often at quite high rates. Typically these heirs have inherited a much smaller amount from an even larger estate.

In short, the strength of the current estate tax system from a fairness perspective is its ability to effectively narrow disparities in inherited income on average. Its weakness is that it is inconsistent in doing so in individual cases.

III. Reforms Worth Consideration

The goal of any reform of the estate tax system should be to more effectively target the tax on the unearned income that inheritances represent. Doing so will ensure that it is based on the ability to pay of the person who actually bears the tax: the heir. It will also ensure that the tax more effectively mitigates the income and wealth disparities and barriers to intergenerational economic mobility that extraordinarily large inheritances exacerbate. If a reform can further this objective while reducing administrative and compliance costs, or strengthening the efficiency of the tax system in other ways, all the better.

As illustrated in Table 2, over the next several years, the estate tax is scheduled to decline in 2009, disappear in 2010, and then return to life with a much lower exemption and higher rate in 2011 and thereafter. The result is sharp changes in the law, vast uncertainty for taxpayers, and gruesome incentives for prospective heirs on the eve of 2011. This untenable situation does, however, create a window of opportunity for reform.

I will discuss two promising approaches to improving the current system.

Table 2. Scheduled Changes to the Estate Tax System

	Tax Rate		Exclusions			Basis Provisions
	Estate & GST	Gift	Annual Gift17	Lifetime Estate & GST	Lifetime Gift	
2008	45%	41-45%	$12,000	$2 million	$1 million	Gifts: Carryover Bequests: Stepped-up
2009	45%	41-45%	$12,000	$3.5 million	$1 million	Same
2010	0%	35%	$12,000	N/A	$1 million	Gifts & Bequests: Carryover. Up to $4.3M capital gains tax-exempt.
2011 & on	41-55% [18]		$12,000	$1 million	$1 million	Gifts: Carryover Bequests: Stepped-up

A Comprehensive Inheritance Tax

The first option, which would be the most ambitious and effective, would be to replace the estate tax system with what I refer to as a "comprehensive inheritance tax." Under a comprehensive inheritance tax, any individual inheriting an extraordinary amount over his lifetime must pay income tax and an additional "surtax" on the portion of his inheritance that exceeds a large lifetime exemption. This reform could be implemented on a revenue-neutral basis by adjusting the exemption amount and surtax level.

Surachai Khitatrakun and I have estimated that a comprehensive inheritance tax would be revenue-neutral relative to 2009 estate tax law (a $3.5 million lifetime exemption) if the first $1.9 million in lifetime inheritances were tax-exempt, and inheritances thereafter were included in income and subject to a flat 15 percent tax. In effect, extraordinary amounts of inherited income would then be taxed at the same rate that families pay on earned income under the income and payroll taxes.

To state the obvious, $1.9 million is a lot of money. An individual who inherits $1.9 million at age eighteen can live off his inheritance for the rest of his life without either he or his spouse ever working, and his annual household income will still be higher than that of nine out of ten American families [19]. Accordingly, a lower exemption amount could be adopted to raise more revenue, or to maintain revenue-neutrality relative to a different baseline.

Table 3 summarizes some alternate possibilities. These estimates assume that any portion of a bequest that is included in income can be spread out over the current year and the previous four years. They also assume that each year $12,000 in gifts and $60,000 in bequests can be disregarded entirely, and do not count toward the lifetime exemption. All of these estimates are very rough and would differ from an actual revenue estimate because they assume no behavioral response [20]. For example, the Joint Committee on Taxation estimates that 2009 estate tax law will raise $21.8 billion and 2011 law will raise $50.7 billion [21].

To understand how this tax would work, imagine a person receives a bequest of $3 million above the annual exemption and has not received inheritances exceeding the annual exemption in any prior year. If the lifetime exemption is $1.9 million and the surtax is 15 percent, this person would only have to include $1.1 million of the bequest in his taxable income. This portion of his inheritance would be taxed under the same rate structure as his other ordinary income plus 15 percentage points. Because the income tax brackets rise with income, this might mean that the taxable portion of his bequest would fall within a higher tax bracket than his earned income because he received it all at once To limit this effect, he could elect to file as if he received $220,000 of taxable inheritance in the current year and the same amount in the previous four years [22].

Table 3. Estimated Revenue Effects of Estate Tax System and Comprehensive Inheritance Tax under Different Revenue Baselines

Estate Tax			Bush Income Tax Cuts	Revenue-Neutral Inheritance Tax		Revenue (billions)
Law	Exemption (millions)	Rate		Exemption (millions)	Surtax	
2009	$3.5	45%	Yes	$1.9	15%	$17.5
2009	$3.5	45%	Yes	$1.6	10%	$17.5
2008	$2.0	45%	Yes	$1.1	15%	$26.2
2008	$2.0	45%	Yes	$1.0	10%	$26.2
2011	$1.0	41-55%*	No	$0.5	15%	$50.2
2011	$1.0	41-55%*	No	$0.4	10%	$50.2
2011	$1.0	41-55%*	Some**	$0.5	15%	$50.2

* Phase-out of lower brackets disregarded.

** Tax cuts to top two income tax brackets eliminated.

From an administrative perspective, the heir should be responsible for filing an annual return reporting cumulative gifts and bequests exceeding the annual exemptions. Because third party reporting is essential for maximizing compliance, donors or their estates should also have to report information on transfers above these annual exemptions and remit a withholding tax. The heir would be responsible for claiming any excess tax withheld and paying any excess tax due if his lifetime reportable inheritances exceeded the lifetime exemption.

Advantages and Estimated Effects

A comprehensive inheritance tax would be substantially more targeted on inherited income than the current estate tax system because the tax rate would turn directly on the amount received. It would also be better attuned to the ability to pay of the individual who bears most of the burden of either tax—the heir.

Theoretically, if an estate and inheritance tax both had the same flat tax rate, there would be no difference in their distributional effects. Because all inheritances come from estates, the aggregate amount subject to tax would be the same, and any differences in how estates were distributed would be irrelevant because of the flat tax rate. Similarly, if all estates were distributed to only one taxable beneficiary and the inheritance tax rate depended solely on the amount inherited, there would be no distributional difference between the two approaches. In practice, however, the estate tax system has a progressive rate structure (due to the lifetime exemption) and estates frequently have more than one taxable beneficiary. As a result, a comprehensive inheritance tax should burden people differently.

Figures 6 through 9 illustrate that a comprehensive inheritance tax would indeed result in different tax burdens, and to a surprisingly large degree. If the 2009 estate tax was replaced with the revenue-neutral comprehensive inheritance tax outlined (with a $1.9 million exemption and 15 percent surtax), the distribution of tax burdens under the new tax would be similar in aggregate. This is true regardless of whether one considers the distribution of burdens by the amount inherited, the heir's economic income, or even the estate size or decedent's income (Figures 6 and 7).

But at an individual level, the new tax would allocate burdens very differently. For example, Figure 8 shows that of all the heirs who would be burdened by either tax in 2009, only 30 percent would be burdened by both. Indeed, a full 63 percent of heirs who are burdened by the estate tax would not bear any tax burden whatsoever under the comprehensive inheritance tax.

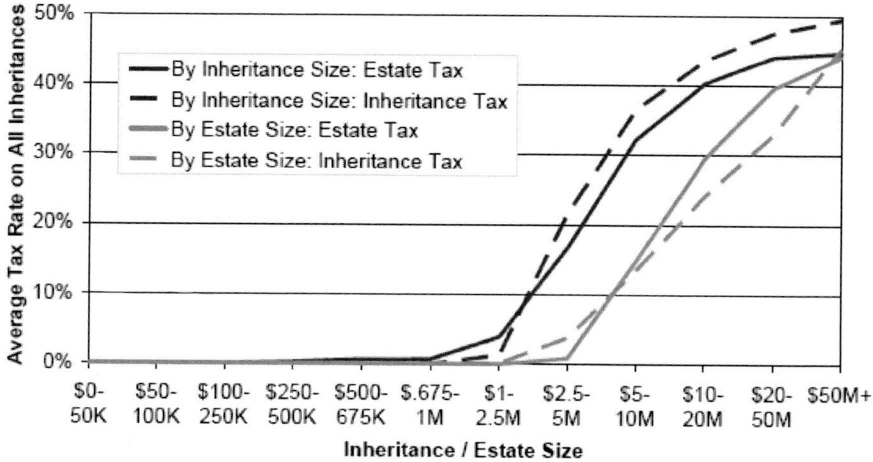

Figure 6. Estimated Average Tax Burden on All Inheritances under 2009 Estate Tax and Revenue-Neutral Comprehensive Inheritance Tax by Inheritance and Estate Size.

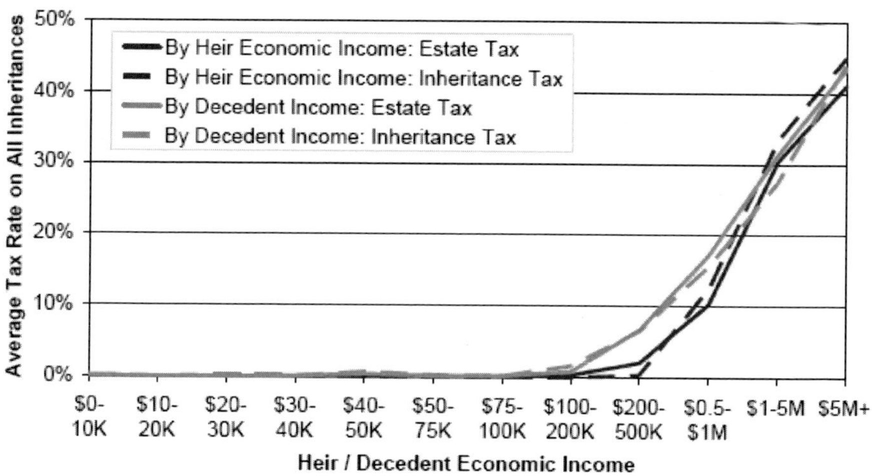

Figure 7. Estimated Average Tax Burden on All Inheritances under 2009 Estate Tax and Revenue-Neutral Comprehensive Inheritance Tax by Heir and Decedent Economic Income.

The essential reason why these differences arise is that all large inheritances do not come from the largest estates, and all smaller inheritances do not come from smaller ones [23].

The differences between the estate tax system and this new tax can be understood still further by considering heirs who would be burdened by both taxes. These heirs do account for the lion's share of revenue raised under either tax (about 90 percent). However, many would be subject to a very different tax rate under the comprehensive inheritance tax. As a result, 30 percent of the burden of the new tax in dollar terms would fall on different heirs. This variance in tax burdens can be seen in Figure 9, which focuses on those heirs who would be burdened by either tax (i.e., in one of the circles in Figure 8) and plots the average estate tax rate and comprehensive inheritance tax rate that each heir would face [24]. On average, the estate tax rate rises with the inheritance tax rate, and vice versa. But Figure 9 illustrates that individual heirs who are burdened by both tax systems often face dramatically different rates under one versus the other.

These substantial distributional differences in the burdens of a comprehensive inheritance tax essentially quantify its fairness benefits relative to the estate tax system. Each time the comprehensive inheritance tax applies a higher or lower tax rate to an heir, it is more accurately measuring inherited income and, in doing so, more effectively narrowing the disparities in economic opportunities and outcomes that stem from extraordinary large inheritances.

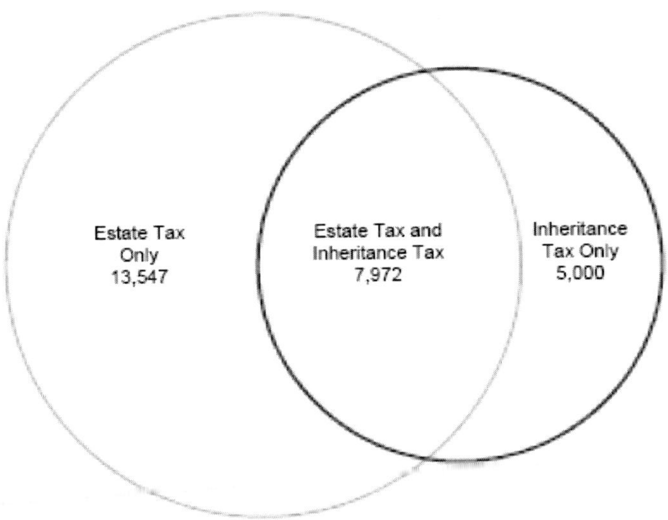

Figure 8. Number of Heirs Burdened by 2009 Estate Tax and Revenue-Neutral Comprehensive Inheritance Tax.

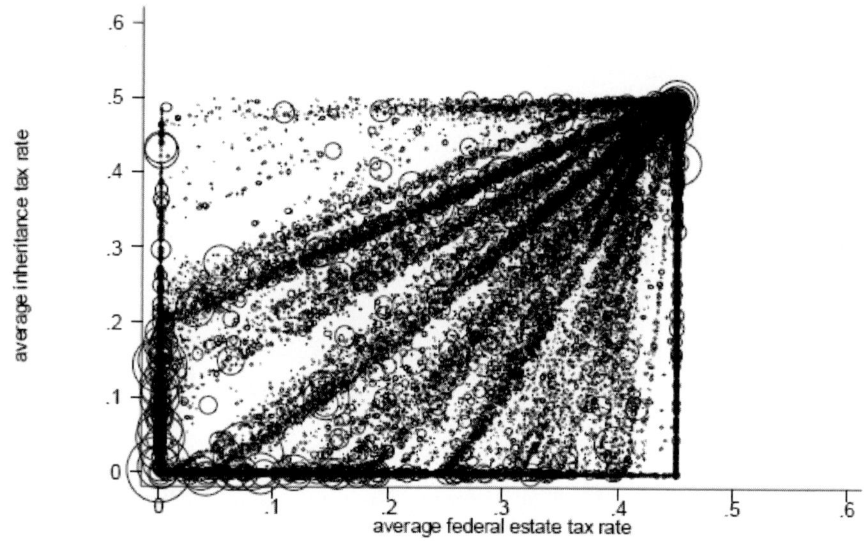

Figure 9. Average Tax Rate on Inheritance of Individual Heirs under 2009 Estate Tax and Revenue-Neutral Comprehensive Inheritance Tax (Weighted by Inheritance Size).

A comprehensive inheritance tax is only one of several alternatives to an estate tax system. As illustrated in Figure 10, jurisdictions currently apply five general approaches to taxing wealth transfers. Some, like the United States, have an estate and gift tax. Others have no wealth transfer tax and therefore disregard inherited income entirely in allocating tax burdens. Most, however, have an inheritance tax of which there are three types.

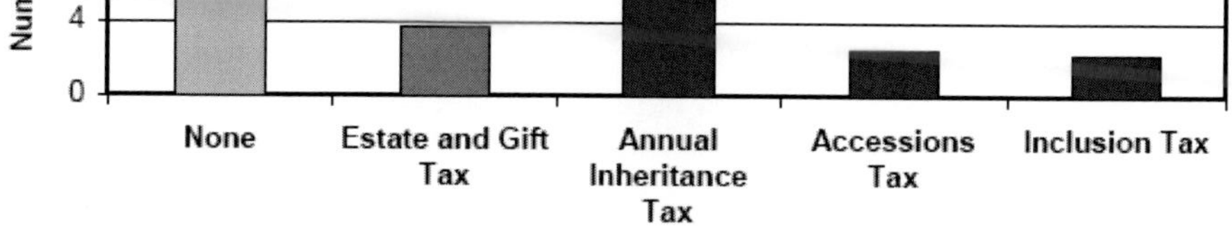

Figure 10. Type of Wealth Transfer Tax in 34 Countries [26].

The rate schedule of an "accessions tax" turns solely on the amount the heir inherits over a long period of time, typically his lifetime. The rate schedule of an "annual inheritance tax" instead turns on the amount inherited each year. Finally, an inclusion tax requires the heir to include inheritances in his income tax base, and the rate schedule therefore turns on both the amount inherited and the heir's other income.

All three traditional types of inheritance taxes have their advantages and have been proposed by a number of commentators [25]. Nevertheless, a comprehensive inheritance tax would be the best approach. Under the current income tax rate schedule, an inclusion tax would result in lower tax burdens on the largest inheritances and thus would be less effective at mitigating the effects of extraordinary large inheritances. Both an inclusion tax and an annual inheritance tax would permit extensive gaming by applying much lower rates if inheritances are spread out over an heir's lifetime. Finally, an annual inheritance tax and accessions tax would not link the tax rate to the ability to pay of the heir, who might have very little earning potential due to a disability or other condition. A comprehensive inheritance tax essentially combines the best features of all three.

Potential Concerns and Responses

Replacing the estate tax system with a different tax system should raise a number of concerns. While the estate tax system is a rough tool for mitigating disparities in inherited income, it is reasonably effective nonetheless. The fairness advantages of a comprehensive inheritance tax should be weighed against the costs of enacting such far- reaching reform. On balance, my view is that these costs are worth the benefits of a more equitable system. Moreover, a comprehensive inheritance tax has advantages along other dimensions by reducing incentives in the current system to engage in costly and complicated tax planning.

Family Farms and Other Illiquid Assets. One concern that may arise is the effect of a comprehensive inheritance tax on family-owned businesses and other illiquid assets. All of the current relief provisions for such property, and others, could be part of a comprehensive inheritance tax.

Given the tendency of this issue to dominate discussion of wealth transfer taxes, one idea worth consideration is replacing the current relief provisions with a single one that would completely eliminate the possibility that an heir would need to sell an inherited family business immediately in order to pay the associated tax liability. This could be accomplished by providing that, to the extent that the tax due on inherited assets exceeded the liquid assets an heir inherited, the heir could defer the tax due on his inherited illiquid assets with interest at a market rate until he sold them. This would eliminate disincentives and (unlike current law) incentives to hold wealth in illiquid forms. However, the advisability of this relief provision would depend critically on it charging interest on any deferred tax, and at a market rate.

State Wealth Transfer Taxes. A second potential concern is the effect of a comprehensive inheritance tax on state wealth transfer taxes and revenue sharing. Prior to 2005 (and under 2011 law and thereafter), the federal government effectively shared estate tax revenues with the states through a wealth transfer tax credit. Under a comprehensive inheritance tax, this and any other form of revenue sharing could also be replicated.

Moreover, if full federal revenue sharing were not reinstated, a comprehensive inheritance tax could leave states freer to retain wealth transfer taxes if they so wish. States would likely act to conform their wealth transfer tax to the inheritance tax model in order to piggyback on the new federal reporting requirements, as they did under the federal estate tax credit (even the states that had an inheritance tax). Because it is generally easier for a retired individual to move to a state with no estate tax than it is for all of her potential heirs to move to states without inheritance taxes, such a shift could reduce the pressure on states to eliminate wealth transfer taxes when competing for wealthy residents.

Giving Patterns and Charitable Contributions. A third potential concern is the effect of shifting to a comprehensive inheritance tax on giving patterns and charitable transfers. While such a shift should not have a large effect on the magnitude of wealth transfers if implemented on a revenue-neutral basis, it could change the identity of individuals receiving inheritances and the amount of charitable contributions.

A comprehensive inheritance tax should induce donors to give slightly more broadly, especially to lower-income heirs or those to whom the donor would not have given previously. These incentives would arise because the tax rate would turn in part on the heir's income tax rate, and because transfers to additional heirs would be exempt if below the heir's remaining lifetime exemption. How much donors would respond to these changed incentives is unclear. Nevertheless, to the extent donors did respond, the fairness benefits of the reform would be magnified as it would further narrow disparities in inherited income. Notably, neither of these incentives exists under current law. A wealthy donor can give to 100 heirs or 1, to Paris Hilton or a foster child, and the tax rate is unaffected.

On the other hand, the reform could affect charitable bequests. In some respects, it would strengthen incentives for charitable giving. For example, contributions to nonprofits that are ineligible for the charitable deduction under the income and estate taxes (e.g., 501(c)(4)s) would be tax-exempt. But the fact that the donor could potentially make more tax-free transfers by giving to more individuals might weaken incentives to make charitable transfers on net. Once again, how much donors would respond to these changed incentives is unclear [27]. To the extent that donors did make fewer charitable transfers, however, it would generally be because they were spreading their wealth transfers out over more individuals.

Administrability and Transition Costs. A fourth potential concern is that replacing the estate tax system with a comprehensive inheritance tax would entail unacceptably high transition costs, or result in an unadministrable system. Experience in other jurisdictions suggests that a comprehensive inheritance tax would be administrable. Each element of the tax has been implemented at a state level or in other countries. Indeed, seven U.S. states have some type of inheritance tax in place, and Figure 10 shows that inheritance taxes are much more common than estate taxes cross-nationally.

Moreover, shifting from the estate tax system to a comprehensive inheritance tax would not require reinventing the wheel. A valuable infrastructure of legal rules and administrative practices has arisen under the estate tax, all of which help to prevent evasion and to promote compliance. Virtually all of these rules and practices could be retained. For example, the existing rules governing when a transfer has occurred, how it is valued, and what transfers are taxable could remain unchanged.

Any large shift in tax policy can result in transition winners and losers. This tendency could be minimized by making the new tax fully effective (with no look-backs) on a date before enactment, such as the date the bill was introduced. Ireland, which is the only jurisdiction I have identified that moved directly from an estate tax to an inheritance tax, applied these transition rules. This approach would limit gaming around the transition by preventing donors from making transfers up to the lifetime gift tax exemption once enactment appears likely. It would also be reasonably equitable. Most individuals receive only one substantial inheritance over their lifetime so disregarding prior inheritances and estate taxes should have little effect. For example, among those who receive a bequest greater than $1.7 million, on average that bequest represents 94 percent of their lifetime inheritances to date.

Compliance Costs and Tax Planning. Finally, one might worry that moving to a comprehensive inheritance tax would increase compliance costs and tax planning after the transition. A wealth transfer tax system can impose direct compliance costs on taxpayers, for example, by requiring them to spend multiple hours reading instructions and filing returns. It also may impose indirect compliance burdens—which are typically more costly—by creating incentives to engage in gaming and tax planning by structuring transfers in ways that are economically identical but taxed more lightly.

If anything, a comprehensive inheritance tax would likely reduce gaming and tax planning incentives relative to the current system for three general reasons. First, it would eliminate the need for careful planning of spousal transfers. Currently spouses can reduce their joint tax liability by making sure that each transfers to their heirs an amount equal to the lifetime exemption, for example, through a credit shelter trust. Some well-advised wealthy donors take advantage of this opportunity; others do not. But under a comprehensive inheritance tax, it would not matter which spouse transfers what. Any tax would be based on the amount the heir receives, regardless of whether it was from the mother or father.

Second, the comprehensive inheritance tax outlined would significantly narrow the current substantial differences in how gifts and bequests are taxed. Unlike the current estate and gift taxes, the same lifetime exemption and the tax rate would apply to the pretax inheritance. Additional features worth consideration could further narrow these differences. For example, indexing the lifetime exemption to inflation would reduce the incentive to transfer (or appear to transfer) wealth earlier in time, when the present value of the exemption is higher. Replacing stepped-up basis for bequests with carryover basis would eliminate the incentive to hold on to appreciated assets until death in order to eliminate the capital gains tax liability—and ensure that all capital income is taxed once regardless of the donor's access to sophisticated tax advice. The associated compliance costs would be minimized if stepped-up basis still applied to bequeathed assets worth less than a certain amount (e.g., $10,000) and not held for the production of income (e.g., jewelry and furniture). Moreover, given that Germany, Japan and Australia have successfully applied carryover basis to bequests, it should be administrable [28].

Finally, moving to a comprehensive inheritance tax would permit a different and simpler method for taxing split or contingent transfers made, for instance, through trusts. In particular, the new tax system could wait to see who gets what before taxing transfers for which the taxable status of the beneficiary is unclear. In the meantime, it could impose a withholding tax. When an heir eventually received his inheritance, he would receive a refund if the amount withheld on his share of the funds was more in present- value terms than the tax he actually owed (using an interest rate equal to the rate of return earned on the transferred assets). Family-owned businesses and other illiquid assets could be treated in a manner I describe below. Essentially, this approach would be economically equivalent to the tax system having perfect foresight regarding which potential beneficiaries will receive what.

This approach would reduce current tax incentives to engage in valuation games. While it would create more valuation points, it would limit incentives to try to shift value to tax-exempt spouses and charities when the ultimate beneficiary is unclear by waiting to see how much is received by whom. As a result, a wide swath of current rules could be eliminated. Indeed, the current rules to address valuation games—including those governing marital trusts, charitable trusts, grantor trusts, and Crummey trusts—compose one-quarter of a leading casebook [29]. An estate tax system cannot adopt this wait-and-see approach. Because its tax rate is based on the amount transferred and not on the amount received, it has to be levied at the time of transfer.

The advantages of shifting to a comprehensive inheritance tax with respect to tax planning should only be partially offset by changes in direct compliance costs. A comprehensive inheritance tax would probably result in about twice as many taxable returns because there are more heirs than estates and the tax filer would be the heir. If it entailed a $1.9 million lifetime exemption and 15 percent surtax, however, there would only be about 13,000 taxable returns annually. The more important source of new direct compliance costs would be information reporting requirements as heirs and donors should have to report (but not pay tax on) gifts and bequests falling above the annual exclusions but below the lifetime exemption.

The reduction in tax planning costs under a comprehensive inheritance tax should substantially exceed any new information reporting and filing costs. Moreover, this reduction should be mirrored at the governmental level. With fewer rules to enforce and fewer tax planning strategies to address, administrative burdens should decline.

A comprehensive inheritance tax would thus strengthen the ability of the estate tax system to achieve its underlying goals with fairly limited downsides. It would be more effective at reducing disparities in inherited income. The tax rate would be based on the ability to pay of the person predominantly bearing the tax: the heir. It could also enhance efficiency and tax simplification. Finally, it would make the income tax more equitable by adopting a more comprehensive measure of the taxpayer's receipts.

Estate Tax Reform

Replacing the estate tax system with a comprehensive inheritance tax has many advantages that cannot be achieved by reforming the current system. Inherently, the estate tax system can only roughly target the unearned income that inheritances represent because the tax rate is based on the amount transferred. It cannot link the tax rate to the amount inherited or to the earnings capacity of the heir. Indeed, even if donors received additional exemptions based on the number of children they have, the estate tax system would not be better targeted on inherited income because the number of donor children is actually a poor proxy for the total number of the donor's heirs and their economic circumstances [30]

Nevertheless, there are a number of ways in which the estate tax system could be improved if replacing it with an inheritance tax is considered too ambitious. In particular, several of the simplification benefits of a comprehensive inheritance tax that I have discussed could be replicated within the estate tax system. Adopting these simplification options and others would better focus the current system on the amount transferred, and limit the extent to which the tax burden depends on the donor's access to sophisticated tax advice. This, in turn, should make the current system better targeted on inherited income because the amount a donor transfers is a proxy, albeit an imperfect one, for the heir's inherited income.

Five simplification options worth consideration are as follows. Each could be adopted on a revenue-neutral basis, and the rate structure could be adjusted to ensure that adoption does not alter the distribution of tax burdens in aggregate.

- . First, and most importantly, the tax rate on wealth transfers over the next several years should be smoothed in order to limit tax planning. The dramatic changes to the top marginal tax rate and exemption amount create incentives for donors and heirs to spend enormous amounts of time and resources making it appear that a gift or bequest occurred in a low-tax year.
- • Second, the benefits of a comprehensive inheritance tax with respect to spousal tax planning could be replicated by permitting a surviving spouse to use any unused lifetime exemption of his or her deceased spouse. Then the tax rate on an inheritance would not depend on whether the donor couple was savvy enough to split their transfers or use spousal trusts in order take full advantage of their lifetime exemptions.
- Third, the complex relief provisions for family-owned businesses could be simplified and made more efficient if replaced with a single new relief provision for all illiquid assets. Specifically, to the extent that the tax due on illiquid assets exceeded the liquid assets that an heir inherited, he could be allowed to defer the tax due with interest at a market rate until he sold the illiquid assets. Such a provision might address concerns about the forced sale of family-owned businesses more effectively even if, as the evidence suggests, no such forced sale has ever occurred [31]. In

addition, if the interest rate were set correctly, it would eliminate both incentives and disincentives to hold wealth in illiquid forms. It is only worth consideration, however, if interest were applied and at a market rate. Otherwise, it could result in substantial gaming by sophisticated donors and heirs who do not need protection.

- Fourth, replacing stepped-up basis for bequests with carryover basis would remove one of the most common traps for the unwary. Many elderly investors sell underperforming appreciated assets without realizing that, in doing so, they are reducing the value of their estate by paying the associated capital gains tax liability. Under current law, the tax due can be avoided forever if the donor instead bequeaths the asset and the heir sells it.
- Finally, the countervailing incentives to inherit wealth transfers as gifts under current law could be mitigated through several changes. Indexing the lifetime exemption to inflation would reduce the incentive to receive inheritances earlier in time when the present value of the exemption is higher. Applying the gift tax on a tax-inclusive basis (like the estate tax) and unifying the gift tax and estate tax lifetime exemptions would further limit tax planning. In addition, reducing the annual gift tax exclusion would limit the incentive to set up complicated tax planning vehicles, such as Crummey trusts, in order to take advantage of each year's exemption.

IV. Conclusion

Inherited income tends to exacerbate existing economic disparities and may be the most important barrier to intergenerational economic mobility. As a result, any equitable tax system should account for whether a household has inherited an extraordinarily large amount when allocating tax burdens. As Franklin D. Roosevelt declared: "inherited economic power is as inconsistent with the ideals of this generation, as inherited political power was inconsistent with the ideals of the generation which established our government" [32].

Presently, the estate tax system is the most important mechanism by which our fiscal system mitigates the effect of inheritances on economic disparities and intergenerational mobility. It is borne largely by a small number of heirs, and, on average, its burdens rise rapidly with the amount inherited. However, the relationship between the heir's financial circumstances and his or her estate tax burden is relatively imprecise. Some individuals who receive extraordinarily large inheritances bear little or no tax burden, while a small number who inherit relatively small amounts bear a substantial tax burden.

The scheduled repeal of the estate tax in 2010 and reinstatement at higher levels in 2011 create an opportunity to better focus the estate tax system on the unearned income that inheritances represent—an opportunity that should not be missed. One reform option worth consideration is simplifying the estate tax system so that it better targets the amount transferred as a proxy for the amount inherited. An even better option would be to replace it with a comprehensive inheritance tax that directly taxes extraordinary amounts of inherited income at the same or higher rates than earned income.

Either way, we should use the upcoming opportunity for change—not to increase inherited economic power by repealing the estate tax or reducing the share of revenue it raises—but to reform it so as to tax inherited income in a more equitable way.

REFERENCES

[1] The views expressed in this testimony are those of the author alone and do not necessarily represent those of NYU School of Law. Portions of this testimony draw upon Lily L. Batchelder, Taxing Privilege More Effectively: Replacing the Estate Tax with an Inheritance Tax, in THE PATH TO PROSPERITY: HAMILTON PROJECT IDEAS ON INCOME SECURITY, EDUCATION AND TAXES (Jason Furman and Jason Bordoff, eds.) (Brookings Institution Press, forthcoming), Lily L. Batchelder and Surachai Khitatrakun, Dead or Alive: An Investigation of the Incidence of Estate Taxes versus Inheritance Taxes (work-in-progress), and Lily L. Batchelder, Taxing Privilege More Effectively: Replacing the Estate Tax with an Inheritance Tax, BROOKINGS INST. HAMILTON PROJECT DISCUSSION PAPER 2007-07 (June, 2007). My co-author also should not be held responsible for the views expressed in this testimony.

[2] This is the case regardless of whether economic income is defined as income from work and saving plus the amount inherited, one-fifth of the amount inherited, or the annuitized value of the amount inherited.

[3] Unless otherwise noted, all estimates in this testimony are based on 2009 law and data, and are derived from Batchelder and Khitatrakun, supra note 1, or Batchelder (2008), *supra note* 1. These estimates are very rough because of data limitations that require multiple levels of imputation and because they rely in part on data from 1992.

[4] Including taxable gifts made by the donor during life would increase the $400 billion figure by an unclear amount. Taxable gifts exclude gifts to spouses and charities, support expenses for minor children, payments for education or health care, and, currently, the first $12,000 in otherwise taxable gifts to a given beneficiary each year ($24,000 per couple). Taxable gifts comprise about 15 percent of the lifetime wealth transfers of donors taxed under the estate tax system. However, the likelihood that a donor will make a taxable gift rises dramatically if the donor is exceptionally wealthy. David Joulfaian & Kathleen McGarry *Estate and Gift Tax Incentives and Inter Vivos Giving,* 57 NAT'L TAX J. 429, 439 tbl.5 (June, 2004)

[5] James B Davies & Anthony F. Shorrocks, The Distribution of Wealth, in HANDBOOK OF INCOME DISTRIBUTION (Anthony B. Atkinson and Francois Bourguignon, eds.) (2001); Wojciech Kopczuk & Joseph P. Lupton, *To Leave or Not to Leave: The Distribution of Bequest Motives*, 74 REV. ECON. 207, note 2 (2007).

[6] Thomas Piketty, *Theories of Persistent Inequality and Intergenerational Mobility,* in HANDBOOK OF INCOME DISTRIBUTION §§ 2.1, 3 (A. Atkinson and F. Bourguignon, eds., 1998). For example, half of sons of fathers in the bottom income decile have earnings below the 30th percentile, while half of sons of fathers in the top decile have earnings above the 80th percentile. Bhashkar Mazumder, *The Apple Falls Even Closer to the Tree than We Thought: New and Revised Estimates of the Intergenerational Inheritance of Earnings*, in UNEQUAL CHANCES: FAMILY BACKGROUND AND ECONOMIC SUCCESS 80 (Samuel Bowles et al, eds., 2005).

[7] Tom Hertz, *Rags, Riches and Race*: *The Intergenerational Economic Mobility of Black and White Families in the United States*, in UNEQUAL CHANCES: FAMILY BACKGROUND AND ECONOMIC SUCCESS 165, 184 (Samuel Bowles et al, eds., 2005).

[8] Samuel Bowles, et al, *Introduction* 1, 18-19, in UNEQUAL CHANCES: FAMILY BACKGROUND AND ECONOMIC SUCCESS 1, 20 (Samuel Bowles et al, eds., 2005).

[9] Id.; Piketty, *supra note* 5; Mazumder, *supra note* 5 at 94

[10] Id. tbls. 2.1 & 2.5 at 31, 45 (2008). Federal revenues include on-budget and off-budget receipts.

[11] In 2006, the estate tax raised $24.653 billion, the gift tax $ 1.628 billion and the generation-skipping transfer tax $0.126 billion. Internal Revenue Service, Statistics on Income, *Estate Tax Returns By Tax Status and Size of Gross Estate,* 2006, available at http://www.irs.gov/pub/irs-

soi/06es01fy.xls; Internal Revenue Service, Statistics on Income, Total Gifts of Donor, Total Gifts, Deductions, Credits, and Net Gift Tax, 2006, available at http://www.irs.gov/pub/irs-soi/06gf01gr.xls.

[12] Office of Management and Budget, Historical Tables, Budget of the United States Government, FY2008, tbl. 2.5 at 45 (2008).

[13] This is because the estate tax serves as an important "backstop" to the income and gift taxes; the Joint Committee on Taxation estimates that estate tax repeal would also lead to income and gift tax revenue losses. See *Joint Committee on Taxation, History, Present Law and Analysis of the Federal Wealth Transfer Tax System* (JCX 108-07) (Nov. 13, 2007); NONA A. NOTTO, ESTATE AND GIFT TAX REVENUES: PAST AND PROJECTED 13 (Congressional Research Service Report for Congress, Aug. 24, 2007).

[14] Even if all donors respond to wealth transfer taxes by increasing their consumption, they may still bear some burden to the extent they value the after-tax amount their heirs receive. However, a surprisingly large share of wealth transfers appear to stem from the donor saving for reasons unrelated to their heirs. Recent studies estimate that these other motives for accumulating wealth that is bequeathed (e.g., precautionary saving for retirement expenses) account for the vast majority of bequests. See e.g., Wojciech Kipczuk & Joseph P. Lupton, *To Leave or Not to Leave: The Distribution of Bequest Motives*, 74 REV. ECON. 207 (2007); John Laitner & F. Thomas Juster, New Evidence of Altruism: A Study of TIAA-CREF Retirees, 86 AM. ECON. REV. 893 (Sept., 2006). In a review of the empirical literature, Douglas Holtz-Eakin concluded that there is no single "smoking gun" explanation for why donors accumulate wealth that is bequeathed, including the explanation that the donor values how much his or her heirs receives. Douglas Holtz-Eakin, *The Uneasy Empirical Case for Abolishing the Estate Tax*, 51 TAX L. REV. 495, 511 (1996).

[15] See David Joulfaian, The Behavioral Response of Wealth Accumulation to Estate Taxation: Time Series Evidence, 59 NAT'L TAX J. 253 (June, 2006); Wojciech Kopczuk & Joel Slemrod, *The Impact of the Estate Tax on Wealth Accumulation and Avoidance Behavior*, in RETHINKING ESTATE AND GIFT TAXATION 299 (William G. Gale, James R. Hines Jr., and Joel Slemrod, eds, 2001) . Kopczuk and Slemrod note any negative relationship between the size of reported estates and the estate tax rate may reflect evasion activity, rather than a change in the amount transferred.

[16] Gregory N. Mankiw, Remarks by Dr. N. Gregory Mankiw, Chairman, Council of Economic Advisers at the National Bureau of Economic

Research Tax Policy and the Economy Meeting (Washington DC: National Press Club) (Nov. 4, 2003), available at http://www.whitehouse.gov/cea/NPressClub20031104.html.

[17] In Figure 4, economic income includes the heir's income from work and saving, and the amount the heir inherits which is spread over five years in order to account for the fact that inheritances typically are not received in equal amounts every year. The figure looks directionally similar if the inheritance is spread over the heir's remaining life expectancy instead.

[18] The exclusion is inflation-adjusted so it may rise above $12,000 after 2008.

[19] For estates between $1 million and $3 million, the marginal tax rate rises from 41% to 55%. For estates above $3 million, the marginal tax rate generally is 55%. However a surtax that eliminates the lower brackets technically results in an effective marginal tax rate of 60% on taxable estates between $10 million and $17.184 million.

[20] Author's calculations based on a 7 percent interest rate and U.S. Census Bureau, Current Population Survey 1968 to 2006 Annual Social and Economic Supplements tbl. A-3, available at www.census.gov/hhes/www/income/histinc/p60no231_tablea3.pdf.

[21] The estimates are very rough due to data limitations, outdated data, and the assumption of no behavioral response to the tax. To the extent that donors respond to the different incentives created by the tax, it is likely that the revenue-neutral exemption would be lower and, as discussed below, that disparities in inherited income on a pre-tax basis would be narrower.

[22] Joint Committee on Taxation, *supra note* 12, tbl.5 at 29.

[23] Inherited income should be spread over prior years in order to limit incentives for the heir to work less in order to obtain a lower tax rate.

[24] For example, consider two taxable estates of $9 million where the donors have not made any prior gifts. Both would be subject to an average estate tax rate of 28 percent. However, one could be left entirely to one heir who is in the top income tax bracket and has received $1 million in prior inheritances, while the other could be left pro rata to six heirs with no prior inheritances. In the former case, the inheritance tax rate would be 45%, but in the latter it would be zero. As a further example taking the opposite perspective, suppose two heirs both have economic income of $1.2 million if one-fifth of bequests are included when measuring economic income. One might have earned $200,000 in income and inherited $5 million from an estate worth $5 million. The other might have the same amount of earned income and inheritance, but have inherited from an estate worth $30 million. Both would bear the same inheritance tax burden of 31 percent. But

the estate tax rate on the former would be 14 percent while the latter's would be 40 percent. In aggregate, if there were roughly the same amount of heirs of both types, the estate and inheritance tax rates would be quite similar, but at an individual level, their tax rates would vary dramatically.

[25] Each point represents an heir and each circle represents multiple heirs. Along the y-axis are heirs who are burdened only the inheritance tax, and along the x-axis are heirs who are burdened only by the estate tax. Every point in between represents the 30 percent of burdened heirs, who account for 90 percent of the revenue, and are burdened by both taxes. The correlation statistic for Figure 9 is 0.71. If the figure is not weighted by inheritance size, the correlation statistic is 0.33.

[26] See e.g., Anne L. Alstott, Equal Opportunity and Inheritance Taxation, 121 HARV. L. REV. (2007); Maya MacGuineas & Ian Davidoff, Tax Inheritance, Not "Death", WASH. POST (July 4, 2006); Gary Becker, Should the Estate Tax Go?, (May 15, 2005), available at www.becker-posnerblog.com/archives/2005/05/should_the_esta.html; David G. Duff, *Taxing Inherited Wealth: A Philosophical Argument.* 6 CAN. J. L. AND JURISPRUDENCE 3 (1993); Joseph M. Dodge, Beyond Estate and Gift Tax Reform: Including Gifts and Bequests in Income, 91 HARV. L. REV. 1177 (1978); William D. Andrews, The Accessions Tax Proposal, 22 TAX L. REV. 589 (1967); HENRY C. SIMONS, PERSONAL INCOME TAXATION (1938); Franklin D. Roosevelt, Message to the Congress on Tax Revision (June 19, 1935), in Public Papers and Addresses of Franklin D. Roosevelt. Vol. 4. (1938); Edwin R. A. Seligman, "*A National Inheritance Tax,*" The New Republic (March 25, 1916).

[27] International Bureau of Fiscal Documentation, Asia-Pacific Tax Surveys (2006); International Bureau of Fiscal Documentation, European Tax Surveys (2006); HUGH J. AULT & BRIAN J. ARNOLD, COMPARATIVE INCOME TAXATION: A STRUCTURAL ANALYSIS (2nd ed., 2004); Ministry of Finance and Economy, Korean Taxation (2007), available at http://english.mofe.go.kr/issues/laws /financial_list.php?sect=laws_tax. The countries included are: Australia, Austria, Belgium, Bulgaria, Canada, Czech Republic, Denmark, Estonia, Finland, France Germany, Greece, Hungary, Iceland, Italy, Ireland, Japan, Korea, Lithuania, Luxembourg, Netherlands, New Zealand, Norway, Poland, Portugal, Russia, Serbia, Slovenia, Spain, Sweden, Switzerland, Turkey, U.K. and the U.S.

[28] Joint Committee on Taxation, *supra note* 12, at 45.

[29] Ault and Arnold, *supra note* 26, at 184.

[30] Paul R. Mcdaniel, James R. Repetti & Paul R. Caron, Federal Wealth Transfer Taxation (5th ed., 2003).

[31] Batchelder & Khitatrakun, *supra note* 1.

[32] For instance, neither the American Farm Bureau nor the New York Times has been able to identify a single instance of a family farm being sold to pay estate taxes. Michael J. Graetz & Ian Shapiro, Death By A Thousand Cuts: The Fight Over Taxing Inherited Wealth 126 (2005).

[33] Franklin D. Roosevelt, *Message to the Congress on Tax Revision* (June 19, 1935), in PUBLIC PAPERS AND ADDRESSES OF FRANKLIN D. ROOSEVELT. VOL. 4. (1938).

In: Estate and Gift Taxes
Editor: Clay B. Apperton

ISBN 978-1-60692-129-6

Chapter 5

ECONOMIC GROWTH AND TAX RELIEF RECONCILIATION ACT OF 2001*

TITLE I—INDIVIDUAL INCOME TAX RATE REDUCTIONS

Sec. 101. Reduction in Income Tax Rates for Individuals

(a) IN GENERAL.—Section 1 (relating to tax imposed) is amended 26 USC 1. by adding at the end the following new subsection:

"(i) RATE REDUCTIONS AFTER 2000.—

"(1) 10-PERCENT RATE BRACKET.—

"(A) IN GENERAL.—In the case of taxable years beginning after December 31, 2000—

(i) the rate of tax under subsections (a), (b), (c), and (d) on taxable income not over the initial bracket amount shall be 10 percent, and

(ii) the 15 percent rate of tax shall apply only to taxable income over the initial bracket amount but not over the maximum dollar amount for the 15-percent rate bracket.

"(B) INITIAL BRACKET AMOUNT.—For purposes of this paragraph, the initial bracket amount is—

(i) $14,000 ($12,000 in the case of taxable years beginning before January 1, 2008) in the case of subsection (a),

(ii) $10,000 in the case of subsection (b), and

* Excerpted from Public Law 107–16 107th Congress.

(iii) 1/2 the amount applicable under clause (i) (after adjustment, if any, under subparagraph (C)) in the case of subsections (c) and (d).

"(C) INFLATION ADJUSTMENT.—In prescribing the tables Applicability. under subsection (f) which apply with respect to taxable years beginning in calendar years after 2000—

(i) the Secretary shall make no adjustment to the initial bracket amount for any taxable year beginning before January 1, 2009,

(ii) the cost-of-living adjustment used in making adjustments to the initial bracket amount for any taxable year beginning after December 31, 2008, shall be determined under subsection (f)(3) by substituting '2007' for '1992' in subparagraph (B) thereof, and

(iii) such adjustment shall not apply to the amount referred to in subparagraph (B)(iii).

If any amount after adjustment under the preceding sentence is not a multiple of $50, such amount shall be rounded to the next lowest multiple of $50.

"(D) COORDINATION WITH ACCELERATION OF 10 PERCENT RATE BRACKET BENEFIT FOR 2001.—This paragraph shall not apply to any taxable year to which section 6428 applies.

"(2) REDUCTIONS IN RATES AFTER JUNE 30, 2001.—In the case of taxable years beginning in a calendar year after 2000, the corresponding percentage specified for such calendar year in the following table shall be substituted for the otherwise applicable tax rate in the tables under subsections (a), (b), (c), (d), and (e)

"In the case of taxable years beginning during calendar year:	**The corresponding percentages shall be substituted for the following percentages:**			
	28%	**31%**	**36%**	**39.6%**
2001	27.5%	30.5%	35.5%	39.1%
2002 and 2003	27.0%	30.0%	35.0%	38.6%
2004 and 2005	26.0%	29.0%	34.0%	37.6%
2006 and thereafter	25.0%	28.0%	33.0%	35.0%

"(3) ADJUSTMENT OF TABLES.—The Secretary shall adjust the tables prescribed under subsection (f) to carry out this subsection.".

(b) ACCELERATION OF 10 PERCENT RATE BRACKET BENEFIT FOR 2001.—

(1) IN GENERAL.—Subchapter B of chapter 65 (relating to abatements, credits, and refunds) is amended by adding at the end the following new section:

"Sec. 6428. Acceleration of 10 Percent Income Tax Rate Bracket Benefit for 2001

"(a) IN GENERAL.—In the case of an eligible individual, there shall be allowed as a credit against the tax imposed by chapter 1 for the taxpayer's first taxable year beginning in 2001 an amount equal to 5 percent of so much of the taxpayer's taxable income as does not exceed the initial bracket amount (as defined in section 1(i)(1)(B)).

"(b) LIMITATION BASED ON AMOUNT OF TAX.—The credit allowed by subsection (a) shall not exceed the excess (if any) of—

"(1) the sum of the regular tax liability (as defined in section 26(b)) plus the tax imposed by section 55, over

"(2) the sum of the credits allowable under part IV of subchapter A of chapter 1 (other than the credits allowable under subpart C thereof, relating to refundable credits).

"(c) ELIGIBLE INDIVIDUAL.—For purposes of this section, the term 'eligible individual' means any individual other than—

"(1) any estate or trust,

"(2) any nonresident alien individual, and

"(3) any individual with respect to whom a deduction under section 151 is allowable to another taxpayer for a taxable year beginning in the calendar year in which the individual's taxable year begins.

"(d) SPECIAL RULES.—

"(1) COORDINATION WITH ADVANCE REFUNDS OF CREDIT.—

"(C) IN GENERAL.—The amount of credit which would (but for this paragraph) be allowable under this section shall be reduced (but not below zero) by the aggregate refunds and credits made or allowed to the taxpayer under subsection (e). Any failure to so reduce the credit shall be treated as arising out of a mathematical or clerical error and assessed according to section 6213(b)(1).

"(D) JOINT RETURNS.—In the case of a refund or credit made or allowed under subsection (e) with respect to a joint return, half of such refund or credit shall be treated as having been made or allowed to each individual filing such return.

"(2) COORDINATION WITH ESTIMATED TAX.—The credit under this section shall be treated for purposes of section 6654(f) in the same manner as a credit under subpart A of part IV of subchapter A of chapter 1.

"(e) ADVANCE REFUNDS OF CREDIT BASED ON PRIOR YEAR DATA.—

"(1) IN GENERAL.—Each individual who was an eligible individual for such individual's first taxable year beginning in 2000 shall be treated as having made a payment against the tax imposed by chapter 1 for such first taxable year in an amount equal to the advance refund amount for such taxable year.

"(2) ADVANCE REFUND AMOUNT.—For purposes of paragraph (1), the advance refund amount is the amount that would have been allowed as a credit under this section for such first taxable year if this section (other than subsection (d) and this subsection) had applied to such taxable year.

"(3) TIMING OF PAYMENTS.—In the case of any overpayment attributable to this subsection, the Secretary shall, subject to the provisions of this title, refund or credit such overpayment as rapidly as possible and, to the extent practicable, before October 1, 2001. No refund or credit shall be made or allowed under this subsection after December 31, 2001.

"(4) NO INTEREST.—No interest shall be allowed on any overpayment attributable to this subsection.".

(2) CLERICAL AMENDMENT.—The table of sections for subchapter B of chapter 65 is amended by adding at the end the following new item:

(c) CONFORMING AMENDMENTS.—

(1) Subparagraph (B) of section 1(g)(7) is amended by 26 USC 1. striking "15 percent" in clause (ii)(II) and inserting "10 percent.".

(2) Section 1(h) is amended—

(A) by striking "28 percent" both places it appears in paragraphs (1)(A)(ii)(I) and (1)(B)(i) and inserting "25 percent", and

(B) by striking paragraph (13).

(3) Section 15 is amended by adding at the end the following new subsection:

"(f) RATE REDUCTIONS ENACTED BY ECONOMIC GROWTH AND TAX RELIEF RECONCILIATION ACT OF 2001.—This section shall not apply to any change in rates under subsection (i) of section 1 (relating to rate reductions after 2000).".

"(1) Section 531 is amended by striking "equal to" and all that follows and inserting "equal to the product of the highest rate of tax under section 1(c) and the accumulated taxable income.".

"(2) Section 541 is amended by striking "equal to" and all that follows and inserting "equal to the product of the highest rate of tax under section 1(c) and the undistributed personal holding company income.".

"(3) Section 3402(p)(1)(B) is amended by striking "7, 15, 28, or 31 percent" and inserting "7 percent, any percentage applicable to any of the 3 lowest income brackets in the table under section 1(c),".

"(4) Section 3402(p)(2) is amended by striking “15 percent”and inserting “10 percent”.

"(5) Section 3402(q)(1) is amended by striking “equal to 28 percent of such payment” and inserting “equal to the product of the third lowest rate of tax applicable under section 1(c) and such payment”.

"(6) Section 3402(r)(3) is amended by striking “31 percent”and inserting “the fourth lowest rate of tax applicable under section 1(c)”.

"(7) Section 3406(a)(1) is amended by striking “equal to 31 percent of such payment” and inserting “equal to the product of the fourth lowest rate of tax applicable under section 1(c) and such payment”.

"(8) Section 13273 of the Revenue Reconciliation Act of 1993 is amended by striking “28 percent” and inserting “the third lowest rate of tax applicable under section 1(c) of the Internal Revenue Code of 1986”.

(d) EFFECTIVE DATES.—

"(1) IN GENERAL.—Except as provided in paragraph (2), the amendments made by this section shall apply to taxable years beginning after December 31, 2000.

"(2) AMENDMENTS TO WITHHOLDING PROVISIONS.—The amendments made by paragraphs (6), (7), (8), (9), (10), and (11) of subsection (c) shall apply to amounts paid after the 60th day after the date of the enactment of this Act. References to income brackets and rates of tax in such paragraphs shall be applied without regard to section 1(i)(1)(D) of the Internal Revenue Code of 1986.

Sec. 102. Repeal of Phaseout of Personal Exemptions

(a) IN GENERAL.—Paragraph (3) of section 15 1(d) (relating to exemption amount) is amended by adding at the end the following new subparagraphs:

“(E) REDUCTION OF PHASEOUT.—

(1) IN GENERAL.—In the case of taxable years beginning after December 31, 2005, and before January 1, 2010, the reduction under subparagraph (A) shall be equal to the applicable fraction of the amount which would (but for this subparagraph) be the amount of such reduction.

(2) APPLICABLE FRACTION.—For purposes of clause (i), the applicable fraction shall be determined in accordance with the following table:

“For taxable years beginning in calendar year	The applicable fraction is
2006 and 2007	2⁄3
2008 and 2009	1⁄3.

"(F) TERMINATION.—This paragraph shall not apply to any taxable year beginning after December 31, 2009.".

(b) EFFECTIVE DATE.—The amendment made by this section shall apply to taxable years beginning after December 31, 2005.

Sec. 103. Phaseout of Overall Limitation on Itemized Deductions

(a) IN GENERAL.—Section 68 is amended by adding at the end the following new subsections:

"(f) PHASEOUT OF LIMITATION.—

"(1) IN GENERAL.—In the case of taxable years beginning after December 31, 2005, and before January 1, 2010, the reduction under subsection (a) shall be equal to the applicable fraction of the amount which would (but for this subsection) be the amount of such reduction.

"(2) APPLICABLE FRACTION.—For purposes of paragraph (1), the applicable fraction shall be determined in accordance with the following table:

"For taxable years beginning in calendar year	The applicable fraction is—
2006 and 2007	2⁄3
2008 and 2009	1⁄3.

"(g) TERMINATION.—This section shall not apply to any taxable year beginning after December 31, 2009.".

(b) EFFECTIVE DATE.—The amendment made by this section shall apply to taxable years beginning after December 31, 2005.

TITLE II—TAX BENEFITS RELATING TO CHILDREN

Sec. 201. Modifications to Child Tax Credit

(a) INCREASE IN PER CHILD AMOUNT.—Subsection (a) of section 24 (relating to child tax credit) is amended to read as follows:

"(a) ALLOWANCE OF CREDIT.—

(1) IN GENERAL.—There shall be allowed as a credit against the tax imposed by this chapter for the taxable year with respect to each qualifying child of the taxpayer an amount equal to the per child amount.

(2) PER CHILD AMOUNT.—For purposes of paragraph (1), the per child amount shall be determined as follows:

"In the case of any taxable year beginning in—	The per child amount is—
2001, 2002, 2003, or 2004	$ 600
2005, 2006, 2007, or 2008	700
2009	800
2010 or thereafter	1,000"

(b) CREDIT ALLOWED AGAINST ALTERNATIVE MINIMUM TAX.—

(1) IN GENERAL.—Subsection (b) of section 24 (relating to child tax credit) is amended by adding at the end the following new paragraph:

"(3) LIMITATION BASED ON AMOUNT OF TAX.—The credit allowed under subsection (a) for any taxable year shall not exceed the excess of—

"(A) the sum of the regular tax liability (as defined in section 26(b)) plus the tax imposed by section 55, over

"(B) the sum of the credits allowable under this subpart (other than this section) and section 27 for the taxable year.".

(2) CONFORMING AMENDMENTS.—

(A) The heading for section 24(b) is amended to read as follows: "LIMITATIONS.—".

(B) The heading for section 24(b)(1) is amended to read as follows: "LIMITATION BASED ON ADJUSTED GROSS INCOME.—".

(C) Section 24(d), as amended by subsection (c), is amended—

(i) by striking "section 26(a)" each place it appears and inserting "subsection (b)(3)", and

(ii) in paragraph (1)(B) by striking "aggregate amount of credits allowed by this subpart" and inserting "amount of credit allowed by this section".

(D) Paragraph (1) of section 26(a) is amended by inserting "(other than section 24)" after "this subpart".

(E) Subsection (c) of section 23 is amended by striking "and section 1400C" and inserting "and sections 24 and 1400C".

(F) Subparagraph (C) of section 25(e)(1) is amended by inserting ", 24," after "sections 23".

(G) Section 904(h) is amended by inserting "(other than section 24)" after "chapter".

(H) Subsection (d) of section 1400C is amended by inserting "and section 24" after "this section".

(c) REFUNDABLE CHILD CREDIT.—

(1) IN GENERAL.—So much of section 24(d) (relating to additional credit for families with 3 or more children) as precedes paragraph (2) is amended to read as follows:

"(d) PORTION OF CREDIT REFUNDABLE.—

"(1) IN GENERAL.—The aggregate credits allowed to a taxpayer under subpart C shall be increased by the lesser of—

"(A) the credit which would be allowed under this section without regard to this subsection and the limitation under section 26(a), or

"(B) the amount by which the amount of credit allowed by this section (determined without regard to this subsection) would increase if the limitation imposed by section 26(a) were increased by the greater of—

"(i) 15 percent (10 percent in the case of taxable years beginning before January 1, 2005) of so much of the taxpayer's earned income (within the meaning of section 32) which is taken into account in computing taxable income for the taxable year as exceeds $10,000, or

"(ii) in the case of a taxpayer with 3 or more qualifying children, the excess (if any) of—

"(I) the taxpayer's social security taxes for the taxable year, over

"(II) the credit allowed under section 32 for the taxable year.

The amount of the credit allowed under this subsection shall not be treated as a credit allowed under this subpart and shall reduce the amount of credit otherwise allowable under subsection (a) without regard to section 26(a).".

(2) INFLATION ADJUSTMENT.—Subsection (d) of section 24 is amended by adding at the end the following new paragraph:

"(4) INFLATION ADJUSTMENT.—In the case of any taxable year beginning in a calendar year after 2001, the $10,000 amount contained in paragraph (1)(B) shall be increased by an amount equal to—

"(A) such dollar amount, multiplied by

"(B) the cost-of-living adjustment determined under section 1(f)(3) for the calendar year in which the taxable year begins, determined by substituting 'calendar year 2000' for 'calendar year 1992' in subparagraph (B) thereof.

Any increase determined under the preceding sentence shall be rounded to the nearest multiple of $50.".

(3) CONFORMING AMENDMENT.—Section 32 is amended by striking subsection (n).

(d) ELIMINATION OF REDUCTION OF CREDIT TO TAXPAYER SUBJECT TO ALTERNATIVE MINIMUM TAX PROVISION.—Section 24(d) is amended—

(1) by striking paragraph (2), and

(2) by redesignating paragraphs (3) and (4) as paragraphs (2) and (3), respectively.

(e) EFFECTIVE DATES.—

(1) IN GENERAL.—Except as provided in paragraph (2), the amendments made by this section shall apply to taxable years beginning after December 31, 2000.

(2) SUBSECTION (b).—The amendments made by subsection (b) shall apply to taxable years beginning after December 31, 2001.

Sec. 202. Expansion of Adoption Credit and Adoption Assistance Programs

(a) IN GENERAL.—

(1) ADOPTION CREDIT.—Section 23(a)(1) (relating to allowance of credit) is amended to read as follows:

"(1) IN GENERAL.—In the case of an individual, there shall be allowed as a credit against the tax imposed by this chapter—

"(A) in the case of an adoption of a child other than a child with special needs, the amount of the qualified adoption expenses paid or incurred by the taxpayer, and

"(B) in the case of an adoption of a child with special needs, $10,000.''.

(2) ADOPTION ASSISTANCE PROGRAMS.—Section 137(a) (relating to adoption assistance programs) is amended to read as follows:

"(a) IN GENERAL.—Gross income of an employee does not include amounts paid or expenses incurred by the employer for adoption expenses in connection with the adoption of a child by an employee if such amounts are furnished pursuant to an adoption assistance program. The amount of the exclusion shall be—

"(1) in the case of an adoption of a child other than a child with special needs, the amount of the qualified adoption expenses paid or incurred by the taxpayer, and

"(2) in the case of an adoption of a child with special needs, $10,000.''.

(b) DOLLAR LIMITATIONS.—

(1) DOLLAR AMOUNT OF ALLOWED EXPENSES.—

(A) ADOPTION EXPENSES.—Section 23(b)(1) (relating to allowance of credit) is amended—

(i) by striking "$5,000'' and inserting "$10,000'',

(ii) by striking "($6,000, in the case of a child with special needs)'', and

(iii) by striking "subsection (a)'' and inserting "subsection (a)(1)(A)''.

(B) ADOPTION ASSISTANCE PROGRAMS.—Section 137(b)(1) (relating to dollar limitations for adoption assistance programs) is amended—

(i) by striking “$5,000'' and inserting “$10,000'', and

(ii) by striking “($6,000, in the case of a child with special needs)'', and

(iii) by striking “subsection (a)” and inserting “subsection (a)(1)”.

(2) PHASE-OUT LIMITATION.—

(A) ADOPTION EXPENSES.—Clause (i) of section 23(b)(2)(A) (relating to income limitation) is amended by striking “$75,000” and inserting “$150,000”.

(B) ADOPTION ASSISTANCE PROGRAMS.—Section 137(b)(2)(A) (relating to income limitation) is amended by striking “$75,000” and inserting “$150,000”.

(c) YEAR CREDIT ALLOWED.—Section 23(a)(2) (relating to year credit allowed) is amended by adding at the end the following new flush sentence:

“In the case of the adoption of a child with special needs, the credit allowed under paragraph (1) shall be allowed for the taxable year in which the adoption becomes final.”.

(d) REPEAL OF TERMINATIONS.—

(1) CHILDREN WITHOUT SPECIAL NEEDS.—Paragraph (2) of section 23(d) (relating to definition of eligible child) is amended to read as follows:

“(2) ELIGIBLE CHILD.—The term ‘eligible child’ means any individual who—

"(A) has not attained age 18, or

"(B) is physically or mentally incapable of caring for himself.”.

(2) ADOPTION ASSISTANCE PROGRAMS.—Section 137 (relating to adoption assistance programs) is amended by striking subsection (f).

(e) ADJUSTMENT OF DOLLAR AND INCOME LIMITATIONS FOR INFLATION.—

(1) ADOPTION CREDIT.—Section 23 (relating to adoption expenses) is amended by redesignating subsection (h) as subsection (i) and by inserting after subsection (g) the following new subsection:

“(h) ADJUSTMENTS FOR INFLATION.—In the case of a taxable year beginning after December 31, 2002, each of the dollar amounts in subsection (a)(1)(B) and paragraphs (1) and (2)(A)(i) of subsection (b) shall be increased by an amount equal to—

"(1) such dollar amount, multiplied by

"(2) the cost-of-living adjustment determined under section 1(f)(3) for the calendar year in which the taxable year begins, determined by substituting ‘calendar year 2001’ for ‘calendar year 1992’ in subparagraph (B) thereof.”.

(2) ADOPTION ASSISTANCE PROGRAMS.—Section 137 (relating to adoption assistance programs), as amended by subsection (d), is amended by adding at the end the following new subsection:

"(f) ADJUSTMENTS FOR INFLATION.—In the case of a taxable year beginning after December 31, 2002, each of the dollar amounts in subsection (a)(2) and paragraphs (1) and (2)(A) of subsection (b) shall be increased by an amount equal to—

"(1) such dollar amount, multiplied by

"(2) the cost-of-living adjustment determined under section 1(f)(3) for the calendar year in which the taxable year begins, determined by substituting 'calendar year 2001' for 'calendar year 1992' in subparagraph (B) thereof.".

(f) CREDIT ALLOWED AGAINST ALTERNATIVE MINIMUM TAX.—
(1) IN GENERAL.—Subsection (b) of section 23 is amended by adding at the end the following new paragraph:

"(4) LIMITATION BASED ON AMOUNT OF TAX.—The credit allowed under subsection (a) for any taxable year shall not exceed the excess of—

"(A) the sum of the regular tax liability (as defined in section 26(b)) plus the tax imposed by section 55, over

"(B) the sum of the credits allowable under this subpart (other than this section) and section 27 for the taxable year.".

(2) CONFORMING AMENDMENTS.—

(A) Section 23(c), as amended by section 20 1(b), is amended—

(i) by striking "section 26(a)" and inserting "subsection (b)(4)", and

(ii) by striking "reduced by the sum of the credits allowable under this subpart (other than this section and sections 24 and 1400C)".

(B) Section 24(b)(3)(B), as added by section 201(b), is amended by striking "this section" and inserting "this section and section 23".

(C) Sections 26(a)(1), 904(h), and 1400C(d), as amended by section 20 1(b), are each amended by striking "section 24" and inserting "sections 23 and 24".

(g) EFFECTIVE DATE.—

(1) IN GENERAL.—Except as provided in paragraph (2), the amendments made by this section shall apply to taxable years beginning after December 31, 2001.

(2) SUBSECTION (a).—The amendments made by subsection (a) shall apply to taxable years beginning after December 31, 2002.

Sec. 203. Refunds Disregarded in the Administration of Federal Programs and Federally Assisted Programs

Any payment considered to have been made to any individual by reason of section 24 of the Internal Revenue Code of 1986, as amended by section 201, shall not be taken into account as income and shall not be taken into account as resources for the month of receipt and the following month, for purposes of determining the eligibility of such individual or any other individual for benefits or assistance, or the amount or extent of benefits or assistance, under any Federal program or under any State or local program financed in whole or in part with Federal funds.

Sec. 204. Dependent Care Credit

(a) INCREASE IN DOLLAR LIMIT.—Subsection (c) of section 21 (relating to expenses for household and dependent care services necessary for gainful employment) is amended—

(1) by striking "$2,400" in paragraph (1) and inserting "$3,000", and

(2) by striking "$4,800" in paragraph (2) and inserting "$6,000".

(b) INCREASE IN APPLICABLE PERCENTAGE.—Section 21(a)(2) (defining applicable percentage) is amended—

(1) by striking "30 percent" and inserting "35 percent", and

(2) by striking "$10,000" and inserting "$15,000"

(c) EFFECTIVE DATE.—The amendments made by this section shall apply to taxable years beginning after December 31, 2002.

Sec. 205. Allowance of Credit for Employer Expenses for Child Care Assistance

(a) IN GENERAL.—Subpart D of part IV of subchapter A of chapter 1 (relating to business related credits), as amended by section 619, is further amended by adding at the end the following:

"Sec. 45f. Employer-Provided Child Care Credit

"(a) IN GENERAL.—For purposes of section 38, the employer- provided child care credit determined under this section for the taxable year is an amount equal to the sum of—

"(1) 25 percent of the qualified child care expenditures, and

"(2) 10 percent of the qualified child care resource and referral expenditures,

of the taxpayer for such taxable year.

"(b) DOLLAR LIMITATION.—The credit allowable under subsection (a) for any taxable year shall not exceed $150,000.

"(c) DEFINITIONS.—For purposes of this section—

"(1) QUALIFIED CHILD CARE EXPENDITURE.—

"(A) IN GENERAL.—The term 'qualified child care expenditure' means any amount paid or incurred—

"(i) to acquire, construct, rehabilitate, or expand property—

"(I) which is to be used as part of a qualified child care facility of the taxpayer,

"(II) with respect to which a deduction for depreciation (or amortization in lieu of depreciation) is allowable, and

"(III) which does not constitute part of the principal residence (within the meaning of section 121) of the taxpayer or any employee of the taxpayer,

"(ii) for the operating costs of a qualified child care facility of the taxpayer, including costs related to the training of employees, to scholarship programs, and to the providing of increased compensation to employees with higher levels of child care training, or

"(iii) under a contract with a qualified child care facility to provide child care services to employees of the taxpayer.

"(B) FAIR MARKET VALUE.—The term 'qualified child care expenditures' shall not include expenses in excess of the fair market value of such care.

"(2) QUALIFIED CHILD CARE FACILITY.—

"(A) IN GENERAL.—The term 'qualified child care facility' means a facility—

"(i) the principal use of which is to provide child care assistance, and

"(ii) which meets the requirements of all applicable laws and regulations of the State or local government in which it is located, including the licensing of the facility as a child care facility.

Clause (i) shall not apply to a facility which is the principal residence (within the meaning of section 121) of the operator of the facility.

"(B) SPECIAL RULES WITH RESPECT TO A TAXPAYER.—

A facility shall not be treated as a qualified child care facility with respect to a taxpayer unless—

"(i) enrollment in the facility is open to employees of the taxpayer during the taxable year,

"(ii) if the facility is the principal trade or business of the taxpayer, at least 30 percent of the enrollees of such facility are dependents of employees of the taxpayer, and "(iii) the use of such facility (or the eligibility to use such facility) does not discriminate in favor of employees of the taxpayer who are highly compensated employees (within the meaning of section 4 14(q)).

"(3) QUALIFIED CHILD CARE RESOURCE AND REFERRAL EXPENDITURE.—

(A) IN GENERAL.—The term 'qualified child care resource and referral expenditure' means any amount paid or incurred under a contract to provide child care resource and referral services to an employee of the taxpayer.

(B) NONDISCRIMINATION.—The services shall not be treated as qualified unless the provision of such services (or the eligibility to use such services) does not discriminate in favor of employees of the taxpayer who are highly compensated employees (within the meaning of section 4 14(q)).

"(d) RECAPTURE OF ACQUISITION AND CONSTRUCTION CREDIT.—

"(1) IN GENERAL.—If, as of the close of any taxable year, there is a recapture event with respect to any qualified child care facility of the taxpayer, then the tax of the taxpayer under this chapter for such taxable year shall be increased by an amount equal to the product of—

"(A) the applicable recapture percentage, and

"(B) the aggregate decrease in the credits allowed under section 38 for all prior taxable years which would have resulted if the qualified child care expenditures of the taxpayer described in subsection (c)(1)(A) with respect to such facility had been zero.

"(2) APPLICABLE RECAPTURE PERCENTAGE.—

"(A) IN GENERAL.—For purposes of this subsection, the applicable recapture percentage shall be determined from the following table:

"If the recapture event occurs in:	The applicable recapture percentage is:
Years 1–3	100
Year 4	85
Year 5	70
Year 6	55
Year 7	40
Year 8	25
Years 9 and 10	10
Years 11 and thereafter	0.

"(B) YEARS.—For purposes of subparagraph (A), year 1 shall begin on the first day of the taxable year in which the qualified child care facility is placed in service by the taxpayer

"(3) RECAPTURE EVENT DEFINED.—For purposes of this subsection, the term 'recapture event' means—

"(A) CESSATION OF OPERATION.—The cessation of the operation of the facility as a qualified child care facility.

"(B) CHANGE IN OWNERSHIP.—

"(i) IN GENERAL.—Except as provided in clause (ii), the disposition of a taxpayer's interest in a qualified child care facility with respect to which the credit described in subsection (a) was allowable.

"(ii) AGREEMENT TO ASSUME RECAPTURE LIABILITY.—Clause (i) shall not apply if the person acquiring such interest in the facility agrees in writing to assume the recapture liability of the person disposing of such interest in effect immediately before such disposition. In the event of such an assumption, the person acquiring the interest in the facility shall be treated as the taxpayer for purposes of assessing any recapture liability (computed as if there had been no change in ownership).

"(4) SPECIAL RULES.—

"(A) TAX BENEFIT RULE.—The tax for the taxable year shall be increased under paragraph (1) only with respect to credits allowed by reason of this section which were used to reduce tax liability. In the case of credits not so used to reduce tax liability, the carryforwards and carrybacks under section 39 shall be appropriately adjusted.

"(B) NO CREDITS AGAINST TAX.—Any increase in tax under this subsection shall not be treated as a tax imposed by this chapter for purposes of determining the amount of any credit under subpart A, B, or D of this part.

"(C) NO RECAPTURE BY REASON OF CASUALTY LOSS.—The increase in tax under this subsection shall not apply to a cessation of operation of the facility as a qualified child care facility by reason of a casualty loss to the extent such loss is restored by reconstruction or replacement within a reasonable period established by the Secretary.

"(e) SPECIAL RULES.—For purposes of this section—

"(1) AGGREGATION RULES.—All persons which are treated as a single employer under subsections (a) and (b) of section 52 shall be treated as a single taxpayer.

"(2) PASS-THRU IN THE CASE OF ESTATES AND TRUSTS.—

"(3) Under regulations prescribed by the Secretary, rules similar to the rules of subsection (d) of section 52 shall apply.

"(4) ALLOCATION IN THE CASE OF PARTNERSHIPS.—In the case of partnerships, the credit shall be allocated among partners under regulations prescribed by the Secretary.

"(f) NO DOUBLE BENEFIT.—

"(1) REDUCTION IN BASIS.—For purposes of this subtitle—

"(A) IN GENERAL.—If a credit is determined under this section with respect to any property by reason of expenditures described in subsection (c)(1)(A), the basis of such property shall be reduced by the amount of the credit so determined.

"(B) CERTAIN DISPOSITIONS.—If, during any taxable year, there is a recapture amount determined with respect to any property the basis of which was reduced under subparagraph (A), the basis of such property (immediately before the event resulting in such recapture) shall be increased by an amount equal to such recapture amount. For purposes of the preceding sentence, the term 'recapture amount' means any increase in tax (or adjustment in carrybacks or carryovers) determined under subsection (d).

"(2) OTHER DEDUCTIONS AND CREDITS.—No deduction or credit shall be allowed under any other provision of this chapter with respect to the amount of the credit determined under this section.".

(b) CONFORMING AMENDMENTS.—

(1) Section 38(b), as amended by section 619, is amended by striking "plus" at the end of paragraph (13), by striking the period at the end of paragraph (14) and inserting ", plus", and by adding at the end the following:

"(15) the employer-provided child care credit determined under section 45F.".

(2) The table of sections for subpart D of part IV of subchapter A of chapter 1 is amended by adding at the end the following:

"Sec. 45F. Employer-provided child care credit."

(3) Section 1016(a) is amended by striking "and" at the end of paragraph (26), by striking the period at the end of paragraph (27) and inserting ", and", and by adding at the end the following:

"(28) in the case of a facility with respect to which a credit was allowed under section 45F, to the extent provided in section 45F(f)(1).".

(c) EFFECTIVE DATE.—The amendments made by this section shall apply to taxable years beginning after December 31, 2001.

TITLE III—MARRIAGE PENALTY RELIEF

Sec. 301. Elimination of Marriage Penalty in Standard Deduction

(a) IN GENERAL.—Paragraph (2) of section 63(c) (relating to standard deduction) is amended—

(1) by striking "$5,000" in subparagraph (A) and inserting "the applicable percentage of the dollar amount in effect under subparagraph (C) for the taxable year";

(2) by adding "or" at the end of subparagraph (B);

(3) by striking "in the case of'' and all that follows in subparagraph (C) and inserting "in any other case."; and

(4) by striking subparagraph (D).

(b) APPLICABLE PERCENTAGE.—Section 63(c) (relating to standard deduction) is amended by adding at the end the following new paragraph:

"(7) APPLICABLE PERCENTAGE.—For purposes of paragraph (2), the applicable percentage shall be determined in accordance with the following table:

"For taxable years beginning in calendar year—	The applicable percentage is—
2005	174
2006	184
2007	187
2008	190
2009 and thereafter	200

(c) TECHNICAL AMENDMENTS.—

"(1) Subparagraph (B) of section 1(f)(6) is amended by striking "(other than with" and all that follows through "shall be applied" and inserting "(other than with respect to sections 63(c)(4) and 151(d)(4)(A)) shall be applied".

"(2) Paragraph (4) of section 63(c) is amended by adding at the end the following flush sentence:

"The preceding sentence shall not apply to the amount referred to in paragraph (2)(A).".

(d) EFFECTIVE DATE.—The amendments made by this section shall apply to taxable years beginning after December 31, 2004.

Sec. 302. Phaseout of Marriage Penalty in 15-Percent Bracket

(a) IN GENERAL.—Section 1(f) (relating to adjustments in tax tables so that inflation will not result in tax increases) is amended by adding at the end the following new paragraph:

"(8) PHASEOUT OF MARRIAGE PENALTY IN 15-PERCENT BRACKET.—

"(A) IN GENERAL.—With respect to taxable years beginning after December 31, 2004, in prescribing the tables under paragraph (1)—

"(i) the maximum taxable income in the 15-percent rate bracket in the table contained in subsection (a) (and the minimum taxable income in the next higher taxable income bracket in such table) shall be the applicable percentage of the maximum taxable income in the 15-percent rate bracket in the table contained in subsection (c) (after any other adjustment under this subsection), and

"(ii) the comparable taxable income amounts in the table contained in subsection (d) shall be 1⁄2 of the amounts determined under clause (i).

"(B) APPLICABLE PERCENTAGE.—For purposes of subparagraph (A), the applicable percentage shall be determined in accordance with the following table:

"For taxable years beginning in calendar year—	The applicable percentage is—
2005	180
2006	187
2007	193
2008 and thereafter	200.

"(C) ROUNDING.—If any amount determined under subparagraph (A)(i) is not a multiple of $50, such amount shall be rounded to the next lowest multiple of $50.".

(b) TECHNICAL AMENDMENTS.—

(1) Subparagraph (A) of section 1(f)(2) is amended by inserting "except as provided in paragraph (8)," before "by increasing".

(2) The heading for subsection (f) of section 1 is amended by inserting "PHASEOUT OF MARRIAGE PENALTY IN 15-PERCENT BRACKET;" before "ADJUSTMENTS".

(c) EFFECTIVE DATE.—The amendments made by this section shall apply to taxable years beginning after December 31, 2004

Sec. 303. Marriage Penalty Relief for Earned Income Credit; Earned Income to Include Only Amounts Includible in Gross Income; Simplification of Earned Income Credit

(a) INCREASED PHASEOUT AMOUNT.—

(1) IN GENERAL.—Section 32(b)(2) (relating to amounts) is amended—

(A) by striking "AMOUNTS.—The earned" and inserting "AMOUNTS.—

"(A) IN GENERAL.—Subject to subparagraph (B), the earned", and

(B) by adding at the end the following new subparagraph:

"(B) JOINT RETURNS.—In the case of a joint return filed by an eligible individual and such individual's spouse, the phaseout amount determined under subparagraph (A) shall be increased by—

"(i) $1,000 in the case of taxable years beginning in 2002, 2003, and 2004,

"(ii) $2,000 in the case of taxable years beginning in 2005, 2006, and 2007, and

"(iii) $3,000 in the case of taxable years beginning after 2007.".

(2) INFLATION ADJUSTMENT.—Paragraph (1)(B) of section 32(j) (relating to inflation adjustments) is amended to read as follows:

"(B) the cost-of-living adjustment determined under section 1(f)(3) for the calendar year in which the taxable year begins, determined—

"(i) in the case of amounts in subsections (b)(2)(A) and (i)(1), by substituting 'calendar year 1995' for 'calendar year 1992' in subparagraph (B) thereof, and

"(ii) in the case of the $3,000 amount in subsection (b)(2)(B)(iii), by substituting 'calendar year 2007' for 'calendar year 1992' in subparagraph (B) of such section 1.".

(3) ROUNDING.—Section 32(j)(2)(A) (relating to rounding) is amended by striking "subsection (b)(2)" and inserting "subsection (b)(2)(A) (after being increased under subparagraph (B) thereof)".

(b) EARNED INCOME TO INCLUDE ONLY AMOUNTS INCLUDIBLE IN GROSS INCOME.—Clause (i) of section 32(c)(2)(A) (defining earned income) is amended by inserting ", but only if such amounts are includible in gross income for the taxable year" after "other employee compensation".

(c) REPEAL OF REDUCTION OF CREDIT TO TAXPAYERS SUBJECT TO ALTERNATIVE MINIMUM TAX.—Section 32(h) is repealed.

(d) REPLACEMENT OF MODIFIED ADJUSTED GROSS INCOME WITH ADJUSTED GROSS INCOME.—

(1) IN GENERAL.—Section 32(a)(2)(B) is amended by striking "modified".

(2) CONFORMING AMENDMENTS.—

(A) Section 32(c) is amended by striking paragraph (5).

(B) Section 32(f)(2)(B) is amended by striking "modified" each place it appears.

(e) RELATIONSHIP TEST.—

(1) IN GENERAL.—Clause (i) of section 32(c)(3)(B) (relating to relationship test) is amended to read as follows:

"(i) IN GENERAL.—An individual bears a relationship to the taxpayer described in this subparagraph if such individual is—

"(I) a son, daughter, stepson, or stepdaughter, or a descendant of any such individual,

"(II) a brother, sister, stepbrother, or stepsister, or a descendant of any such individual, who the taxpayer cares for as the taxpayer's own child, or

"(III) an eligible foster child of the taxpayer.".

(2) ELIGIBLE FOSTER CHILD.—

(A) IN GENERAL.—Clause (iii) of section 32(c)(3)(B) is amended to read as follows:

"(iii) ELIGIBLE FOSTER CHILD.—For purposes of clause (i), the term 'eligible foster child' means an individual not described in subclause (I) or (II) of clause (i) who—

"(I) is placed with the taxpayer by an authorized placement agency, and

"(II) the taxpayer cares for as the taxpayer's own child.".

(B) CONFORMING AMENDMENT.—Section 32(c)(3)(A)(ii) is amended by striking "except as provided in subparagraph (B)(iii),".

(f) 2 OR MORE CLAIMING QUALIFYING CHILD.—Section 32(c)(1)(C) is amended to read as follows:

"(C) 2 OR MORE CLAIMING QUALIFYING CHILD.—

"(i) IN GENERAL.—Except as provided in clause (ii), if (but for this paragraph) an individual may be claimed, and is claimed, as a qualifying child by 2 or more taxpayers for a taxable year beginning in the same calendar year, such individual shall be treated as the qualifying child of the taxpayer who is—

"(I) a parent of the individual, or

"(II) if subclause (I) does not apply, the taxpayer with the highest adjusted gross income for such taxable year.

"(ii) MORE THAN 1 CLAIMING CREDIT.—If the parents claiming the credit with respect to any qualifying child do not file a joint return together, such child shall be treated as the qualifying child of—

"(I) the parent with whom the child resided for the longest period of time during the taxable year, or

"(II) if the child resides with both parents for the same amount of time during such taxable year, the parent with the highest adjusted gross income.".

(g) EXPANSION OF MATHEMATICAL ERROR AUTHORITY.—Paragraph (2) of section 6213(g) is amended by striking "and" at the end of subparagraph (K), by striking the period at the end of subparagraph (L) and inserting ", and", and by inserting after subparagraph (L) the following new subparagraph:

"(M) the entry on the return claiming the credit under section 32 with respect to a child if, according to the Federal Case Registry of Child Support Orders established under section 453(h) of the Social Security Act, the taxpayer is a noncustodial parent of such child.".

(h) CLERICAL AMENDMENT.—Subparagraph (E) of section 32(c)(3) is amended by striking "subparagraphs (A)(ii) and 26 USC 32. (B)(iii)(II)" and inserting "subparagraph (A)(ii)".

(i) EFFECTIVE DATES.—

(1) IN GENERAL.—Except as provided in paragraph (2), the Applicability. amendments made by this section shall apply to taxable years beginning after December 31, 2001.

(2) SUBSECTION (g).—The amendment made by subsection (g) shall take effect on January 1, 2004.

TITLE IV—AFFORDABLE EDUCATION PROVISIONS

Subtitle A—Education Savings Incentives

Sec. 401. Modifications to Education Individual Retirement Accounts

(a) MAXIMUM ANNUAL CONTRIBUTIONS.—

(1) IN GENERAL.—Section 530(b)(1)(A)(iii) (defining education individual retirement account) is amended by striking "$500" and inserting "$2,000".

(2) CONFORMING AMENDMENT.—Section 4973(e)(1)(A) is amended by striking "$500" and inserting "$2,000".

(b) MODIFICATION OF AGI LIMITS TO REMOVE MARRIAGE PENALTY.—Section 530(c)(1) (relating to reduction in permitted contributions based on adjusted gross income) is amended—

(1) by striking "$150,000" in subparagraph (A)(ii) and inserting "$190,000", and

(2) by striking “$10,000” in subparagraph (B) and inserting “$30,000”.

(c) TAX-FREE EXPENDITURES FOR ELEMENTARY AND SECONDARY SCHOOL EXPENSES.—

(1) IN GENERAL.—Section 530(b)(2) (defining qualified higher education expenses) is amended to read as follows:

“(2) QUALIFIED EDUCATION EXPENSES.—

“(A) IN GENERAL.—The term ‘qualified education expenses’ means—

"(i) qualified higher education expenses (as defined in section 529(e)(3)), and

"(ii) qualified elementary and secondary education expenses (as defined in paragraph (4)).

“(B) QUALIFIED STATE TUITION PROGRAMS.—Such term shall include any contribution to a qualified State tuition program (as defined in section 529(b)) on behalf of the designated beneficiary (as defined in section 529(e)(1)); but there shall be no increase in the investment in the contract for purposes of applying section 72 by reason of any portion of such contribution which is not includible in gross income by reason of subsection (d)(2).”

(2) QUALIFIED ELEMENTARY AND SECONDARY EDUCATION EXPENSES.—Section 530(b) (relating to definitions and special rules) is amended by adding at the end the following new paragraph:

“(4) QUALIFIED ELEMENTARY AND SECONDARY EDUCATION EXPENSES.—

“(A) IN GENERAL.—The term ‘qualified elementary and secondary education expenses’ means—

"(i) expenses for tuition, fees, academic tutoring, special needs services in the case of a special needs beneficiary, books, supplies, and other equipment which are incurred in connection with the enrollment or attendance of the designated beneficiary of the trust as an elementary or secondary school student at a public, private, or religious school,

"(ii) expenses for room and board, uniforms, transportation, and supplementary items and services (including extended day programs) which are required or provided by a public, private, or religious school in connection with such enrollment or attendance, and

"(iii) expenses for the purchase of any computer technology or equipment (as defined in section 170(e)(6)(F)(i)) or Internet access and related services, if such technology, equipment, or services are to be used by the beneficiary and the beneficiary’s family during any of the years the beneficiary is in school.

Clause (iii) shall not include expenses for computer software designed for sports, games, or hobbies unless the software is predominantly educational in nature.

"(B) SCHOOL.—The term 'school' means any school which provides elementary education or secondary education (kindergarten through grade 12), as determined under State law.".

(3) CONFORMING AMENDMENTS.—Section 530 is amended—

(A) by striking "higher" each place it appears in subsections (b)(1) and (d)(2), and

(B) by striking "HIGHER" in the heading for subsection (d)(2).

(d) WAIVER OF AGE LIMITATIONS FOR CHILDREN WITH SPECIAL NEEDS.—Section 530(b)(1) (defining education individual retirement account) is amended by adding at the end the following flush sentence:

"The age limitations in subparagraphs (A)(ii) and (E), and paragraphs (5) and (6) of subsection (d), shall not apply to any designated beneficiary with special needs (as determined under regulations prescribed by the Secretary).".

(e) ENTITIES PERMITTED TO CONTRIBUTE TO ACCOUNTS.—Section 530(c)(1) (relating to reduction in permitted contributions based on adjusted gross income) is amended by striking "The maximum amount which a contributor" and inserting "In the case of a contributor who is an individual, the maximum amount the contributor".

(f) TIME WHEN CONTRIBUTIONS DEEMED MADE.—

(1) IN GENERAL.—Section 530(b) (relating to definitions and special rules), as amended by subsection (c)(2), is amended by adding at the end the following new paragraph:

"(5) TIME WHEN CONTRIBUTIONS DEEMED MADE.—An individual shall be deemed to have made a contribution to an education individual retirement account on the last day of the preceding taxable year if the contribution is made on account of such taxable year and is made not later than the time prescribed by law for filing the return for such taxable year (not including extensions thereof).".

(2) EXTENSION OF TIME TO RETURN EXCESS CONTRIBUTIONS.—Subparagraph (C) of section 530(d)(4) (relating to addi 26 USC 530. tional tax for distributions not used for educational expenses) is amended—

(A) by striking clause (i) and inserting the following new clause:

"(i) such distribution is made before the first day of the sixth month of the taxable year following the taxable year, and", and

(B) by striking "DUE DATE OF RETURN" in the heading and inserting "CERTAIN DATE".

(g) COORDINATION WITH HOPE AND LIFETIME LEARNING CREDITS AND QUALIFIED TUITION PROGRAMS.—

(1) IN GENERAL.—Section 530(d)(2)(C) is amended to read as follows:

"(C) COORDINATION WITH HOPE AND LIFETIME LEARNING CREDITS AND QUALIFIED TUITION PROGRAMS.—For purposes of subparagraph (A)—

"(i) CREDIT COORDINATION.—The total amount of qualified higher education expenses with respect to an individual for the taxable year shall be reduced—

"(I) as provided in section 25A(g)(2), and

"(II) by the amount of such expenses which were taken into account in determining the credit allowed to the taxpayer or any other person under section 25A.

"(ii) COORDINATION WITH QUALIFIED TUITION PROGRAMS.—If, with respect to an individual for any taxable year—

"(I) the aggregate distributions during such year to which subparagraph (A) and section 529(c)(3)(B) apply, exceed

"(II) the total amount of qualified education expenses (after the application of clause (i)) for such year,

the taxpayer shall allocate such expenses among such distributions for purposes of determining the amount of the exclusion under subparagraph (A) and section 529(c)(3)(B).".

(2) CONFORMING AMENDMENTS.—

(A) Subsection (e) of section 25A is amended to read as follows:

"(e) ELECTION NOT TO HAVESECTION APPLY.—A taxpayer may elect not to have this section apply with respect to the qualified tuition and related expenses of an individual for any taxable year.".

(B) Section 135(d)(2)(A) is amended by striking "allowable" and inserting "allowed".

(C) Section 530(d)(2)(D) is amended—

(i) by striking "or credit" and inserting ", credit, or exclusion", and (ii) by striking "CREDIT OR DEDUCTION" in the heading and inserting "DEDUCTION, CREDIT, OR EXCLUSION".

(D) Section 4973(e)(1) is amended by adding "and"at the end of subparagraph (A), by striking subparagraph

(B), and by redesignating subparagraph (C) as subparagraph (B).

(h) EFFECTIVE DATE.—The amendments made by this section shall apply to taxable years beginning after December 31, 2001.

Sec. 402. Modifications to Qualified Tuition Programs

(a) ELIGIBLE EDUCATIONAL INSTITUTIONS PERMITTED TO MAINTAIN QUALIFIED TUITION PROGRAMS.—

(1) IN GENERAL.—Section 529(b)(1) (defining qualified State tuition program) is amended—

(A) by inserting "or by 1 or more eligible educational institutions" after "maintained by a State or agency or instrumentality thereof" in the matter preceding subparagraph (A), and

(B) by adding at the end the following new flush sentence:

"Except to the extent provided in regulations, a program established and maintained by 1 or more eligible educational institutions shall not be treated as a qualified tuition program unless such program provides that amounts are held in a qualified trust and such program has received a ruling or determination that such program meets the applicable requirements for a qualified tuition program. For purposes of the preceding sentence, the term 'qualified trust' means a trust which is created or organized in the United States for the exclusive benefit of designated beneficiaries and with respect to which the requirements of paragraphs (2) and (5) of section 408(a) are met.".

(2) PRIVATE QUALIFIED TUITION PROGRAMS LIMITED TO BENEFIT PLANS.—Clause (ii) of section 529(b)(1)(A) is amended by inserting "in the case of a program established and maintained by a State or agency or instrumentality thereof," before "may make".

(3) ADDITIONAL TAX ON NONQUALIFIED WITHDRAWALS.—Section 529 is amended—

(A) by striking paragraph (3) of subsection (b) and by redesignating paragraphs (4), (5), (6), and (7) of such subsection as paragraphs (3), (4), (5), and (6), respectively, and

(B) by adding at the end of subsection (c) the following new paragraph:

"(6) ADDITIONAL TAX.—The tax imposed by section 530(d)(4) shall apply to any payment or distribution from a qualified tuition program in the same manner as such tax applies to a payment or distribution from an education individual retirement account. This paragraph shall not apply to any payment or distribution in any taxable year beginning before January 1, 2004, which is includible in gross income but used for qualified higher education expenses of the designated beneficiary.".

(4) CONFORMING AMENDMENTS.—

(A) Sections 72(e)(9), 135(c)(2)(C), 135(d)(1)(D), 529, 530(b)(2)(B), 4973(e), and 6693(a)(2)(C) are amended by striking "qualified State tuition" each place it appears and inserting "qualified tuition".

(B) The headings for sections 72(e)(9) and 135(c)(2)(C) are amended by striking "QUALIFIED STATE TUITION" each place it appears and inserting "QUALIFIED TUITION".

(C) The headings for sections 529(b) and 530(b)(2)(B) are amended by striking "QUALIFIED STATE TUITION" each place it appears and inserting "QUALIFIED TUITION".

(D) The heading for section 529 is amended by striking "STATE".

(E) The item relating to section 529 in the table of sections for part VIII of subchapter F of chapter 1 is amended by striking "State".

(b) EXCLUSION FROM GROSS INCOME OF EDUCATION DISTRIBUTIONS FROM QUALIFIED TUITION PROGRAMS.—

(1) IN GENERAL.—Section 529(c)(3)(B) (relating to distributions) is amended to read as follows:

"(B) DISTRIBUTIONS FOR QUALIFIED HIGHER EDUCATION EXPENSES.—For purposes of this paragraph—

"(i) IN-KIND DISTRIBUTIONS.—No amount shall be includible in gross income under subparagraph (A) by reason of a distribution which consists of providing a benefit to the distributee which, if paid for by the distributee, would constitute payment of a qualified higher education expense.

"(ii) CASH DISTRIBUTIONS.—In the case of distributions not described in clause (i), if—

"(I) such distributions do not exceed the qualified higher education expenses (reduced by expenses described in clause (i)), no amount shall be includible in gross income, and

"(II) in any other case, the amount otherwise includible in gross income shall be reduced by an amount which bears the same ratio to such amount as such expenses bear to such distributions.

"(iii) EXCEPTION FOR INSTITUTIONAL PROGRAMS.— In the case of any taxable year beginning before January 1, 2004, clauses (i) and (ii) shall not apply with respect to any distribution during such taxable year under a qualified tuition program established and maintained by 1 or more eligible educational institutions.

"(iv) TREATMENT AS DISTRIBUTIONS.—Any benefit furnished to a designated beneficiary under a qualified tuition program shall be treated as a distribution to the beneficiary for purposes of this paragraph.

"(v) COORDINATION WITH HOPE AND LIFETIME LEARNING CREDITS.—The total amount of qualified higher education expenses with respect to an individual for the taxable year shall be reduced—

"(I) as provided in section 25A(g)(2), and

"(II) by the amount of such expenses which were taken into account in determining the credit allowed to the taxpayer or any other person under section 25A

"(vi) COORDINATION WITH EDUCATION INDIVIDUAL RETIREMENT ACCOUNTS.—If, with respect to an individual for any taxable year—

"(I) the aggregate distributions to which clauses (i) and (ii) and section530(d)(2)(A) apply, exceed

"(II) the total amount of qualified higher education expenses otherwise taken into account under clauses (i) and (ii) (after the application of clause (v)) for such year, the taxpayer shall allocate such expenses among such distributions for purposes of determining the amount of the exclusion under clauses (i) and (ii) and section 530(d)(2)(A).".

(2) CONFORMING AMENDMENTS.—

(A) Section 135(d)(2)(B) is amended by striking "the exclusion under section 530(d)(2)" and inserting "the exclusions under sections 529(c)(3)(B) and 530(d)(2)".

(B) Section 221(e)(2)(A) is amended by inserting "529,"after "135,".

(c) ROLLOVER TO DIFFERENT PROGRAM FOR BENEFIT OF SAME DESIGNATED BENEFICIARY.—Section 529(c)(3)(C) (relating to change in beneficiaries) is amended—

(1) by striking "transferred to the credit" in clause (i) and inserting "transferred—

"(I) to another qualified tuition program for the benefit of the designated beneficiary, or

"(II) to the credit",

(2) by adding at the end the following new clause:

"(iii) LIMITATION ON CERTAIN ROLLOVERS.—Clause (i)(I) shall not apply to any transfer if such transfer occurs within 12 months from the date of a previous transfer to any qualified tuition program for the benefit of the designated beneficiary.", and

(3) by inserting "OR PROGRAMS" after "BENEFICIARIES" in the heading.

(d) MEMBER OF FAMILY INCLUDES FIRST COUSIN.—Section 529(e)(2) (defining member of family) is amended by striking "and"at the end of subparagraph (B), by striking the period at the end of subparagraph (C) and by inserting "; and", and by adding at the end the following new subparagraph:

"(D) any first cousin of such beneficiary.".

(e) ADJUSTMENT OF LIMITATION ON ROOM AND BOARD DISTRIBUTIONS.—Section 529(e)(3)(B)(ii) is amended to read as follows:

"(ii) LIMITATION.—The amount treated as qualified higher education expenses by reason of clause (i) shall not exceed—

"(I) the allowance (applicable to the student) for room and board included in the cost of attendance (as defined in section 472 of the Higher Education Act of 1965 (20 U.S.C. 1087ll), as in effect on the date of the enactment of the Economic Growth and Tax Relief Reconciliation Act of 2001) as determined by the eligible educational institution for such period, or

"(II) if greater, the actual invoice amount the student residing in housing owned or operated by the eligible educational institution is charged by such institution for room and board costs for such period.".

(f) SPECIAL NEEDS SERVICES.—Subparagraph (A) of section 529(e)(3) (defining qualified higher education expenses) is amended 26 USC 529. to read as follows:

"(A) IN GENERAL.—The term 'qualified higher education expenses' means—

"(i) tuition, fees, books, supplies, and equipment required for the enrollment or attendance of a designated beneficiary at an eligible educational institution; and

"(ii) expenses for special needs services in the case of a special needs beneficiary which are incurred in connection with such enrollment or attendance.".

(g) TECHNICAL AMENDMENTS.—Section 529(c)(3)(D) is amended—

(1) by inserting "except to the extent provided by the Secretary," before "all distributions" in clause (ii), and

(2) by inserting "except to the extent provided by the Secretary," before "the value" in clause (iii).

(h) EFFECTIVE DATE.—The amendments made by this section Applicability. shall apply to taxable years beginning after December 31, 2001. 26 USC 72 note.

Subtitle B—Educational Assistance

Sec. 411. Extension of Exclusion for Employer-Provided Educational Assistance

(a) IN GENERAL.—Section 127 (relating to exclusion for educational assistance programs) is amended by striking subsection (d) and by redesignating subsection (e) as subsection (d).

(b) REPEAL OF LIMITATION ON GRADUATE EDUCATION.—The last sentence of section 127(c)(1) is amended by striking ", and such term also does not include any payment for, or the provision of any benefits with respect to, any graduate level course of a kind normally taken by an individual pursuing a program leading to a law, business, medical, or other advanced academic or professional degree".

(c) CONFORMING AMENDMENT.—Section 51A(b)(5)(B)(iii) is amended by striking "or would be so excludable but for section 127(d)".

(d) EFFECTIVE DATE.—The amendments made by this section Applicability. shall apply with respect to expenses relating to courses beginning 26 USC 51A note. after December 31, 2001.

Sec. 412. Elimination of 60-Month Limit and Increase in Income Limitation on Student Loan Interest Deduction

(a) ELIMINATION OF 60-MONTH LIMIT.—

(1) IN GENERAL.—Section 221 (relating to interest on education loans), as amended by section 402(b)(2)(B), is amended by striking subsection (d) and by redesignating subsections (e), (f), and (g) as subsections (d), (e), and (f), respectively.

(2) CONFORMING AMENDMENT.—Section 6050S(e) is amended by striking "section 221(e)(1)" and inserting "section 221(d)(1)"

(3) EFFECTIVE DATE.—The amendments made by this subsection shall apply with respect to any loan interest paid after December 31, 2001, in taxable years ending after such date.

(b) INCREASE IN INCOME LIMITATION.—

(1) IN GENERAL.—Section 221(b)(2)(B) (relating to amount of reduction) is amended by striking clauses (i) and (ii) and inserting the following:

"(i) the excess of—

"(I) the taxpayer's modified adjusted gross income for such taxable year, over

"(II) $50,000 ($100,000 in the case of a joint return), bears to

"(ii) $15,000 ($30,000 in the case of a joint return).".

(2) CONFORMING AMENDMENT.—Section 221(g)(1) is amended by striking "$40,000 and $60,000 amounts" and inserting "$50,000 and $100,000 amounts".

(3) EFFECTIVE DATE.—The amendments made by this subsection shall apply to taxable years ending after December 31, 2001.

Sec. 413. Exclusion of Certain Amounts Received under the National Health Service Corps Scholarship Program and the F. Edward Hebert Armed Forces Health Professions Scholarship and Financial Assistance Program

(a) IN GENERAL.—Section 117(c) (relating to the exclusion from gross income amounts received as a qualified scholarship) is amended—

(1) by striking "Subsections (a)" and inserting the following:

"(1) IN GENERAL.—Except as provided in paragraph (2), subsections (a)", and

(2) by adding at the end the following new paragraph:

"(2) EXCEPTIONS.—Paragraph (1) shall not apply to any amount received by an individual under—

"(A) the National Health Service Corps Scholarship Program under section 338A(g)(1)(A) of the Public Health Service Act, or

"(B) the Armed Forces Health Professions Scholarship and Financial Assistance program under subchapter I of chapter 105 of title 10, United States Code.".

(b) EFFECTIVE DATE.—The amendments made by subsection (a) shall apply to amounts received in taxable years beginning after December 31, 2001.

Subtitle C—Liberalization of Tax-Exempt Financing Rules for Public School Construction

Sec. 421. Additional Increase in Arbitrage Rebate Exception for Governmental Bonds Used to Finance Educational Facilities

(a) IN GENERAL.—Section 148(f)(4)(D)(vii) (relating to increase in exception for bonds financing public school capital expenditures is amended by striking "$5,000,000" the second place it appears and inserting "$10,000,000".

(b) EFFECTIVE DATE.—The amendment made by subsection (a) shall apply to obligations issued in calendar years beginning after December 31, 2001.

Sec. 422. Treatment of Qualified Public Educational Facility Bonds as Exempt Facility Bonds

(a) TREATMENT AS EXEMPT FACILITY BOND.—Subsection (a) of section 142 (relating to exempt facility bond) is amended by striking "or" at the end of paragraph (11), by striking the period at the end of paragraph (12) and inserting ", or", and by adding at the end the following new paragraph: 26 USC

"(13) qualified public educational facilities.".

(b) QUALIFIED PUBLIC EDUCATIONAL FACILITIES.—Section 142 (relating to exempt facility bond) is amended by adding at the end the following new subsection:

"(k) QUALIFIED PUBLIC EDUCATIONAL FACILITIES.—

"(1) IN GENERAL.—For purposes of subsection (a)(13), the term 'qualified public educational facility' means any school facility which is—

"(A) part of a public elementary school or a public secondary school, and

"(B) owned by a private, for-profit corporation pursuant to a public-private partnership agreement with a State or local educational agency described in paragraph (2).

"(2) PUBLIC-PRIVATE PARTNERSHIP AGREEMENT DESCRIBED.—A public-private partnership agreement is described in this paragraph if it is an agreement—

"(A) under which the corporation agrees—

"(i) to do 1 or more of the following: construct, rehabilitate, refurbish, or equip a school facility, and

"(ii) at the end of the term of the agreement, to transfer the school facility to such agency for no additional consideration, and

"(B) the term of which does not exceed the term of the issue to be used to provide the school facility.

"(3) SCHOOL FACILITY.—For purposes of this subsection, the term 'school facility' means—

"(A) any school building,

"(B) any functionally related and subordinate facility and land with respect to such building, including any stadium or other facility primarily used for school events, and

"(C) any property, to which section 168 applies (or would apply but for section 179), for use in a facility described in subparagraph (A) or (B).

"(4) PUBLIC SCHOOLS.—For purposes of this subsection, the terms 'elementary school' and 'secondary school' have the meanings given such terms by section 14101 of the Elementary and Secondary Education Act of 1965 (20 U.S.C. 8801), as in effect on the date of the enactment of this subsection.

"(5) ANNUAL AGGREGATE FACE AMOUNT OF TAX-EXEMPT FINANCING.—

"(A) IN GENERAL.—An issue shall not be treated as an issue described in subsection (a)(13) if the aggregate face amount of bonds issued by the State pursuant thereto (when added to the aggregate face amount of bonds previously so issued during the calendar year) exceeds an amount equal to the greater of—

"(i) $10 multiplied by the State population, or

"(ii) $5,000,000.

"(B) ALLOCATION RULES.—

"(i) IN GENERAL.—Except as otherwise provided in this subparagraph, the State may allocate the amount described in subparagraph (A) for any calendar year in such manner as the State determines appropriate.

"(ii) RULES FOR CARRYFORWARD OF UNUSED LIMITATION.—A State may elect to carry forward an unused limitation for any calendar year for 3 calendar years following the calendar year in which the unused limitation arose under rules similar to the rules of section 146(f), except that the only purpose for which the carryforward may be elected is the issuance of exempt facility bonds described in subsection (a)(13).".

(c) EXEMPTION FROM GENERAL STATE VOLUME CAPS.—Paragraph (3) of section 146(g) (relating to exception for certain bonds) is amended—

(1) by striking "or (12)" and inserting "(12), or (13)", and

(2) by striking "and environmental enhancements of hydroelectric generating facilities" and inserting "environmental enhancements of hydroelectric generating facilities, and qualified public educational facilities".

(d) EXEMPTION FROM LIMITATION ON USE FOR LAND ACQUISITION.—Section 147(h) (relating to certain rules not to apply to mortgage revenue bonds, qualified student loan bonds, and qualified 501(c)(3) bonds) is amended by adding at the end the following new paragraph:

"(3) EXEMPT FACILITY BONDS FOR QUALIFIED PUBLIC-PRIVATE SCHOOLS.—Subsection (c) shall not apply to any exempt facility bond issued as part of an issue described in section 142(a)(13) (relating to qualified public educational facilities).".

(e) CONFORMING AMENDMENT.—The heading for section 147(h) is amended by striking "MORTGAGE REVENUE BONDS, QUALIFIED STUDENT LOAN BONDS, AND QUALIFIED 501(c)(3) BONDS" and inserting "CERTAIN BONDS".

(f) EFFECTIVE DATE.—The amendments made by this section shall apply to bonds issued after December 31, 2001.

Subtitle D—Other Provisions

Sec. 431. Deduction for Higher Education Expenses

(a) DEDUCTION ALLOWED.—Part VII of subchapter B of chapter 1 (relating to additional itemized deductions for individuals) is amended by redesignating section 222 as section 223 and by inserting after section 221 the following:

"Sec. 222. Qualified Tuition and Related Expenses

"(a) ALLOWANCE OF DEDUCTION.—In the case of an individual, there shall be allowed as a deduction an amount equal to the qualified tuition and related expenses paid by the taxpayer during the taxable year

"(b) DOLLAR LIMITATIONS.—

"(1) IN GENERAL.—The amount allowed as a deduction under subsection (a) with respect to the taxpayer for any taxable year shall not exceed the applicable dollar limit.

"(2) APPLICABLE DOLLAR LIMIT.—

"(A) 2002 AND 2003.—In the case of a taxable year beginning in 2002 or 2003, the applicable dollar limit shall be equal to—

"(i) in the case of a taxpayer whose adjusted gross income for the taxable year does not exceed $65,000 ($130,000 in the case of a joint return), $3,000, and—

"(ii) in the case of any other taxpayer, zero.

"(B) 2004 AND 2005.—In the case of a taxable year beginning in 2004 or 2005, the applicable dollar amount shall be equal to—

"(i) in the case of a taxpayer whose adjusted gross income for the taxable year does not exceed $65,000 ($130,000 in the case of a joint return), $4,000,

"(ii) in the case of a taxpayer not described in clause (i) whose adjusted gross income for the taxable year does not exceed $80,000 ($160,000 in the case of a joint return), $2,000, and

"(iii) in the case of any other taxpayer, zero.

"(C) ADJUSTED GROSS INCOME.—For purposes of this paragraph, adjusted gross income shall be determined—

"(i) without regard to this section and sections 911, 931, and 933, and

"(ii) after application of sections 86, 135, 137, 219, 221, and 469.

"(c) NO DOUBLE BENEFIT.—

"(1) IN GENERAL.—No deduction shall be allowed under subsection (a) for any expense for which a deduction is allowed to the taxpayer under any other provision of this chapter.

"(2) COORDINATION WITH OTHER EDUCATION INCENTIVES.—

"(A) DENIAL OF DEDUCTION IF CREDIT ELECTED.—No deduction shall be allowed under subsection (a) for a taxable year with respect to the qualified tuition and related expenses with respect to an individual if the taxpayer or any other person elects to have section 25A apply with respect to such individual for such year.

"(B) COORDINATION WITH EXCLUSIONS.—The total amount of qualified tuition and related expenses shall be reduced by the amount of such expenses taken into account in determining any amount excluded under section 135, 529(c)(1), or 530(d)(2). For purposes of the preceding sentence, the amount taken into account in determining the amount excluded under section 529(c)(1) shall not include that portion of the distribution which represents a return of any contributions to the plan.

"(3) DEPENDENTS.—No deduction shall be allowed under subsection (a) to any individual with respect to whom a deduction under section 151 is allowable to another taxpayer for a taxable year beginning in the calendar year in which such individual's taxable year begins.

"(d) DEFINITIONS AND SPECIAL RULES.—For purposes of this section—

"(1) QUALIFIED TUITION AND RELATED EXPENSES.—The term 'qualified tuition and related expenses' has the meaning given such term by section 25A(f). Such expenses shall be reduced in the same manner as under section 25A(g)(2).

"(2) IDENTIFICATION REQUIREMENT.—No deduction shall be allowed under subsection (a) to a taxpayer with respect to the qualified tuition and related expenses of an individual unless the taxpayer includes the name and taxpayer identification number of the individual on the return of tax for the taxable year.

"(3) LIMITATION ON TAXABLE YEAR OF DEDUCTION.—

"(A) IN GENERAL.—A deduction shall be allowed under subsection (a) for qualified tuition and related expenses for any taxable year only to the extent such expenses are in connection with enrollment at an institution of higher education during the taxable year.

"(B) CERTAIN PREPAYMENTS ALLOWED.—Subparagraph (A) shall not apply to qualified tuition and related expenses paid during a taxable year if such expenses are in connection with an academic term beginning during such taxable year or during the first 3 months of the next taxable year.

"(4) NO DEDUCTION FOR MARRIED INDIVIDUALS FILING SEPARATE RETURNS.—If the taxpayer is a married individual (within the meaning of section 7703), this section shall apply only if the taxpayer and the taxpayer's spouse file a joint return for the taxable year.

"(5) NONRESIDENT ALIENS.—If the taxpayer is a nonresident alien individual for any portion of the taxable year, this section shall apply only if such individual is treated as a resident alien of the United States for purposes of this chapter by reason of an election under subsection (g) or (h) of section 6013.

"(6) REGULATIONS.—The Secretary may prescribe such regulations as may be necessary or appropriate to carry out this section, including regulations requiring recordkeeping and information reporting.

"(e) TERMINATION.—This section shall not apply to taxable years beginning after December 31, 2005.".

(b) DEDUCTION ALLOWED IN COMPUTING ADJUSTED GROSS INCOME.—Section 62(a) is amended by inserting after paragraph (17) the following:

"(18) HIGHER EDUCATION EXPENSES.—The deduction allowed by section 222.".

CONFORMING AMENDMENTS.—

(1) Sections 86(b)(2), 135(c)(4), 137(b)(3), and 219(g)(3) are each amended by inserting "222," after "221,".
(2) Section 221(b)(2)(C) is amended by inserting "222,"before "911".
(3) Section 469(i)(3)(F) is amended by striking "and 221"and inserting ", 221, and 222".
(4) The table of sections for part VII of subchapter B of chapter 1 is amended by striking the item relating to section 222 and inserting the following:

"Sec. 222. Qualified tuition and related expenses.

"Sec. 223. Cross reference.".

(d) EFFECTIVE DATE.—The amendments made by this section shall apply to payments made in taxable years beginning after December 31, 2001.

TITLE V—ESTATE, GIFT, AND GENERATION-SKIPPING TRANSFER TAX PROVISIONS

Subtitle A—Repeal of Estate and Generation-Skipping Transfer Taxes

Sec. 501. Repeal of Estate and Generation-Skipping Transfer Taxes

(a) ESTATE TAX REPEAL.—Subchapter C of chapter 11 of subtitle B (relating to miscellaneous) is amended by adding at the end the following new section:

"Sec. 2210. Termination

"(a) IN GENERAL.—Except as provided in subsection (b), this chapter shall not apply to the estates of decedents dying after December 31, 2009.

"(b) CERTAIN DISTRIBUTIONS FROM QUALIFIED DOMESTIC TRUSTS.—In applying section 2056A with respect to the surviving spouse of a decedent dying before January 1, 2010—

"(1) section 2056A(b)(1)(A) shall not apply to distributions made after December 31, 2020, and

"(2) section 2056A(b)(1)(B) shall not apply after December 31, 2009.".

(b) GENERATION-SKIPPING TRANSFER TAX REPEAL.—Subchapter G of chapter 13 of subtitle B (relating to administration) is amended by adding at the end the following new section:

"Sec. 2664. Termination

"This chapter shall not apply to generation-skipping transfers after December 31, 2009.".

(c) CONFORMING AMENDMENTS.—

"(1) The table of sections for subchapter C of chapter 11 is amended by adding at the end the following new item:

"Sec. 2210. Termination.".

"(2) The table of sections for subchapter G of chapter 13 is amended by adding at the end the following new item:

"Sec. 2664. Termination.".

(d) EFFECTIVE DATE.—The amendments made by this section shall apply to the estates of decedents dying, and generation-skipping transfers, after December 31, 2009.

Subtitle B—Reductions of Estate and Gift Tax Rates

Sec. 511. Additional Reductions f Estate and Gift Tax Rates

(a) MAXIMUM RATE OF TAX REDUCED TO 50 PERCENT.—The table contained in section 200 1(c)(1) is amended by striking the two highest brackets and inserting the following:

"Over $2,500,000 $1 ,025,800, plus 50% of the excess over $2,500,000.".

(b) REPEAL OF PHASEOUT OF GRADUATED RATES.—Subsection

(c) of section 2001 is amended by striking paragraph (2).

(c) ADDITIONAL REDUCTIONS OF MAXIMUM RATE OF TAX.—Subsection (c) of section 2001, as amended by subsection (b), is amended by adding at the end the following new paragraph:

"(2) PHASEDOWN OF MAXIMUM RATE OF TAX.—

"(A) IN GENERAL.—In the case of estates of decedents dying, and gifts made, in calendar years after 2002 and before 2010, the tentative tax under this subsection shall be determined by using a table prescribed by the Secretary (in lieu of using the table contained in paragraph (1)) which is the same as such table; except that—

"(1) the maximum rate of tax for any calendar year shall be determined in the table under subparagraph (B), and

"(2) the brackets and the amounts setting forth the tax shall be adjusted to the extent necessary to reflect the adjustments under subparagraph (A).

"(B) MAXIMUM RATE.—

"In calendar year:	The maximum rate is:
2003	49 percent
2004	48 percent
2005	47 percent
2006	46 percent
2007, 2008, and 2009	45 percent.".

(d) MAXIMUM GIFT TAX RATE REDUCED TO MAXIMUM INDIVIDUAL RATE AFTER 2009.—Subsection (a) of section 2502 (relating to rate of tax) is amended to read as follows:

"(a) COMPUTATION OF TAX.—

"(1) IN GENERAL.—The tax imposed by section 2501 for each calendar year shall be an amount equal to the excess of—

"(A) a tentative tax, computed under paragraph (2), on the aggregate sum of the taxable gifts for such calendar year and for each of the preceding calendar periods, over

"(B) a tentative tax, computed under paragraph (2), on the aggregate sum of the taxable gifts for each of the preceding calendar periods.

"(2) RATE SCHEDULE.—

"If the amount with respect to which the tentative tax to be computed is:

Not over $10,000	18% of such amount.
Over $10,000 but not over $20,000	$1 ,800, plus 20% of the excess over $10,000.
Over $20,000 but not over $40,000	$3,800, plus 22% of the excess over $20,000

"If the amount with respect to which the tentative tax to be computed is:	The tentative tax is:
Over $40,000 but not over $60,000	$8,200, plus 24% of the excess over $40,000.
Over $60,000 but not over $80,000	$13,000, plus 26% of the excess over $60,000.
Over $80,000 but not over $100,000	$18,200, plus 28% of the excess over $80,000.
Over $100,000 but not over $150,000	$23,800, plus 30% of the excess over $100,000.
Over $150,000 but not over $250,000	$38,800, plus 32% of the excess over $150,000.
Over $250,000 but not over $500,000	$70,800, plus 34% of the excess over $250,000.
Over $500,000	$155,800, plus 35% of the excess over $500,000."

(e) TREATMENT OF CERTAIN TRANSFERS IN TRUST.—Section 2511 (relating to transfers in general) is amended by adding at the end the following new subsection:

"(c) TREATMENT OF CERTAIN TRANSFERS IN TRUST.—Notwithstanding any other provision of this section and except as provided in regulations, a transfer in trust shall be treated as a taxable gift under section 2503, unless the trust is treated as wholly owned by the donor or the donor's spouse under subpart E of part I of subchapter J of chapter 1.".

(f) EFFECTIVE DATES.—

(1) SUBSECTIONS (a) AND (b).—The amendments made by subsections (a) and (b) shall apply to estates of decedents dying, and gifts made, after December 31, 2001.

(2) SUBSECTION (c).—The amendment made by subsection

(c) shall apply to estates of decedents dying, and gifts made, after December 31, 2002.

(3) SUBSECTIONS (d) AND (e).—The amendments made by subsections (d) and (e) shall apply to gifts made after December 31, 2009.

Subtitle C—Increase in Exemption Amounts

Sec. 521. Increase in Exemption Equivalent of Unified Credit, Lifetime Gifts Exemption, and Gst Exemption Amounts

(a) IN GENERAL.—Subsection (c) of section 2010 (relating to applicable credit amount) is amended by striking the table and inserting the following new table:

"In the case of estates of decedents dying during:	The applicable exclusion amount is:
2002 and 2003	$1,000,000
2004 and 2005	$1,500,000
2006, 2007, and 2008	$2,000,000
2009	$3,500,000.".

(b) LIFETIME GIFT EXEMPTION INCREASED TO $ 1,000,000.—

(1) FOR PERIODS BEFORE ESTATE TAX REPEAL.—Paragraph

(1) of section 2505(a) (relating to unified credit against gift tax) is amended by inserting "(determined as if the applicable

exclusion amount were $1,000,000)" after "calendar year".

(2) FOR PERIODS AFTER ESTATE TAX REPEAL.—Paragraph (1) of section 2505(a) (relating to unified credit against gift tax), as amended by paragraph (1), is amended to read as follows:

"(1) the amount of the tentative tax which would be determined under the rate schedule set forth in section 2502(a)(2) if the amount with respect to which such tentative tax is to be computed were $1,000,000, reduced by".

(c) GST EXEMPTION.—

(1) IN GENERAL.—Subsection (a) of 2631 (relating to GST exemption) is amended by striking "of $1,000,000" and inserting "amount".

(2) EXEMPTION AMOUNT.—Subsection (c) of section 2631 is amended to read as follows:

"(c) GST EXEMPTION AMOUNT.—For purposes of subsection (a), the GST exemption amount for any calendar year shall be equal to the applicable exclusion amount under section 20 10(c) for such calendar year.".

(d) REPEAL OF SPECIAL BENEFIT FOR FAMILY-OWNED BUSINESS INTERESTS.—Section 2057 (relating to family-owned business interests) is amended by adding at the end the following new subsection:

"(j) TERMINATION.—This section shall not apply to the estates of decedents dying after December 31, 2003.".

(e) EFFECTIVE DATES.—

(1) IN GENERAL.—Except as provided in paragraphs (2) and (3), the amendments made by this section shall apply to estates of decedents dying, and gifts made, after December 31, 2001.

(2) SUBSECTION (b)(2).—The amendments made by subsection (b)(2) shall apply to gifts made after December 31, 2009.

(3) SUBSECTIONS (c) AND (d).—The amendments made by subsections (c) and (d) shall apply to estates of decedents dying, and generation-skipping transfers, after December 31, 2003.

Subtitle D—Credit for State Death Taxes

Sec. 531. Reduction of Credit for State Death Taxes

(a) IN GENERAL.—Section 2011(b) (relating to amount of credit) is amended—

(1) by striking "CREDIT.—The credit allowed" and inserting "CREDIT.—

"(1) IN GENERAL.—Except as provided in paragraph (2), the credit allowed",

(2) by striking "For purposes" and inserting the following:

"(3) ADJUSTED TAXABLE ESTATE.—For purposes", and

(3) by inserting after paragraph (1) the following new paragraph:

"(2) REDUCTION OF MAXIMUM CREDIT.—

"(1) IN GENERAL.—In the case of estates of decedents dying after December 31, 2001, the credit allowed by this section shall not exceed the applicable percentage of the credit otherwise determined under paragraph (1).

"(B) APPLICABLE PERCENTAGE.—

"In the case of estates of decedents dying during:	The applicable percentage is:
2003	50 percent
2004	25 percent.".

(b) EFFECTIVE DATE.—The amendments made by this subsection shall apply to estates of decedents dying after December 31, 2001.

Sec. 532. Credit for State Death Taxes Replaced with Deduction for Such Taxes

(a) REPEAL OF CREDIT.—Section 2011 (relating to credit for 26 USC 2011. State death taxes) is amended by adding at the end the following new subsection:

"(g) TERMINATION.—This section shall not apply to the estates of decedents dying after December 31, 2004.".

(b) DEDUCTION FOR STATE DEATH TAXES.—Part IV of subchapter A of chapter 11 is amended by adding at the end the following new section:

"Sec. 2058. State Death Taxes

"(a) ALLOWANCE OF DEDUCTION.—For purposes of the tax imposed by section 2001, the value of the taxable estate shall be determined by deducting from the value of the gross estate the amount of any estate, inheritance, legacy, or succession taxes actually paid to any State or the District of Columbia, in respect of any property included in the gross estate (not including any such taxes paid with respect to the estate of a person other than the decedent).

"(b) PERIOD OF LIMITATIONS.—The deduction allowed by this section shall include only such taxes as were actually paid and deduction therefor claimed before the later of—

"(1) 4 years after the filing of the return required by section 6018, or

"(2) if—

"(A) a petition for redetermination of a deficiency has been filed with the Tax Court within the time prescribed in section 62 13(a), the expiration of 60 days after the decision of the Tax Court becomes final,

"(B) an extension of time has been granted under section 6161 or 6166 for payment of the tax shown on the return, or of a deficiency, the date of the expiration of the period of the extension, or

"(C) a claim for refund or credit of an overpayment of tax imposed by this chapter has been filed within the time prescribed in section 6511, the latest of the expiration of—

"(1) 60 days from the date of mailing by certified mail or registered mail by the Secretary to the taxpayer of a notice of the disallowance of any part of such claim,

"(2) 60 days after a decision by any court of competent jurisdiction becomes final with respect to a timely suit instituted upon such claim, or

"(3) 2 years after a notice of the waiver of disallowance is filed under section 6532(a)(3).

Notwithstanding sections 6511 and 6512, refund based on the deduction may be made if the claim for refund is filed within the period provided in the preceding sentence. Any such refund shall be made without interest.".

(c) CONFORMING AMENDMENTS.— (1) Subsection (a) of section 2012 is amended by striking "the credit for State death taxes provided by section 2011 and"

(2) Subparagraph (A) of section 2013(c)(1) is amended by striking "2011,".

(3) Paragraph (2) of section 2014(b) is amended by striking ", 2011,".

(4) Sections 2015 and 2016 are each amended by striking "2011 or".

(5) Subsection (d) of section 2053 is amended to read as follows:

"(d) CERTAIN FOREIGN DEATH TAXES.—

"(1) IN GENERAL.—Notwithstanding the provisions of subsection (c)(1)(B), for purposes of the tax imposed by section 2001, the value of the taxable estate may be determined, if the executor so elects before the expiration of the period of limitation for assessment provided in section 6501, by deducting from the value of the gross estate the amount (as determined in accordance with regulations prescribed by the Secretary) of any estate, succession, legacy, or inheritance tax imposed by and actually paid to any foreign country, in respect of any property situated within such foreign country and included in the gross estate of a citizen or resident of the United States, upon a transfer by the decedent for public, charitable, or religious uses described in section 2055. The determination under this paragraph of the country within which property is situated shall be made in accordance with the rules applicable under subchapter B (sec. 2101 and following) in determining whether property is situated within or without the United States. Any election under this paragraph shall be exercised in accordance with regulations prescribed by the Secretary.

"(2) CONDITION FOR ALLOWANCE OF DEDUCTION.—No deduction shall be allowed under paragraph (1) for a foreign death tax specified therein unless the decrease in the tax imposed by section 2001 which results from the deduction provided in paragraph (1) will inure solely for the benefit of the public, charitable, or religious transferees described in section 2055 or section 2106(a)(2).

In any case where the tax imposed by section 2001 is equitably apportioned among all the transferees of property included in the gross estate, including those described in sections 2055 and 2106(a)(2) (taking into account any exemptions, credits, or deductions allowed by this chapter), in determining such decrease, there shall be disregarded any decrease in the Federal estate tax which any transferees other than those described in sections 2055 and 2106(a)(2) are required to pay.

"(3) EFFECT ON CREDIT FOR FOREIGN DEATH TAXES OF DEDUCTION UNDER THIS SUBSECTION.—

"(A) ELECTION.—An election under this subsection shall be deemed a waiver of the right to claim a credit, against the Federal estate tax, under a death tax convention with any foreign country for any tax or portion thereof in respect of which a deduction is taken under this subsection.

"(B) CROSS REFERENCE.—

"See Section 2014(f) For the Effect of a Deduction Taken under This Paragraph on the Credit for Foreign Death Taxes"

(6) Subparagraph (A) of section 2056A(b)(10) is amended—

(A) by striking "2011,", and

(B) by inserting "2058," after "2056,".

(7)(A) Subsection (a) of section 2102 is amended to read 26 USC 2102. as follows:

"(a) IN GENERAL.—The tax imposed by section 2101 shall be credited with the amounts determined in accordance with sections 2012 and 2013 (relating to gift tax and tax on prior transfers).".

(B) Section 2102 is amended by striking subsection (b) and by redesignating subsection (c) as subsection (b).

(C) Section 2102(b)(5) (as redesignated by subparagraph (B)) and section 2107(c)(3) are each amended by striking "2011 to 2013, inclusive," and inserting "2012 and 2013".

(8) Subsection (a) of section 2106 is amended by adding at the end the following new paragraph:

"(4) STATE DEATH TAXES.—The amount which bears the same ratio to the State death taxes as the value of the property, as determined for purposes of this chapter, upon which State death taxes were paid and which is included in the gross estate under section 2103 bears to the value of the total gross estate under section 2103. For purposes of this paragraph, the term 'State death taxes' means the taxes described in section 2011(a).".

(9) Section 2201 is amended—

(A) by striking "as defined in section 2011(d)", and

(B) by adding at the end the following new flush sentence:

"For purposes of this section, the additional estate tax is the difference between the tax imposed by section 2001 or 2101 and the amount equal to 125 percent of the maximum credit provided by section 2011(b), as in effect before its repeal by the Economic Growth and Tax Relief Reconciliation Act of 2001.".

(10) Section 2604 (relating to credit for certain State taxes) is amended by adding at the end the following new subsection: "(c) TERMINATION.—This section shall not apply to the generation-skipping transfers after December 31, 2004.".

(11) Paragraph (2) of section 6511(i) is amended by striking "2011(c), 2014(b)," and inserting "2014(b)".

(12) Subsection (c) of section 6612 is amended by striking "section 2011(c) (relating to refunds due to credit for State taxes),".

(13) The table of sections for part II of subchapter A of chapter 11 is amended by striking the item relating to section 2011.

(14) The table of sections for part IV of subchapter A of chapter 11 is amended by adding at the end the following new item:

"Sec. 2058. State death taxes.".

(15) The table of sections for subchapter A of chapter 13 is amended by striking the item relating to section 2604.

(d) EFFECTIVE DATE.—The amendments made by this section shall apply to estates of decedents dying, and generation-skipping transfers, after December 31, 2004.

Subtitle E—Carryover Basis at Death; Other Changes Taking Effect with Repeal

Sec. 541. Termination of Step-Up in Basis at Death

Section 1014 (relating to basis of property acquired from a decedent) is amended by adding at the end the following new subsection:

"(f) TERMINATION.—This section shall not apply with respect to decedents dying after December 31, 2009."

Sec. 542. Treatment of Property Acquired from a Decedent Dying after December 31, 2009.

(a) GENERAL RULE.—Part II of subchapter O of chapter 1 (relating to basis rules of general application) is amended by inserting after section 1021 the following new section:

"Sec. 1022. Treatment of Property Acquired from a Decedent Dying after December 31, 2009

"(a) IN GENERAL.—Except as otherwise provided in this section—

"(1) property acquired from a decedent dying after December 31, 2009, shall be treated for purposes of this subtitle as transferred by gift, and

"(2) the basis of the person acquiring property from such a decedent shall be the lesser of—

"(A) the adjusted basis of the decedent, or

"(B) the fair market value of the property at the date of the decedent's death.

"(b) BASIS INCREASE FOR CERTAIN PROPERTY.—

"(1) IN GENERAL.—In the case of property to which this subsection applies, the basis of such property under subsection (a) shall be increased by its basis increase under this subsection.

"(2) BASIS INCREASE.—For purposes of this subsection—

"(A) IN GENERAL.—The basis increase under this subsection for any property is the portion of the aggregate basis increase which is allocated to the property pursuant to this section.

"(B) AGGREGATE BASIS INCREASE.—In the case of any estate, the aggregate basis increase under this subsection is $1,300,000.

"(C) LIMIT INCREASED BY UNUSED BUILT-IN LOSSES AND LOSS CARRYOVERS.—The limitation under subparagraph (B) shall be increased by—

"(i) the sum of the amount of any capital loss carryover under section 1212(b), and the amount of any net operating loss carryover under section 172, which would (but for the decedent's death) be carried from the decedent's last taxable year to a later taxable year of the decedent, plus

"(ii) the sum of the amount of any losses that would have been allowable under section 165 if the property acquired from the decedent had been sold at fair market value immediately before the decedent's death

"(3) DECEDENT NONRESIDENTS WHO ARE NOT CITIZENS OF THE UNITED STATES.—In the case of a decedent nonresident not a citizen of the United States—

"(A) paragraph (2)(B) shall be applied by substituting '$60,000' for '$1,300,000', and

"(B) paragraph (2)(C) shall not apply.

"(c) ADDITIONAL BASIS INCREASE FOR PROPERTY ACQUIRED BY SURVIVING SPOUSE.—

"(1) IN GENERAL.—In the case of property to which this subsection applies and which is qualified spousal property, the basis of such property under subsection (a) (as increased under subsection (b)) shall be increased by its spousal property basis increase.

"(2) SPOUSAL PROPERTY BASIS INCREASE.—For purposes of this subsection—

"(A) IN GENERAL.—The spousal property basis increase for property referred to in paragraph (1) is the portion of the aggregate spousal property basis increase which is allocated to the property pursuant to this section.

"(B) AGGREGATE SPOUSAL PROPERTY BASIS INCREASE.—

In the case of any estate, the aggregate spousal property basis increase is $3,000,000.

"(3) QUALIFIED SPOUSAL PROPERTY.—For purposes of this subsection, the term 'qualified spousal property' means—

"(A) outright transfer property, and

"(B) qualified terminable interest property.

"(4) OUTRIGHT TRANSFER PROPERTY.—For purposes of this subsection—

"(A) IN GENERAL.—The term 'outright transfer property' means any interest in property acquired from the decedent by the decedent's surviving spouse.

"(B) EXCEPTION.—Subparagraph (A) shall not apply where, on the lapse of time, on the occurrence of an event or contingency, or on the failure of an event or contingency to occur, an interest passing to the surviving spouse will terminate or fail—

"(i)(I) if an interest in such property passes or has passed (for less than an adequate and full consideration in money or money's worth) from the decedent to any person other than such surviving spouse (or the estate of such spouse), and

"(II) if by reason of such passing such person (or his heirs or assigns) may possess or enjoy any part of such property after such termination or failure of the interest so passing to the surviving spouse, or

"(ii) if such interest is to be acquired for the surviving spouse, pursuant to directions of the decedent, by his executor or by the trustee of a trust.

For purposes of this subparagraph, an interest shall not be considered as an interest which will terminate or fail merely because it is the ownership of a bond, note, or similar contractual obligation, the discharge of which would not have the effect of an annuity for life or for a term.

"(C) INTEREST OF SPOUSE CONDITIONAL ON SURVIVAL FOR LIMITED PERIOD.—For purposes of this paragraph, an interest passing to the surviving spouse shall not be consid considered as an interest which will terminate or fail on the death of such spouse if—

"(i) such death will cause a termination or failure of such interest only if it occurs within a period not exceeding 6 months after the decedent's death, or only if it occurs as a result of a common disaster resulting in the death of the decedent and the surviving spouse, or only if it occurs in the case of either such event, and

"(ii) such termination or failure does not in fact occur.

"(5) QUALIFIED TERMINABLE INTEREST PROPERTY.—For purposes of this subsection—

"(A) IN GENERAL.—The term 'qualified terminable interest property' means property—

"(i) which passes from the decedent, and

"(ii) in which the surviving spouse has a qualifying income interest for life.

"(B) QUALIFYING INCOME INTEREST FOR LIFE.—The surviving spouse has a qualifying income interest for life if—

"(i) the surviving spouse is entitled to all the income from the property, payable annually or at more frequent intervals, or has a usufruct interest for life in the property, and

"(ii) no person has a power to appoint any part of the property to any person other than the surviving spouse.

Clause (ii) shall not apply to a power exercisable only at or after the death of the surviving spouse. To the extent provided in regulations, an annuity shall be treated in a manner similar to an income interest in property (regardless of whether the property from which the annuity is payable can be separately identified).

"(C) PROPERTY INCLUDES INTEREST THEREIN.—The term 'property' includes an interest in property.

"(D) SPECIFIC PORTION TREATED AS SEPARATE PROPERTY.—A specific portion of property shall be treated as separate property. For purposes of the preceding sentence, the term 'specific portion' only includes a portion determined on a fractional or percentage basis.

“(d) DEFINITIONS AND SPECIAL RULES FOR APPLICATION OF SUBSECTIONS (b) AND (c).—

“(1) PROPERTY TO WHICH SUBSECTIONS (b) AND (c) APPLY.—

“(A) IN GENERAL.—The basis of property acquired from a decedent may be increased under subsection (b) or (c) only if the property was owned by the decedent at the time of death.

“(B) RULES RELATING TO OWNERSHIP.—

“(i) JOINTLY HELD PROPERTY.—In the case of property which was owned by the decedent and another person as joint tenants with right of survivorship or tenants by the entirety—

“(I) if the only such other person is the surviving spouse, the decedent shall be treated as the owner of only 50 percent of the property

“(II) in any case (to which subclause (I) does not apply) in which the decedent furnished consideration for the acquisition of the property, the decedent shall be treated as the owner to the extent of the portion of the property which is proportionate to such consideration, and

“(III) in any case (to which subclause (I) does not apply) in which the property has been acquired by gift, bequest, devise, or inheritance by the decedent and any other person as joint tenants with right of survivorship and their interests are not otherwise specified or fixed by law, the decedent shall be treated as the owner to the extent of the value of a fractional part to be determined by dividing the value of the property by the number of joint tenants with right of survivorship.

"(ii) REVOCABLE TRUSTS.—The decedent shall be treated as owning property transferred by the decedent during life to a qualified revocable trust (as defined in section 645(b)(1)).

"(iii) POWERS OF APPOINTMENT.—The decedent shall not be treated as owning any property by reason of holding a power of appointment with respect to such property.

"(iv) COMMUNITY PROPERTY.—Property which represents the surviving spouse’s one-half share of community property held by the decedent and the surviving spouse under the community property laws of any State or possession of the United States or any foreign country shall be treated for purposes of this section as owned by, and acquired from, the decedent if at least one-half of the whole of the community interest in such property is treated as owned by, and acquired from, the decedent without regard to this clause.

“(C) PROPERTY ACQUIRED BY DECEDENT BY GIFT WITHIN 3 YEARS OF DEATH.—

"(i) IN GENERAL.—Subsections (b) and (c) shall not apply to property acquired by the decedent by gift or by inter vivos transfer for less than adequate and full consideration in money or money's worth during the 3-year period ending on the date of the decedent's death.

"(ii) EXCEPTION FOR CERTAIN GIFTS FROM SPOUSE.—

Clause (i) shall not apply to property acquired by the decedent from the decedent's spouse unless, during such 3-year period, such spouse acquired the property in whole or in part by gift or by inter vivos transfer for less than adequate and full consideration in money or money's worth.

"(D) STOCK OF CERTAIN ENTITIES.—Subsections (b) and (c) shall not apply to—

"(i) stock or securities of a foreign personal holding company,

"(ii) stock of a DISC or former DISC,

"(iii) stock of a foreign investment company, or

"(iv) stock of a passive foreign investment company unless such company is a qualified electing fund (as defined in section 1295) with respect to the decedent.

"(2) FAIR MARKET VALUE LIMITATION.—The adjustments under subsections (b) and (c) shall not increase the basis of any interest in property acquired from the decedent above its fair market value in the hands of the decedent as of the date of the decedent's death.

"(3) ALLOCATION RULES.—

"(A) IN GENERAL.—The executor shall allocate the adjustments under subsections (b) and (c) on the return required by section 6018.

"(B) CHANGES IN ALLOCATION.—Any allocation made pursuant to subparagraph (A) may be changed only as provided by the Secretary.

"(4)INFLATION ADJUSTMENT OF BASIS ADJUSTMENT AMOUNTS.—

"(A) IN GENERAL.—In the case of decedents dying in a calendar year after 2010, the $1,300,000, $60,000, and $3,000,000 dollar amounts in subsections (b) and (c)(2)(B) shall each be increased by an amount equal to the product of—

"(i) such dollar amount, and

"(ii) the cost-of-living adjustment determined under section 1(f)(3) for such calendar year, determined by substituting '2009' for '1992' in subparagraph (B) thereof.

"(B) ROUNDING.—If any increase determined under subparagraph (A) is not a multiple of—

"(i) $100,000 in the case of the $1,300,000 amount,

"(ii) $5,000 in the case of the $60,000 amount,

and

"(iii) $250,000 in the case of the $3,000,000 amount,

such increase shall be rounded to the next lowest multiple thereof.

"(e) PROPERTY ACQUIRED FROM THE DECEDENT.—For purposes of this section, the following property shall be considered to have been acquired from the decedent:

"(1) Property acquired by bequest, devise, or inheritance, or by the decedent's estate from the decedent.

"(2) Property transferred by the decedent during his lifetime—

"(i) to a qualified revocable trust (as defined in section 645(b)(1)), or

"(ii) to any other trust with respect to which the decedent reserved the right to make any change in the enjoyment thereof through the exercise of a power to alter, amend, or terminate the trust.

"(3) Any other property passing from the decedent by reason of death to the extent that such property passed without consideration.

"(f) COORDINATION WITH SECTION 691.—This section shall not apply to property which constitutes a right to receive an item of income in respect of a decedent under section 691.

"(g) CERTAIN LIABILITIES DISREGARDED.—

"(1) IN GENERAL.—In determining whether gain is recognized on the acquisition of property—

"(A) from a decedent by a decedent's estate or any beneficiary other than a tax-exempt beneficiary, and

"(B) from the decedent's estate by any beneficiary other than a tax-exempt beneficiary, and in determining the adjusted basis of such property, liabilities in excess of basis shall be disregarded.

"(2) TAX-EXEMPT BENEFICIARY.—For purposes of paragraph (1), the term 'tax-exempt beneficiary' means—

"(A) the United States, any State or political subdivision thereof, any possession of the United States, any Indian tribal government (within the meaning of section 7871), or any agency or instrumentality of any of the foregoing,

"(B) an organization (other than a cooperative described in section 521) which is exempt from tax imposed by chapter 1,

"(C) any foreign person or entity (within the meaning of section 168(h)(2)), and

"(D) to the extent provided in regulations, any person to whom property is transferred for the principal purpose of tax avoidance.

"(h) REGULATIONS.—The Secretary shall prescribe such regulations as may be necessary to carry out the purposes of this section.".

(b) INFORMATION RETURNS, ETC.—

(1) LARGE TRANSFERS AT DEATH.—So much of subpart C of part II of subchapter A of chapter 61 as precedes section 6019 is amended to read as follows:

"Subpart C—Returns Relating to Transfers During Life or at Death

"Sec. 6018. Returns relating to large transfers at death

"Sec. 6019. Gift tax returns

"SEC. 6018. RETURNS RELATING TO LARGE TRANSFERS AT DEATH.

"(a) IN GENERAL.—If this section applies to property acquired from a decedent, the executor of the estate of such decedent shall make a return containing the information specified in subsection (c) with respect to such property.

"(b) PROPERTY TO WHICH SECTION APPLIES.—

"(1) LARGE TRANSFERS.—This section shall apply to all property (other than cash) acquired from a decedent if the fair market value of such property acquired from the decedent exceeds the dollar amount applicable under section 1022(b)(2)(B) (without regard to section 1022(b)(2)(C)).

"(2) TRANSFERS OF CERTAIN GIFTS RECEIVED BY DECEDENT WITHIN 3 YEARS OF DEATH.—This section shall apply to any appreciated property acquired from the decedent if—

"(A) subsections (b) and (c) of section 1022 do not apply to such property by reason of section 1022(d)(1)(C), and

"(B) such property was required to be included on a return required to be filed under section 6019.

"(3) NONRESIDENTS NOT CITIZENS OF THE UNITED STATES.—

In the case of a decedent who is a nonresident not a citizen of the United States, paragraphs (1) and (2) shall be applied—"(A) by taking into account only—

"(i) tangible property situated in the United States,

and

"(ii) other property acquired from the decedent by a United States person, and

"(B) by substituting the dollar amount applicable under section 1022(b)(3) for the dollar amount referred to in paragraph (1).

"(4) RETURNS BY TRUSTEES OR BENEFICIARIES.—If the executor is unable to make a complete return as to any property acquired from or passing from the decedent, the executor shall include in the return a description of such property and the name of every person holding a legal or beneficial interest therein. Upon notice from the Secretary, such person shall in like manner make a return as to such property.

"(c) INFORMATION REQUIRED TO BE FURNISHED.—The information specified in this subsection with respect to any property acquired from the decedent is—

"(1) the name and TIN of the recipient of such property,

"(2) an accurate description of such property,

"(3) the adjusted basis of such property in the hands of the decedent and its fair market value at the time of death,

"(4) the decedent's holding period for such property,

"(5) sufficient information to determine whether any gain on the sale of the property would be treated as ordinary income,

"(6) the amount of basis increase allocated to the property under subsection (b) or (c) of section 1022, and

"(7) such other information as the Secretary may by regulations prescribe.

"(d) PROPERTY ACQUIRED FROM DECEDENT.—For purposes of this section, section 1022 shall apply for purposes of determining the property acquired from a decedent.

"(e) STATEMENTS TO BE FURNISHED TO CERTAIN PERSONS.—Every person required to make a return under subsection (a) shall furnish to each person whose name is required to be set forth in such return (other than the person required to make such return) a written statement showing—

"(1) the name, address, and phone number of the person required to make such return, and

"(2) the information specified in subsection (c) with respect to property acquired from, or passing from, the decedent to the person required to receive such statement.

The written statement required under the preceding sentence shall be furnished not later than 30 days after the date that the return required by subsection (a) is filed.".

(2) GIFTS.—Section 6019 (relating to gift tax returns) is amended—

(A) by striking "Any individual" and inserting "(a) IN GENERAL.—Any individual", and

(B) by adding at the end the following new subsection:

"(b) STATEMENTS TO BE FURNISHED TO CERTAIN PERSONS.—Every person required to make a return under subsection (a) shall furnish to each person whose name is required to be set forth in such return (other than the person required to make such return) a written statement showing—

"(1) the name, address, and phone number of the person required to make such return, and "(2) the information specified in such return with respect to property received by the person required to receive such statement.

The written statement required under the preceding sentence shall Deadline. be furnished not later than 30 days after the date that the return required by subsection (a) is filed.".

(3) TIME FOR FILING SECTION 6018 RETURNS.—

(A) RETURNS RELATING TO LARGE TRANSFERS AT DEATH.—Subsection (a) of section 6075 is amended to read 26 USC 6075. as follows:

"(a) RETURNS RELATING TO LARGE TRANSFERS AT DEATH.— The return required by section 6018 with respect to a decedent shall be filed with the return of the tax imposed by chapter 1 for the decedent's last taxable year or such later date specified in regulations prescribed by the Secretary.".

(B) CONFORMING AMENDMENTS.—Paragraph (3) of section 6075(b) is amended—

(i) by striking "ESTATE TAX RETURN" in the heading and inserting "SECTION 6018 RETURN", and

(ii) by striking "(relating to estate tax returns)"and inserting "(relating to returns relating to large transfers at death)".

(4) PENALTIES.—Part I of subchapter B of chapter 68 (relating to assessable penalties) is amended by adding at the end the following new section:

"Sec. 6716. Failure to File Information with Respect to Certain Transfers at Death and Gifts

"(a) INFORMATION REQUIRED TO BE FURNISHED TO THE SECRETARY.—Any person required to furnish any information under section 6018 who fails to furnish such information on the date prescribed therefor (determined with regard to any extension of time for filing) shall pay a penalty of $10,000 ($500 in the case of information required to be furnished under section 60 18(b)(2)) for each such failure.

"(b) INFORMATION REQUIRED TO BE FURNISHED TO BENEFICIARIES.—Any person required to furnish in writing to each person described in section 6018(e) or 6019(b) the information required under such section who fails to furnish such information shall pay a penalty of $50 for each such failure.

"(c) REASONABLE CAUSE EXCEPTION.—No penalty shall be imposed under subsection (a) or (b) with respect to any failure if it is shown that such failure is due to reasonable cause.

"(d) INTENTIONAL DISREGARD.—If any failure under subsection (a) or (b) is due to intentional disregard of the requirements under sections 6018 and 6019(b), the penalty under such subsection shall be 5 percent of the fair market value (as of the date of death or, in the case of section 60 19(b), the date of the gift) of the property with respect to which the information is required.

"(e) DEFICIENCY PROCEDURES NOT TO APPLY.—Subchapter B of chapter 63 (relating to deficiency procedures for income, estate, gift, and certain excise taxes) shall not apply in respect of the assessment or collection of any penalty imposed by this section.".

(5) CLERICAL AMENDMENTS.—

(A) The table of sections for part I of subchapter B of chapter 68 is amended by adding at the end the following new item:

"Sec. 6716. Failure to file information with respect to certain transfers at death and gifts.".

(B) The item relating to subpart C in the table of subparts for part II of subchapter A of chapter 61 is amended to read as follows:

"Subpart C. Returns relating to transfers during life or at death.".

(c) EXCLUSION OF GAIN ON SALE OF PRINCIPAL RESIDENCE MADE AVAILABLE TO HEIR OF DECEDENT IN CERTAIN CASES.—Subsection

(d) of section 121 (relating to exclusion of gain from sale of principal residence) is amended by adding at the end the following new paragraph:

"(9) PROPERTY ACQUIRED FROM A DECEDENT.—The exclusion under this section shall apply to property sold by—

"(A) the estate of a decedent,

"(B) any individual who acquired such property from the decedent (within the meaning of section 1022), and

"(C) a trust which, immediately before the death of the decedent, was a qualified revocable trust (as defined in section 645(b)(1)) established by the decedent, determined by taking into account the ownership and use by the decedent.".

(d) TRANSFERS OF APPRECIATED CARRYOVER BASIS PROPERTY TO SATISFY PECUNIARY BEQUEST.—

(1) IN GENERAL.—Section 1040 (relating to transfer of certain farm, etc., real property) is amended to read as follows:

"Sec. 1040. Use of Appreciated Carryover Basis Property to Satisfy Pecuniary Bequest

"(a) IN GENERAL.—If the executor of the estate of any decedent satisfies the right of any person to receive a pecuniary bequest with appreciated property, then gain on such exchange shall be recognized to the estate only to the extent that, on the date of such exchange, the fair market value of such property exceeds such value on the date of death.

"(b) SIMILAR RULE FOR CERTAIN TRUSTS.—To the extent provided in regulations prescribed by the Secretary, a rule similar to the rule provided in subsection (a) shall apply where—

"(1) by reason of the death of the decedent, a person has a right to receive from a trust a specific dollar amount which is the equivalent of a pecuniary bequest, and

"(2) the trustee of a trust satisfies such right with property.

"(c) BASIS OF PROPERTY ACQUIRED IN EXCHANGE DESCRIBED IN SUBSECTION (a) OR (b).—The basis of property acquired in an exchange with respect to which gain realized is not recognized by reason of subsection (a) or (b) shall be the basis of such property immediately before the exchange increased by the amount of the gain recognized to the estate or trust on the exchange.".

(2) The item relating to section 1040 in the table of sections for part III of subchapter O of chapter 1 is amended to read as follows:

"Sec. 1040. Use of appreciated carryover basis property to satisfy pecuniary bequest.".

AMENDMENTS RELATED TO CARRYOVER BASIS.—

(1) RECOGNITION OF GAIN ON TRANSFERS TO NONRESIDENTS.—

(A) Subsection (a) of section 684 is amended by 26 USC 684. inserting "or to a nonresident alien" after "or trust".

(B) Subsection (b) of section 684 is amended to read as follows:

"(b) EXCEPTIONS.—

"(1) TRANSFERS TO CERTAIN TRUSTS.—Subsection (a) shall not apply to a transfer to a trust by a United States person to the extent that any United States person is treated as the owner of such trust under section 671.

"(2) LIFETIME TRANSFERS TO NONRESIDENT ALIENS.—Subsection (a) shall not apply to a lifetime transfer to a nonresident alien.".

(C) The section heading for section 684 is amended by inserting "AND NONRESIDENT ALIENS" after "ESTATES".

(D) The item relating to section 684 in the table of sections for subpart F of part I of subchapter J of chapter 1 is amended by inserting "and nonresident aliens" after "estates".

(2) CAPITAL GAIN TREATMENT FOR INHERITED ART WORK OR SIMILAR PROPERTY.—

(A) IN GENERAL.—Subparagraph (C) of section 1221(a)(3) (defining capital asset) is amended by inserting "(other than by reason of section 1022)" after "is determined".

(B) COORDINATION WITH SECTION 170.—Paragraph (1) of section 170(e) (relating to certain contributions of ordinary income and capital gain property) is amended by adding at the end the following: "For purposes of this paragraph, the determination of whether property is a capital asset shall be made without regard to the exception contained in section 1221(a)(3)(C) for basis determined under section 1022.".

(3) DEFINITION OF EXECUTOR.—Section 7701(a) (relating to definitions) is amended by adding at the end the following:

"(47) EXECUTOR.—The term 'executor' means the executor or administrator of the decedent, or, if there is no executor or administrator appointed, qualified, and acting within the United States, then any person in actual or constructive possession of any property of the decedent.".

(4) CERTAIN TRUSTS.—Subparagraph (A) of section 4947(a)(2) is
26 USC amended by inserting "642(c)," after "170(f)(2)(B),".

(5) OTHER AMENDMENTS.—

(A) Section 1246 is amended by striking subsection (e).

(B) Subsection (e) of section 1291 is amended—

(i) by striking "(e),"; and

(ii) by striking "; except that" and all that follows and inserting a period.

(C) Section 1296 is amended by striking subsection (i) (6) CLERICAL AMENDMENT.—The table of sections for part II of subchapter O of chapter 1 is amended by inserting after the item relating to section 1021 the following new item:

"Sec. 1022. Treatment of property acquired from a decedent dying after December 31, 2009.".

(f) EFFECTIVE DATE.—

(1) IN GENERAL.—Except as provided in paragraph (2), the amendments made by this section shall apply to estates of decedents dying after December 31, 2009.

(2) TRANSFERS TO NONRESIDENTS.—The amendments made by subsection (e)(1) shall apply to transfers after December 31, 2009.

(3) SECTION 4947.—The amendment made by subsection (e)(4) shall apply to deductions for taxable years beginning after December 31, 2009.

Subtitle F—Conservation Easements

Sec. 551. Expansion of Estate Tax Rule for Conservation Easements

(a) REPEAL OF CERTAIN RESTRICTIONS ON WHERE LAND IS LOCATED.—Clause (i) of section 203 1(c)(8)(A) (defining land subject to a qualified conservation easement) is amended to read as follows:

"(i) which is located in the United States or any
possession of the United States,".

(b) CLARIFICATION OF DATE FOR DETERMINING VALUE OF LAND AND EASEMENT.—Section 203 1(c)(2) (defining applicable percentage) is amended by adding at the end the following new sentence: "The values taken into account under the preceding sentence shall be such values as of the date of the contribution referred to in paragraph (8)(B).".

(c) EFFECTIVE DATE.—The amendments made by this section shall apply to estates of decedents dying after December 31, 2000.

Subtitle G—Modifications of Generation-Skipping Transfer Tax

Sec. 561. Deemed Allocation of GST Exemption to Lifetime Transfers to Trusts; Retroactive Allocations

(a) IN GENERAL.—Section 2632 (relating to special rules for allocation of GST exemption) is amended by redesignating subsection (c) as subsection (e) and by inserting after subsection (b) the following new subsections:

"(c) DEEMED ALLOCATION TO CERTAIN LIFETIME TRANSFERS TO GST TRUSTS.—

"(1) IN GENERAL.—If any individual makes an indirect skip during such individual's lifetime, any unused portion of such individual's GST exemption shall be allocated to the property transferred to the extent necessary to make the inclusion ratio for such property zero. If the amount of the indirect skip exceeds such unused portion, the entire unused portion shall be allocated to the property transferred "(2) UNUSED PORTION.—For purposes of paragraph (1), the unused portion of an individual's GST exemption is that portion of such exemption which has not previously been—

"(A) allocated by such individual,

"(B) treated as allocated under subsection (b) with respect to a direct skip occurring during or before the calendar year in which the indirect skip is made, or

"(C) treated as allocated under paragraph (1) with respect to a prior indirect skip.

"(3) DEFINITIONS.—

INDIRECT SKIP.—For purposes of this subsection, the term 'indirect skip' means any transfer of property (other than a direct skip) subject to the tax imposed by chapter 12 made to a GST trust.

GST TRUST.—The term 'GST trust' means a trust that could have a generation-skipping transfer with respect to the transferor unless—

"(i) the trust instrument provides that more than 25 percent of the trust corpus must be distributed to or may be withdrawn by one or more individuals who are non-skip persons—

"(I) before the date that the individual attains age 46,

"(II) on or before one or more dates specified in the trust instrument that will occur before the date that such individual attains age 46, or

"(III) upon the occurrence of an event that, in accordance with regulations prescribed by the Secretary, may reasonably be expected to occur before the date that such individual attains age 46,

"(ii) the trust instrument provides that more than 25 percent of the trust corpus must be distributed to or may be withdrawn by one or more individuals who are non-skip persons and who are living on the date of death of another person identified in the instrument (by name or by class) who is more than 10 years older than such individuals,

"(iii) the trust instrument provides that, if one or more individuals who are non-skip persons die on or before a date or event described in clause (i) or (ii), more than 25 percent of the trust corpus either must be distributed to the estate or estates of one or more of such individuals or is subject to a general power of appointment exercisable by one or more of such individuals,

"(iv) the trust is a trust any portion of which would be included in the gross estate of a non-skip person (other than the transferor) if such person died immediately after the transfer,

"(v) the trust is a charitable lead annuity trust (within the meaning of section 2642(e)(3)(A)) or a charitable remainder annuity trust or a charitable remainder unitrust (within the meaning of section 664(d)), or

"(vi) the trust is a trust with respect to which a deduction was allowed under section 2522 for the amount of an interest in the form of the right to receive annual payments of a fixed percentage of the net fair market value of the trust property (determined yearly) and which is required to pay principal to a non-skip person if such person is alive when the yearly payments for which the deduction was allowed terminate.

For purposes of this subparagraph, the value of transferred property shall not be considered to be includible in the gross estate of a non-skip person or subject to a right of withdrawal by reason of such person holding a right to withdraw so much of such property as does not exceed the amount referred to in section 2503(b) with respect to any transferor, and it shall be assumed that powers of appointment held by non-skip persons will not be exercised.

"(4) AUTOMATIC ALLOCATIONS TO CERTAIN GST TRUSTS.—

For purposes of this subsection, an indirect skip to which section 2642(f) applies shall be deemed to have been made only at the close of the estate tax inclusion period. The fair market value of such transfer shall be the fair market value of the trust property at the close of the estate tax inclusion period.

"(5) APPLICABILITY AND EFFECT.—

"(A) IN GENERAL.—An individual—

"(i) may elect to have this subsection not apply to—

"(I) an indirect skip, or

"(II) any or all transfers made by such individual to a particular trust, and 26 USC

"(ii) may elect to treat any trust as a GST trust for purposes of this subsection with respect to any or all transfers made by such individual to such trust.

"(B) ELECTIONS.—

"(i) ELECTIONS WITH RESPECT TO INDIRECT SKIPS.—

An election under subparagraph (A)(i)(I) shall be deemed to be timely if filed on a timely filed gift tax return for the calendar year in which the transfer was made or deemed to have been made pursuant to paragraph (4) or on such later date or dates as may be prescribed by the Secretary.

"(ii) OTHER ELECTIONS.—An election under clause (i)(II) or (ii) of subparagraph (A) may be made on a timely filed gift tax return for the calendar year for which the election is to become effective.

"(d) RETROACTIVE ALLOCATIONS.—

"(1) IN GENERAL.—If—

"(A) a non-skip person has an interest or a future interest in a trust to which any transfer has been made,

"(B) such person—

"(i) is a lineal descendant of a grandparent of the transferor or of a grandparent of the transferor's spouse or former spouse, and

"(ii) is assigned to a generation below the generation assignment of the transferor, and

"(C) such person predeceases the transferor then the transferor may make an allocation of any of such transferor's unused GST exemption to any previous transfer or transfers to the trust on a chronological basis.

"(2) SPECIAL RULES.—If the allocation under paragraph (1) by the transferor is made on a gift tax return filed on or before the date prescribed by section 6075(b) for gifts made within the calendar year within which the non-skip person's death occurred—

"(A) the value of such transfer or transfers for purposes of section 2642(a) shall be determined as if such allocation had been made on a timely filed gift tax return for each calendar year within which each transfer was made,

"(B) such allocation shall be effective immediately before such death, and

"(C) the amount of the transferor's unused GST exemption available to be allocated shall be determined immediately before such death.

"(3) FUTURE INTEREST.—For purposes of this subsection, a person has a future interest in a trust if the trust may permit income or corpus to be paid to such person on a date or dates in the future.".

(b) CONFORMING AMENDMENT.—Paragraph (2) of section 2632(b) is amended by striking "with respect to a prior direct skip" and inserting "or subsection (c)(1)".

(c) EFFECTIVE DATES.—

(1) DEEMED ALLOCATION.—Section 2632(c) of the Internal Revenue Code of 1986 (as added by subsection (a)), and the amendment made by subsection (b), shall apply to transfers subject to chapter 11 or 12 made after December 31, 2000, and to estate tax inclusion periods ending after December 31, 2000.

(2) RETROACTIVE ALLOCATIONS.—Section 2632(d) of the Internal Revenue Code of 1986 (as added by subsection (a)) shall apply to deaths of non-skip persons occurring after December 31, 2000.

Sec. 562. Severing of Trusts

(a) INGENERAL.—Subsection (a) of section 2642 (relating to inclusion ratio) is amended by adding at the end the following new paragraph:

"(3) SEVERING OF TRUSTS.—

"(A) IN GENERAL. If a trust is severed in a qualified severance, the trusts resulting from such severance shall be treated as separate trusts thereafter for purposes of this chapter.

"(B) QUALIFIED SEVERANCE.—For purposes of subparagraph (A)—

"(i) IN GENERAL.—The term 'qualified severance' means the division of a single trust and the creation (by any means available under the governing instrument or under local law) of two or more trusts if—

"(I) the single trust was divided on a fractional basis, and

"(II) the terms of the new trusts, in the aggregate, provide for the same succession of interests of beneficiaries as are provided in the original trust.

"(ii) TRUSTS WITH INCLUSION RATIO GREATER THAN ZERO.—If a trust has an inclusion ratio of greater than zero and less than 1, a severance is a qualified severance only if the single trust is divided into two trusts, one of which receives a fractional share of the total value of all trust assets equal to the applicable fraction of the single trust immediately before the severance. In such case, the trust receiving such fractional share shall have an inclusion ratio of zero and the other trust shall have an inclusion ratio of 1.

"(iii) REGULATIONS.—The term 'qualified severance' includes any other severance permitted under regulations prescribed by the Secretary.

"(C) TIMING AND MANNER OF SEVERANCES.—A severance pursuant to this paragraph may be made at any time. The Secretary shall prescribe by forms or regulations the manner in which the qualified severance shall be reported to the Secretary.".

(b) EFFECTIVE DATE.—The amendment made by this section shall apply to severances after December 31, 2000.

Sec. 563. Modification of Certain Valuation Rules

(a) GIFTS FOR WHICH GIFT TAX RETURN FILED OR DEEMED ALLOCATION MADE.—Paragraph (1) of section 2642(b) (relating to valuation rules, etc.) is amended to read as follows:

"(1) GIFTS FOR WHICH GIFT TAX RETURN FILED OR DEEMED ALLOCATION MADE.—If the allocation of the GST exemption to any transfers of property is made on a gift tax return filed on or before the date prescribed by section 6075(b) for such transfer or is deemed to be made under section 2632 (b)(1) or (c)(1)—

"(A) the value of such property for purposes of subsection (a) shall be its value as finally determined for purposes of chapter 12 (within the meaning of section 200 1(f)(2)), or, in the case of an allocation deemed to have been made at the close of an estate tax inclusion period, its value at the time of the close of the estate tax inclusion period, and

"(B) such allocation shall be effective on and after the date of such transfer, or, in the case of an allocation deemed to have been made at the close of an estate tax inclusion period, on and after the close of such estate tax inclusion period.".

(b) TRANSFERS AT DEATH.—Subparagraph (A) of section 2642(b)(2) is amended to read as follows:

"(A) TRANSFERS AT DEATH.—If property is transferred as a result of the death of the transferor, the value of such property for purposes of subsection (a) shall be its value as finally determined for purposes of chapter 11; except that, if the requirements prescribed by the Secretary respecting allocation of post-death changes in value are not met, the value of such property shall be determined as of the time of the distribution concerned.".

(c) EFFECTIVE DATE.—The amendments made by this section shall apply to transfers subject to chapter 11 or 12 of the Internal Revenue Code of 1986 made after December 31, 2000.

Sec. 564. Relief Provisions

(a) IN GENERAL.—Section 2642 is amended by adding at the 26 USC 2642. end the following new subsection:

"(g) RELIEF PROVISIONS.—

"(1) RELIEF FROM LATE ELECTIONS.—

"(A) IN GENERAL.—The Secretary shall by regulation Regulations. prescribe such circumstances and procedures under which extensions of time will be granted to make—

"(i) an allocation of GST exemption described in paragraph (1) or (2) of subsection (b), and

"(ii) an election under subsection (b)(3) or (c)(5) of section 2632.

Such regulations shall include procedures for requesting comparable relief with respect to transfers made before the date of the enactment of this paragraph.

"(B) BASIS FOR DETERMINATIONS.—In determining whether to grant relief under this paragraph, the Secretary shall take into account all relevant circumstances, including evidence of intent contained in the trust instrument or instrument of transfer and such other factors as the Secretary deems relevant. For purposes of determining whether to grant relief under this paragraph, the time for making the allocation (or election) shall be treated as if not expressly prescribed by statute.

"(2) SUBSTANTIAL COMPLIANCE.—An allocation of GST exemption under section 2632 that demonstrates an intent to have the lowest possible inclusion ratio with respect to a transfer or a trust shall be deemed to be an allocation of so much of the transferor's unused GST exemption as produces the lowest possible inclusion ratio. In determining whether there has been substantial compliance, all relevant circumstances shall be taken into account, including evidence of intent contained in the trust instrument or instrument of transfer and such other factors as the Secretary deems relevant.".

(b) EFFECTIVE DATES.— Applicability.

the Internal Revenue Code of 1986 (as added by subsection

(1) RELIEF FROM LATE ELECTIONS.—Section 2642(g)(1) of 26 USC 2642 note.

(a)) shall apply to requests pending on, or filed after, December 31, 2000.

(2) SUBSTANTIAL COMPLIANCE.—Section 2642(g)(2) of such Code (as so added) shall apply to transfers subject to chapter 11 or 12 of the Internal Revenue Code of 1986 made after December 31, 2000. No implication is intended with respect to the availability of relief from late elections or the application of a rule of substantial compliance on or before such date.

Subtitle H—Extension of Time for Payment of Estate Tax

Sec. 571. Increase in Number of Allowable Partners and Shareholders in Closely Held Businesses

(a) IN GENERAL.—Paragraphs (1)(B)(ii), (1)(C)(ii), and (9)(B)(iii)(I) of section 6166(b) (relating to definitions and special rules) are each amended by striking "15" and inserting "45".

(b) EFFECTIVE DATE.—The amendments made by this section shall apply to estates of decedents dying after December 31, 2001.

Sec. 572. Expansion of Availability of Installment Payment for Estates with Interests Qualifying Lending and Finance Businesses

(a) IN GENERAL.—Section 6 166(b) (relating to definitions and special rules) is amended by adding at the end the following new paragraph:

"(10) STOCK IN QUALIFYING LENDING AND FINANCE BUSINESS TREATED AS STOCK IN AN ACTIVE TRADE OR BUSINESS COMPANY.—

"(A) IN GENERAL.—If the executor elects the benefits of this paragraph, then—

"(i) STOCK IN QUALIFYING LENDING AND FINANCE BUSINESS TREATED AS STOCK IN AN ACTIVE TRADE OR BUSINESS COMPANY.—For purposes of this section, any asset used in a qualifying lending and finance business shall be treated as an asset which is used in carrying on a trade or business.

"(ii) 5-YEAR DEFERRAL FOR PRINCIPAL NOT TO APPLY.—The executor shall be treated as having selected under subsection (a)(3) the date prescribed by section 615 1(a).

"(iii) 5 EQUAL INSTALLMENTS ALLOWED.—For purposes of applying subsection (a)(1), '5' shall be substituted for '10'.

"(B) DEFINITIONS.—For purposes of this paragraph—

"(i) QUALIFYING LENDING AND FINANCE BUSINESS.—
The term 'qualifying lending and finance business'
means a lending and finance business, if—

"(I) based on all the facts and circumstances immediately before the date of the decedent's death, there was substantial activity with respect to the lending and finance business, or

"(II) during at least 3 of the 5 taxable years ending before the date of the decedent's death, such business had at least 1 full-time employee substantially all of whose services were the active management of such business, 10 full-time, non- owner employees substantially all of whose services were directly related to such business, and $5,000,000 in gross receipts from activities described in clause (ii).

"(ii) LENDING AND FINANCE BUSINESS.—The term 'lending and finance business' means a trade or business of—

"(I) making loans,

"(II) purchasing or discounting accounts receivable, notes, or installment obligations,

"(III) engaging in rental and leasing of real and tangible personal property, including entering into leases and purchasing, servicing, and disposing of leases and leased assets, rendering services or making facilities available in the ordinary course of a lending or finance business, and

"(IV) rendering services or making facilities available in connection with activities described in subclauses (I) through (IV) carried on by the corporation

"(V) rendering services or making facilities available, or another corporation which is a member of the same affiliated group (as defined in section 1504 without regard to section 1504(b)(3)).

"(iii) LIMITATION.—The term 'qualifying lending and finance business' shall not include any interest in an entity, if the stock or debt of such entity or a controlled group (as defined in section 267(f)(1)) of which such entity was a member was readily tradable on an established securities market or secondary market (as defined by the Secretary) at any time within 3 years before the date of the decedent's death.".

(b) EFFECTIVE DATE.—The amendment made by this section
shall apply to estates of decedents dying after December 31, 2001.

Sec. 573. Clarification of Availability of Installment Payment

(a) IN GENERAL.—Subparagraph (B) of section 6166(b)(8) (relating to all stock must be non-readily-tradable stock) is amended to read as follows:

"(B) ALL STOCK MUST BE NON-READILY-TRADABLE STOCK.—

"(I) IN GENERAL.—No stock shall be taken into account for purposes of applying this paragraph unless it is non-readily-tradable stock (within the meaning of paragraph (7)(B)).

"(II) SPECIAL APPLICATION WHERE ONLY HOLDING COMPANY STOCK IS NON-READILY-TRADABLE STOCK.—If the requirements of clause (i) are not met, but all of the stock of each holding company taken into account is non-readily-tradable, then this paragraph shall apply, but subsection (a)(1) shall be applied by substituting '5' for '10'.".

(b) EFFECTIVE DATE.—The amendment made by this section shall apply to estates of decedents dying after December 31, 2001.

Subtitle I—Other Provisions

Sec. 581. Waiver of Statute of Limitation for Taxes on Certain Farm Valuations

If on the date of the enactment of this Act (or at any time within 1 year after the date of the enactment) a refund or credit of any overpayment of tax resulting from the application of section 2032A(c)(7)(E) of the Internal Revenue Code of 1986 is barred by any law or rule of law, the refund or credit of such overpayment shall, nevertheless, be made or allowed if claim therefor is filed before the date 1 year after the date of the enactment of this Act.

Title VI—Pension and Individual Retirement Arrangement Provisions

Subtitle A—Individual Retirement Accounts

Sec. 601. Modification of IRA Contribution Limits

(a) INCREASE IN CONTRIBUTION LIMIT.—

(1) IN GENERAL.—Paragraph (1)(A) of section 219(b) (relating to maximum amount of deduction) is amended by striking "$2,000" and inserting "the deductible amount".

(2) DEDUCTIBLE AMOUNT.—Section 2 19(b) is amended by adding at the end the following new paragraph:

"(5) DEDUCTIBLE AMOUNT.—For purposes of paragraph (1)(A)—

"(A) IN GENERAL.—The deductible amount shall be determined in accordance with the following table:

"For taxable years beginning in:	The deductible amount is:
2002 through 2004	$3,000
2005 through 2007	$4,000
2008 and thereafter	$5,000.

"(B) CATCH-UP CONTRIBUTIONS FOR INDIVIDUALS 50 OR OLDER.—

(i) IN GENERAL.—In the case of an individual who has attained the age of 50 before the close of the taxable year, the deductible amount for such taxable year shall be increased by the applicable amount.

(ii) APPLICABLE AMOUNT.—For purposes of clause (i), the applicable amount shall be the amount determined in accordance with the following table:

''For taxable years beginning in:	The applicable amount is:
2002 through 2005	$500
2006 and thereafter	$1,000.

"(C) COST-OF-LIVING ADJUSTMENT.—

"(i) IN GENERAL.—In the case of any taxable year beginning in a calendar year after 2008, the $5,000 amount under subparagraph (A) shall be increased by an amount equal to—

"(I) such dollar amount, multiplied by

"(II) the cost-of-living adjustment determined under section 1(f)(3) for the calendar year in which the taxable year begins, determined by substituting 'calendar year 2007' for 'calendar year 1992' in subparagraph (B) thereof.

"(ii) ROUNDING RULES.—If any amount after adjustment under clause (i) is not a multiple of $500, such amount shall be rounded to the next lower multiple of $500.".

(b) CONFORMING AMENDMENTS.—

(1) Section 408(a)(1) is amended by striking "in excess of $2,000 on behalf of any individual" and inserting "on behalf of any individual in excess of the amount in effect for such taxable year under section 219(b)(1)(A)".

(2) Section 408(b)(2)(B) is amended by striking "$2,000"and inserting "the dollar amount in effect under section 219(b)(1)(A)".

(3) Section 408(b) is amended by striking "$2,000" in the matter following paragraph (4) and inserting "the dollar amount in effect under section 219(b)(1)(A)".

(4) Section 408(j) is amended by striking "$2,000".

(5) Section 408(p)(8) is amended by striking "$2,000" and inserting "the dollar amount in effect under section 219(b)(1)(A)".

(c) EFFECTIVE DATE.—The amendments made by this section shall apply to taxable years beginning after December 31, 2001.

Sec. 602. Deemed IRAs under Employer Plans

(a) IN GENERAL.—Section 408 (relating to individual retirement accounts) is amended by redesignating subsection (q) as subsection (r) and by inserting after subsection (p) the following new subsection:

"(q) DEEMED IRAS UNDER QUALIFIED EMPLOYER PLANS.—

"(1) GENERAL RULE.—If—

"(A) a qualified employer plan elects to allow employees to make voluntary employee contributions to a separate account or annuity established under the plan, and

"(B) under the terms of the qualified employer plan, such account or annuity meets the applicable requirements of this section or section 408A for an individual retirement account or annuity, then such account or annuity shall be treated for purposes of this title in the same manner as an individual retirement plan and not as a qualified employer plan (and contributions to such account or annuity as contributions to an individual retirement plan and not to the qualified employer plan). For purposes of subparagraph (B), the requirements of subsection (a)(5) shall not apply.

"(2) SPECIAL RULES FOR QUALIFIED EMPLOYER PLANS.—For purposes of this title, a qualified employer plan shall not fail to meet any requirement of this title solely by reason of establishing and maintaining a program described in paragraph (1).

"(3) DEFINITIONS.—For purposes of this subsection—

"(A) QUALIFIED EMPLOYER PLAN.—The term 'qualified employer plan' has the meaning given such term by section 72(p)(4); except such term shall not include a government plan which is not a qualified plan unless the plan is an eligible deferred compensation plan (as defined in section 457(b)).

"(B) VOLUNTARY EMPLOYEE CONTRIBUTION.—The term 'voluntary employee contribution' means any contribution (other than a mandatory contribution within the meaning of section 411(c)(2)(C))—

"(i) which is made by an individual as an employee under a qualified employer plan which allows employees to elect to make contributions described in paragraph (1), and

"(ii) with respect to which the individual has designated the contribution as a contribution to which this subsection applies.''.

(b) AMENDMENT OF ERISA.—

(1) IN GENERAL.—Section 4 of the Employee Retirement Income Security Act of 1974 (29 U.S.C. 1003) is amended by adding at the end the following new subsection:

"(c) If a pension plan allows an employee to elect to make voluntary employee contributions to accounts and annuities as provided in section 408(q) of the Internal Revenue Code of 1986, such accounts and annuities (and contributions thereto) shall not be treated as part of such plan (or as a separate pension plan) for purposes of any provision of this title other than section 403(c), 404, or 405 (relating to exclusive benefit, and fiduciary and co- fiduciary responsibilities).''

(2) CONFORMING AMENDMENT.—Section 4(a) of such Act (29 U.S.C. 1003(a)) is amended by inserting "or (c)'' after "subsection (b)''

(c) EFFECTIVE DATE.—The amendments made by this section shall apply to plan years beginning after December 31, 2002

Subtitle B—Expanding Coverage

Sec. 611. Increase in Benefit and Contribution Limits

(a) DEFINED BENEFIT PLANS.—

(1) DOLLAR LIMIT.—

(A) Subparagraph (A) of section 415(b)(1) (relating to limitation for defined benefit plans) is amended by striking "$90,000'' and inserting "$160,000''.

(B) Subparagraphs (C) and (D) of section 415(b)(2) are each amended in the headings and the text, by striking "$90,000'' and inserting "$160,000'',

(C) Paragraph (7) of section 415(b) (relating to benefits under certain collectively bargained plans) is amended by striking "the greater of $68,212 or one-half the amount otherwise applicable for such year under paragraph (1)(A) for '$90,000''' and inserting "one-half the amount otherwise applicable for such year under paragraph (1)(A) for '$160,000'

(2) LIMIT REDUCED WHEN BENEFIT BEGINS BEFORE AGE 62.—

Subparagraph (C) of section 415(b)(2) is amended by striking "the social security retirement age'' each place it appears in the heading and text and inserting "age 62'' and by striking the second sentence.

(3) LIMIT INCREASED WHEN BENEFIT BEGINS AFTER AGE 65.—

Subparagraph (D) of section 415(b)(2) is amended by striking "the social security retirement age'' each place it appears in the heading and text and inserting "age 65''.

(4) COST-OF-LIVING ADJUSTMENTS.—Subsection (d) of section 415 (related to cost-of-living adjustments) is amended—

(A) by striking "$90,000'' in paragraph (1)(A) and inserting "$160,000''; and (B) in paragraph (3)(A)—

(B) by striking "$90,000" in the heading and inserting "$160,000"; and by striking "October 1, 1986" and inserting "July 1, 2001".

(5) CONFORMING AMENDMENTS.—

(A) Section 415(b)(2) is amended by striking subparagraph (F). 26

(B) Section 415(b)(9) is amended to read as follows:

"(9) SPECIAL RULE FOR COMMERCIAL AIRLINE PILOTS.—

"(A) IN GENERAL.—Except as provided in subparagraph (B), in the case of any participant who is a commercial airline pilot, if, as of the time of the participant's retirement, regulations prescribed by the Federal Aviation Administration require an individual to separate from service as a commercial airline pilot after attaining any age occurring on or after age 60 and before age 62, paragraph (2)(C) shall be applied by substituting such age for age 62.

"(B) INDIVIDUALS WHO SEPARATE FROM SERVICE BEFORE AGE 60.—If a participant described in subparagraph (A) separates from service before age 60, the rules of paragraph (2)(C) shall apply.".

(C) Section 415(b)(10)(C)(i) is amended by striking "applied without regard to paragraph (2)(F)".

(b) DEFINED CONTRIBUTION PLANS.—

(1) DOLLAR LIMIT.—Subparagraph (A) of section 415(c)(1) (relating to limitation for defined contribution plans) is amended by striking "$30,000" and inserting "$40,000".

(2) COST-OF-LIVING ADJUSTMENTS.—Subsection (d) of section 415 (related to cost-of-living adjustments) is amended—

by striking "$30,000" in paragraph (1)(C) and inserting "$40,000"; and

(B) in paragraph (3)(D)—

(i) by striking "$30,000" in the heading and inserting "$40,000"; and

(ii) by striking "October 1, 1993" and inserting "July 1, 2001".

(c) QUALIFIED TRUSTS.—

(1) COMPENSATION LIMIT.—Sections 401(a)(17), 404(l),

(2) 408(k), and 505(b)(7) are each amended by striking "$150,000"each place it appears and inserting "$200,000".

(3) BASE PERIOD AND ROUNDING OF COST-OF-LIVING ADJUSTMENT.—Subparagraph (B) of section 401(a)(17) is amended—

(A) by striking "October 1, 1993" and inserting "July 1, 2001"; and

(B) by striking "$10,000" both places it appears and inserting "$5,000".

(d) ELECTIVE DEFERRALS.—

(1) IN GENERAL.—Paragraph (1) of section 402(g) (relating to limitation on exclusion for elective deferrals) is amended to read as follows:

"(1) IN GENERAL.—

"(A) LIMITATION.—Notwithstanding subsections (e)(3) and (h)(1)(B), the elective deferrals of any individual for any taxable year shall be included in such individual's gross income to the extent the amount of such deferrals for the taxable year exceeds the applicable dollar amount.

"(B) APPLICABLE DOLLAR AMOUNT.—For purposes of subparagraph (A), the applicable dollar amount shall be the amount determined in accordance with the following table:

"For taxable years beginning in calendar year:	The applicable dollar amount:
2002	$11,000
2003	$12,000
2004	$13,000
2005	$14,000
2006 or thereafter	$15,000"

COST-OF-LIVING ADJUSTMENT.—Paragraph (5) of section 402(g) is amended to read as follows:

"(5) COST-OF-LIVING ADJUSTMENT.—In the case of taxable years beginning after December 31, 2006, the Secretary shall adjust the $15,000 amount under paragraph (1)(B) at the same time and in the same manner as under section 4 15(d), except that the base period shall be the calendar quarter beginning July 1, 2005, and any increase under this paragraph which is not a multiple of $500 shall be rounded to the next lowest multiple of $500.".

(3) CONFORMING AMENDMENTS.—

(A) Section 402(g) (relating to limitation on exclusion for elective deferrals), as amended by paragraphs (1) and (2), is further amended by striking paragraph (4) and redesignating paragraphs (5), (6), (7), (8), and (9) as paragraphs (4), (5), (6), (7), and (8), respectively.

(B) Paragraph (2) of section 457(c) is amended by striking "402(g)(8)(A)(iii)" and inserting "402(g)(7)(A)(iii)".

(C) Clause (iii) of section 501(c)(18)(D) is amended by striking "(other than paragraph (4) thereof)".

(e) DEFERRED COMPENSATION PLANS OF STATE AND LOCAL GOVERNMENTS AND TAX-EXEMPT ORGANIZATIONS.—

(1) IN GENERAL.—Section 457 (relating to deferred compensation plans of State and local governments and tax-exempt organizations) is amended—

(A) in subsections (b)(2)(A) and (c)(1) by striking "$7,500" each place it appears and inserting "the applicable dollar amount"; and

(B) in subsection (b)(3)(A) by striking "$15,000" and inserting "twice the dollar amount in effect under subsection (b)(2)(A)".

(2) APPLICABLE DOLLAR AMOUNT; COST-OF-LIVING ADJUSTMENT.—Paragraph (15) of section 457(e) is amended to read as follows:

"(15) APPLICABLE DOLLAR AMOUNT.—

"(A) IN GENERAL.—The applicable dollar amount shall be the amount determined in accordance with the following table:

''For taxable years beginning in calendar year:	The applicable dollar amount:
2002	$11,000
2003	$12,000
2004	$13,
2005	$14,000
2006 or thereafter	$15,000.

"(B) COST-OF-LIVING ADJUSTMENTS.—In the case of taxable years beginning after December 31, 2006, the Secretary shall adjust the $15,000 amount under subparagraph (A) at the same time and in the same manner as under section 4 15(d), except that the base period shall be the calendar quarter beginning July 1, 2005, and any increase under this paragraph which is not a multiple of $500 shall be rounded to the next lowest multiple of $500.".

(f) SIMPLE RETIREMENT ACCOUNTS.—

(1) LIMITATION.—Clause (ii) of section 408(p)(2)(A) (relating to general rule for qualified salary reduction arrangement) is amended by striking "$6,000" and inserting "the applicable dollar amount".

(2) APPLICABLE DOLLAR AMOUNT.—Subparagraph (E) of 408(p)(2) is amended to read as follows:

"(E) APPLICABLE DOLLAR AMOUNT; COST-OF-LIVING ADJUSTMENT.—

IN GENERAL.—For purposes of subparagraph (A)(ii), the applicable dollar amount shall be the amount determined in accordance with the following table:

"For years beginning in calendar year:	The applicable dollar amount:
2002	$7,000
2003	$8,000
2004	$9,000
2005 or thereafter	$10,000

COST-OF-LIVING ADJUSTMENT.—In the case of a year beginning after December 31, 2005, the Secretary shall adjust the $10,000 amount under clause (i) at the same time and in the same manner as under section 415(d), except that the base period taken into account shall be the calendar quarter beginning July 1, 2004, and any increase under this subparagraph which is not a multiple of $500 shall be rounded to the next lower multiple of $500.".

(3) CONFORMING AMENDMENTS.—

(A) Subclause (I) of section 401(k)(1 1)(B)(i) is amended by striking "$6,000" and inserting "the amount in effect under section 408(p)(2)(A)(ii)".

(B) Section 401(k)(11) is amended by striking subparagraph (E).

(g) CERTAIN COMPENSATION LIMITS.—

(1) IN GENERAL.—Subparagraph (A) of section 401(c)(2) (defining earned income) is amended by adding at the end thereof the following new sentence: "For purposes of this part only (other than sections 419 and 419A), this subparagraph shall be applied as if the term 'trade or business' for purposes of section 1402 included service described in section 1402(c)(6).".

(2) SIMPLE RETIREMENT ACCOUNTS.—Clause (ii) of section 408(p)(6)(A) (defining self-employed) is amended by adding at the end the following new sentence: "The preceding sentence shall be applied as if the term 'trade or business' for purposes of section 1402 included service described in section 1402(c)(6).".

(h) ROUNDING RULE RELATING TO DEFINED BENEFIT PLANS AND DEFINED CONTRIBUTION PLANS.—Paragraph (4) of section 4 15(d) is amended to read as follows:

"(4) ROUNDING.—

"(A) $160,000 AMOUNT.—Any increase under subparagraph (A) of paragraph (1) which is not a multiple of $5,000 shall be rounded to the next lowest multiple of $5,000.

"(B) $40,000 AMOUNT.—Any increase under subparagraph (C) of paragraph (1) which is not a multiple of $1,000 shall be rounded to the next lowest multiple of $1,000.".

(i) EFFECTIVE DATES.—

(1) IN GENERAL.—The amendments made by this section shall apply to years beginning after December 31, 2001.

(2) DEFINED BENEFIT PLANS.—The amendments made by subsection (a) shall apply to years ending after December 31, 2001.

Sec. 612. Plan Loans for Subchapter S Owners, Partners, and Sole Proprietors

(a) IN GENERAL.—Subparagraph (B) of section 4975(f)(6) (relating to exemptions not to apply to certain transactions) is amended by adding at the end the following new clause:

"(iii) LOAN EXCEPTION.—For purposes of subparagraph (A)(i), the term 'owner-employee' shall only include a person described in subclause (II) or (III) of clause (i).".

(b) AMENDMENT OF ERISA.—Section 408(d)(2) of the Employee Retirement Income Security Act of 1974 (29 U.S.C. 1108(d)(2)) is amended by adding at the end the following new subparagraph:

"(C) For purposes of paragraph (1)(A), the term 'owner- employee' shall only include a person described in clause (ii) or (iii) of subparagraph (A).".

(c) EFFECTIVE DATE.—The amendment made by this section shall apply to years beginning after December 31, 2001.

Sec. 613. Modification of Top-Heavy Rules

(a) SIMPLIFICATION OF DEFINITION OF KEY EMPLOYEE.—

(1) IN GENERAL.—Section 416(i)(1)(A) (defining key employee) is amended—

(A) by striking "or any of the 4 preceding plan years"in the matter preceding clause (i);

(B) by striking clause (i) and inserting the following: "(i) an officer of the employer having an annual compensation greater than $130,000,";

(C) by striking clause (ii) and redesignating clauses (iii) and (iv) as clauses (ii) and (iii), respectively; and

(D) by striking the second sentence in the matter following clause (iii), as redesignated by subparagraph (C), and by inserting the following: "in the case of plan years beginning after December 31, 2002, the $130,000 amount in clause (i) shall be adjusted at the same time and in the same manner as under section 4 15(d), except that the base period shall be the calendar quarter beginning July 1, 2001, and any increase under this sentence which is not a multiple of $5,000 shall be rounded to the next lower multiple of $5,000.".

(2) CONFORMING AMENDMENT.—Section 416(i)(1)(B)(iii) is amended by striking "and subparagraph (A)(ii)".

(b) MATCHING CONTRIBUTIONS TAKEN INTO ACCOUNT FOR MINIMUM CONTRIBUTION REQUIREMENTS.—Section 416(c)(2)(A) (relating to defined contribution plans) is amended by adding at the end the following: "Employer matching contributions (as defined in section 401(m)(4)(A)) shall be taken into account for purposes of this subparagraph (and any reduction under this sentence shall not be taken into account in determining whether section 401(k)(4)(A) applies)"

(c) DISTRIBUTIONS DURING LAST YEAR BEFORE DETERMINATION DATE TAKEN INTO ACCOUNT.—

(1) IN GENERAL.—Paragraph (3) of section 416(g) is amended to read as follows:

"(3) DISTRIBUTIONS DURING LAST YEAR BEFORE DETERMINATION DATE TAKEN INTO ACCOUNT.—

"(A) IN GENERAL.—For purposes of determining—

"(i) the present value of the cumulative accrued benefit for any employee, or

"(ii) the amount of the account of any employee, such present value or amount shall be increased by the aggregate distributions made with respect to such employee under the plan during the 1-year period ending on the determination date. The preceding sentence shall also apply to distributions under a terminated plan which if it had not been terminated would have been required to be included in an aggregation group.

"(B) 5-YEAR PERIOD IN CASE OF IN-SERVICE DISTRIBUTION.—In the case of any distribution made for a reason other than separation from service, death, or disability, subparagraph (A) shall be applied by substituting '5-year period' for '1-year period'.".

(2) BENEFITS NOT TAKEN INTO ACCOUNT.—Subparagraph (E) of section 416(g)(4) is amended—

(A) by striking "LAST 5 YEARS" in the heading and inserting "LAST YEAR BEFORE DETERMINATION DATE"; and

(B) by striking "5-year period" and inserting "1-year period".

(d) DEFINITION OF TOP-HEAVY PLANS.—Paragraph (4) of section 4 16(g) (relating to other special rules for top-heavy plans) is amended by adding at the end the following new subparagraph:

"(H) CASH OR DEFERRED ARRANGEMENTS USING ALTERNATIVE METHODS OF MEETING NONDISCRIMINATION REQUIRE-

MENTS.—The term 'top-heavy plan' shall not include a plan which consists solely of—

"(i) a cash or deferred arrangement which meets the requirements of section 401(k)(12), and

"(ii) matching contributions with respect to which the requirements of section 401(m)(11) are met.

If, but for this subparagraph, a plan would be treated as a top-heavy plan because it is a member of an aggregation group which is a top-heavy group, contributions under the plan may be taken into account in determining whether any other plan in the group meets the requirements of subsection (c)(2)."

(e) FROZEN PLAN EXEMPT FROM MINIMUM BENEFIT REQUIREMENT.—Subparagraph (C) of section 416(c)(1) (relating to defined benefit plans) is amended—

(A) by striking "clause (ii)" in clause (i) and inserting "clause (ii) or (iii)"; and

(B) by adding at the end the following:

"(iii) EXCEPTION FOR FROZEN PLAN.—For purposes of determining an employee's years of service with the employer, any service with the employer shall be disregarded to the extent that such service occurs during a plan year when the plan benefits (within the meaning of section 4 10(b)) no key employee or former key employee.".

(f) EFFECTIVE DATE.—The amendments made by this section shall apply to years beginning after December 31, 2001.

Sec. 614. Elective Deferrals Not Taken into Account for Purposes of Deduction Limits

(a) IN GENERAL.—Section 404 (relating to deduction for contributions of an employer to an employees' trust or annuity plan and compensation under a deferred payment plan) is amended by adding at the end the following new subsection:

"(n) ELECTIVE DEFERRALS NOT TAKEN INTO ACCOUNT FOR PURPOSES OF DEDUCTION LIMITS.—Elective deferrals (as defined in section 402(g)(3)) shall not be subject to any limitation contained in paragraph (3), (7), or (9) of subsection (a), and such elective deferrals shall not be taken into account in applying any such limitation to any other contributions.".

(b) EFFECTIVE DATE.—The amendment made by this section shall apply to years beginning after December 31, 2001.

Sec. 615. Repeal of Coordination Requirements for Deferred Compensation Plans of State and Local Governments and Tax-Exempt Organizations

(a) IN GENERAL.—Subsection (c) of section 457 (relating to deferred compensation plans of State and local governments and tax-exempt organizations), as amended by section 611, is amended to read as follows:

"(c) LIMITATION.—The maximum amount of the compensation of any one individual which may be deferred under subsection (a) during any taxable year shall not exceed the amount in effect under subsection (b)(2)(A) (as modified by any adjustment provided under subsection (b)(3)).".

(b) EFFECTIVE DATE.—The amendment made by subsection (a) shall apply to years beginning after December 31, 2001.

Sec. 616. Deduction Limits

(a) MODIFICATION OF LIMITS.—

(1) STOCK BONUS AND PROFIT SHARING TRUSTS.—

(A) IN GENERAL.—Subclause (I) of section 404(a)(3)(A)(i) (relating to stock bonus and profit sharing trusts) is amended by striking "15 percent" and inserting "25 percent".

(B) CONFORMING AMENDMENT.—Subparagraph (C) of section 404(h)(1) is amended by striking "15 percent" each place it appears and inserting "25 percent".

(2) DEFINED CONTRIBUTION PLANS.—

(A) IN GENERAL.—Clause (v) of section 404(a)(3)(A) (relating to stock bonus and profit sharing trusts) is amended to read as follows:

"(v) DEFINED CONTRIBUTION PLANS SUBJECT TO THE FUNDING STANDARDS.—Except as provided by the Secretary, a defined contribution plan which is subject to the funding standards of section 412 shall be treated in the same manner as a stock bonus or profit-sharing plan for purposes of this subparagraph.".

(B) CONFORMING AMENDMENTS.—

(i) Section 404(a)(1)(A) is amended by inserting

(ii) "(other than a trust to which paragraph (3) applies)"after "pension trust".

(iii) Section 404(h)(2) is amended by striking "stock bonus or profit-sharing trust" and inserting "trust subject to subsection (a)(3)(A)".

(iv) The heading of section 404(h)(2) is amended by striking "STOCK BONUS AND PROFIT-SHARING TRUST"and inserting "CERTAIN TRUSTS".

(b) COMPENSATION.—

(1) IN GENERAL.—Section 404(a) (relating to general rule) is amended by adding at the end the following:

"(12) DEFINITION OF COMPENSATION.—For purposes of paragraphs (3), (7), (8), and (9), the term 'compensation' shall include amounts treated as 'participant's compensation' under subparagraph (C) or (D) of section 415(c)(3).".

(2) CONFORMING AMENDMENTS.—

(A) Subparagraph (B) of section 404(a)(3) is amended by striking the last sentence thereof.

(B) Clause (i) of section 4972(c)(6)(B) is amended by striking "(within the meaning of section 404(a))" and inserting "(within the meaning of section 404(a) and as adjusted under section 404(a)(12))".

(c) EFFECTIVE DATE.—The amendments made by this section shall apply to years beginning after December 31, 2001.

Sec. 617. Option to Treat Elective Deferrals as After-Tax Roth Contributions

(a) IN GENERAL.—Subpart A of part I of subchapter D of chapter 1 (relating to deferred compensation, etc.) is amended by inserting after section 402 the following new section:

"Sec. 402a. Optional Treatment of Elective Deferrals as Roth Contributions

"(a) GENERAL RULE.—If an applicable retirement plan includes a qualified Roth contribution program—

"(1) any designated Roth contribution made by an employee pursuant to the program shall be treated as an elective deferral for purposes of this chapter, except that such contribution shall not be excludable from gross income, and

"(2) such plan (and any arrangement which is part of such plan) shall not be treated as failing to meet any requirement of this chapter solely by reason of including such program.

"(b) QUALIFIED ROTH CONTRIBUTION PROGRAM.—For purposes of this section—

"(1) IN GENERAL.—The term 'qualified Roth contribution program' means a program under which an employee may elect to make designated Roth contributions in lieu of all or a portion of elective deferrals the employee is otherwise eligible to make under the applicable retirement plan.

"(2) SEPARATE ACCOUNTING REQUIRED.—A program shall not be treated as a qualified Roth contribution program unless the applicable retirement plan—

"(A) establishes separate accounts ('designated Roth accounts') for the designated Roth contributions of each employee and any earnings properly allocable to the contributions, and

"(B) maintains separate recordkeeping with respect to each account.

"(c) DEFINITIONS AND RULES RELATING TO DESIGNATED ROTH CONTRIBUTIONS.—For purposes of this section—

"(1) DESIGNATED ROTH CONTRIBUTION.—The term 'designated Roth contribution' means any elective deferral which—

"(A) is excludable from gross income of an employee without regard to this section, and

"(B) the employee designates (at such time and in such manner as the Secretary may prescribe) as not being so excludable.

"(2) DESIGNATION LIMITS.—The amount of elective deferrals which an employee may designate under paragraph (1) shall not exceed the excess (if any) of—

"(A) the maximum amount of elective deferrals excludable from gross income of the employee for the taxable year (without regard to this section), over

"(B) the aggregate amount of elective deferrals of the employee for the taxable year which the employee does not designate under paragraph (1).

"(3) ROLLOVER CONTRIBUTIONS.—

"(A) IN GENERAL.—A rollover contribution of any payment or distribution from a designated Roth account which is otherwise allowable under this chapter may be made only if the contribution is to—

"(i) another designated Roth account of the individual from whose account the payment or distribution was made, or

"(ii) a Roth IRA of such individual.

"(B) COORDINATION WITH LIMIT.—Any rollover contribution to a designated Roth account under subparagraph (A) shall not be taken into account for purposes of paragraph (1).

"(d) DISTRIBUTION RULES.—For purposes of this title—

"(1) EXCLUSION.—Any qualified distribution from a designated Roth account shall not be includible in gross income.

"(2) QUALIFIED DISTRIBUTION.—For purposes of this subsection—

"(A) IN GENERAL.—The term 'qualified distribution' has the meaning given such term by section 408A(d)(2)(A) (without regard to clause (iv) thereof).

"(B) DISTRIBUTIONS WITHIN NONEXCLUSION PERIOD.—A payment or distribution from a designated Roth account shall not be treated as a qualified distribution if such payment or distribution is made within the 5-taxable-year period beginning with the earlier of—

"(i) the first taxable year for which the individual made a designated Roth contribution to any designated Roth account established for such individual under the same applicable retirement plan, or

"(ii) if a rollover contribution was made to such designated Roth account from a designated Roth account previously established for such individual under another applicable retirement plan, the first taxable year for which the individual made a designated Roth contribution to such previously established account.

"(C) DISTRIBUTIONS OF EXCESS DEFERRALS AND CONTRIBUTIONS AND EARNINGS THEREON.—The term 'qualified distribution' shall not include any distribution of any excess deferral under section 402(g)(2) or any excess contribution under section 401(k)(8), and any income on the excess deferral or contribution.

"(3) TREATMENT OF DISTRIBUTIONS OF CERTAIN EXCESS DEFERRALS.—Notwithstanding section 72, if any excess deferral under section 402(g)(2) attributable to a designated Roth contribution is not distributed on or before the 1st April 15 following the close of the taxable year in which such excess deferral is made, the amount of such excess deferral shall—

"(A) not be treated as investment in the contract, and

"(B) be included in gross income for the taxable year in which such excess is distributed.

"(4) AGGREGATION RULES.—Section 72 shall be applied separately with respect to distributions and payments from a designated Roth account and other distributions and payments from the plan.

"(e) OTHER DEFINITIONS.—For purposes of this section—

"(1) APPLICABLE RETIREMENT PLAN.—The term 'applicable retirement plan' means—

"(A) an employees' trust described in section 40 1(a) which is exempt from tax under section 50 1(a), and

"(B) a plan under which amounts are contributed by an individual's employer for an annuity contract described in section 403(b).

"(2) ELECTIVE DEFERRAL.—The term 'elective deferral' means any elective deferral described in subparagraph (A) or (C) of section 402(g)(3)."

(b) EXCESS DEFERRALS.—Section 402(g) (relating to limitation 26 USC 402. on exclusion for elective deferrals) is amended—

(1) by adding at the end of paragraph (1)(A) (as added by section 201(c)(1)) the following new sentence: "The preceding sentence shall not apply the portion of such excess as does not exceed the designated Roth contributions of the individual for the taxable year."; and

(2) by inserting "(or would be included but for the last sentence thereof)" after "paragraph (1)" in paragraph (2)(A).

(c) ROLLOVERS.—Subparagraph (B) of section 402(c)(8) is amended by adding at the end the following:

"If any portion of an eligible rollover distribution is attributable to payments or distributions from a designated Roth account (as defined in section 402A), an eligible retirement plan with respect to such portion shall include only another designated Roth account and a Roth IRA.".

(d) REPORTING REQUIREMENTS.—

(1) W–2 INFORMATION.—Section 605 1(a)(8) is amended by inserting ", including the amount of designated Roth contributions (as defined in section 402A)" before the comma at the end.

(2) INFORMATION.—Section 6047 is amended by redesignating subsection (f) as subsection (g) and by inserting after subsection (e) the following new subsection:

"(f) DESIGNATED ROTH CONTRIBUTIONS.—The Secretary shall require the plan administrator of each applicable retirement plan (as defined in section 402A) to make such returns and reports regarding designated Roth contributions (as defined in section 402A) to the Secretary, participants and beneficiaries of the plan, and such other persons as the Secretary may prescribe.".

(e) CONFORMING AMENDMENTS.—

(1) Section 408A(e) is amended by adding after the first sentence the following new sentence: "Such term includes a rollover contribution described in section 402A(c)(3)(A).".

(2) The table of sections for subpart A of part I of subchapter D of chapter 1 is amended by inserting after the item relating to section 402 the following new item:

"Sec. 402A. Optional treatment of elective deferrals as Roth contributions.".

(f) EFFECTIVE DATE.—The amendments made by this section shall apply to taxable years beginning after December 31, 2005.

Sec. 618. Nonrefundable Credit to Certain Individuals for Elective Deferrals and IRA Contributions

(a) IN GENERAL.—Subpart A of part IV of subchapter A of chapter 1 (relating to nonrefundable personal credits) is amended by inserting after section 25A the following new section:

"Sec. 25b. Elective Deferrals and IRA Contributions by Certain Individuals

"(a) ALLOWANCE OF CREDIT.—In the case of an eligible individual, there shall be allowed as a credit against the tax imposed by this subtitle for the taxable year an amount equal to the applicable percentage of so much of the qualified retirement savings contributions of the eligible individual for the taxable year as do not exceed $2,000.

"(b) APPLICABLE PERCENTAGE.—For purposes of this section, the applicable percentage is the percentage determined in accordance with the following table:

Adjusted Gross Income						Applicable percentage
Joint return		Head of a household		All other cases		
Over	Not over	Over	Not over	Over	Not over	
	$30,000		$22,500		$15,000	50
30,000	32,500	22,500	24,375	15,000	16,250	20
32,500	50,000	24,375	37,500	16,250	25,000	10
50,000		37,500		25,000		0

"(c) ELIGIBLE INDIVIDUAL.—For purposes of this section—

"(1) IN GENERAL.—The term 'eligible individual' means any individual if such individual has attained the age of 18 as of the close of the taxable year "(2) DEPENDENTS AND FULL-TIME STUDENTS NOT ELIGIBLE.—

The term 'eligible individual' shall not include—

"(A) any individual with respect to whom a deduction under section 151 is allowed to another taxpayer for a taxable year beginning in the calendar year in which such individual's taxable year begins, and

"(B) any individual who is a student (as defined in section 151(c)(4)).

"(d) QUALIFIED RETIREMENT SAVINGS CONTRIBUTIONS.—For purposes of this section—

"(1) IN GENERAL.—The term 'qualified retirement savings contributions' means, with respect to any taxable year, the sum of—

"(A) the amount of the qualified retirement contributions (as defined in section 2 19(e)) made by the eligible individual,

"(B) the amount of—

"(i) any elective deferrals (as defined in section 402(g)(3)) of such individual, and

"(ii) any elective deferral of compensation by such individual under an eligible deferred compensation plan (as defined in section 45 7(b)) of an eligible employer described in section 457(e)(1)(A), and

"(C) the amount of voluntary employee contributions by such individual to any qualified retirement plan (as defined in section 4974(c)).

"(2) REDUCTION FOR CERTAIN DISTRIBUTIONS.—

"(A) IN GENERAL.—The qualified retirement savings contributions determined under paragraph (1) shall be reduced (but not below zero) by the sum of—

"(i) any distribution from a qualified retirement plan (as defined in section 4974(c)), or from an eligible deferred compensation plan (as defined in section 457(b)), received by the individual during the testing period which is includible in gross income, and

"(ii) any distribution from a Roth IRA or a Roth account received by the individual during the testing period which is not a qualified rollover contribution (as defined in section 408A(e)) to a Roth IRA or a rollover under section 402(c)(8)(B) to a Roth account.

"(B) TESTING PERIOD.—For purposes of subparagraph (A), the testing period, with respect to a taxable year, is the period which includes—

"(i) such taxable year,

"(ii) the 2 preceding taxable years, and

"(iii) the period after such taxable year and before the due date (including extensions) for filing the return of tax for such taxable year.

"(C) EXCEPTED DISTRIBUTIONS.—There shall not be taken into account under subparagraph (A)—

"(i) any distribution referred to in section 72(p), 401(k)(8), 401(m)(6), 402(g)(2), 404(k), or 408(d)(4), and

"(ii) any distribution to which section 408A(d)(3) applies.

"(D) TREATMENT OF DISTRIBUTIONS RECEIVED BY SPOUSE OF INDIVIDUAL.—For purposes of determining distributions received by an individual under subparagraph

(A) for any taxable year, any distribution received by the spouse of such individual shall be treated as received by such individual if such individual and spouse file a joint return for such taxable year and for the taxable year during which the spouse receives the distribution.

"(e) ADJUSTED GROSS INCOME.—For purposes of this section, adjusted gross income shall be determined without regard to sections 911, 931, and 933.

"(f) INVESTMENT IN THE CONTRACT.—Notwithstanding any other provision of law, a qualified retirement savings contribution shall not fail to be included in determining the investment in the contract for purposes of section 72 by reason of the credit under this section.

"(g) TERMINATION.—This section shall not apply to taxable years beginning after December 31, 2006.".

(b) CREDIT ALLOWED AGAINST REGULAR TAX AND ALTERNATIVE MINIMUM TAX.—

(1) IN GENERAL.—Section 25B, as added by subsection (a), is amended by inserting after subsection (f) the following new subsection:

"(g) LIMITATION BASED ON AMOUNT OF TAX.—The credit allowed under subsection (a) for the taxable year shall not exceed the excess of—

"(1) the sum of the regular tax liability (as defined in section 26(b)) plus the tax imposed by section 55, over

"(2) the sum of the credits allowable under this subpart (other than this section and section 23) and section 27 for the taxable year.".

(2) CONFORMING AMENDMENTS.—

(A) Section 24(b)(3)(B), as amended by sections 201(b) and 203(d), is amended by striking "section 23" and inserting "sections 23 and 25B".

(B) Section 25(e)(1)(C), as amended by section 201(b), is amended by inserting "25B," after "24,".

(C) Section 26(a)(1), as amended by sections 201(b) and 203, is amended by striking "and 24" and inserting ", 24, and 25B".

(D) Section 904(h), as amended by sections 201(b) and 203, is amended by striking “and 24” and inserting “, 24, and 25B”.

(E) Section 1400C(d), as amended by sections 201(b) and 203, is amended by striking “and 24” and inserting “, 24, and 25B”.

(c) CONFORMING AMENDMENT.—The table of sections for subpart A of part IV of subchapter A of chapter 1, as amended by section 432, is amended by inserting after the item relating to section 25A the following new item:

“Sec. 25B. Elective deferrals and IRA contributions by certain individuals.”.

(e) EFFECTIVE DATE.—The amendments made by this section shall apply to taxable years beginning after December 31, 2001.

Sec. 619. Credit for Pension Plan Startup Costs of Small Employers

(a) IN GENERAL.—Subpart D of part IV of subchapter A of chapter 1 (relating to business related credits) is amended by adding at the end the following new section:

“Sec. 45e. Small Employer Pension Plan Startup Costs

“(a) GENERAL RULE.—For purposes of section 38, in the case of an eligible employer, the small employer pension plan startup cost credit determined under this section for any taxable year is an amount equal to 50 percent of the qualified startup costs paid or incurred by the taxpayer during the taxable year.

“(b) DOLLARLIMITATION.—The amount of the credit determined under this section for any taxable year shall not exceed—

"(1) $500 for the first credit year and each of the 2 taxable years immediately following the first credit year, and

"(2) zero for any other taxable year.

“(c) ELIGIBLE EMPLOYER.—For purposes of this section—

"(1) IN GENERAL.—The term ‘eligible employer’ has the meaning given such term by section 408(p)(2)(C)(i).

"(2) REQUIREMENT FOR NEW QUALIFIED EMPLOYER PLANS.—Such term shall not include an employer if, during the 3- taxable year period immediately preceding the 1st taxable year for which the credit under this section is otherwise allowable for a qualified employer plan of the employer, the employer or any member of any controlled group including the employer (or any predecessor of either) established or maintained a qualified employer plan with respect to which contributions were made, or benefits were accrued, for substantially the same employees as are in the qualified employer plan.

“(d) OTHER DEFINITIONS.—For purposes of this section—

“(1) QUALIFIED STARTUP COSTS.—

"(A) IN GENERAL.—The term 'qualified startup costs' means any ordinary and necessary expenses of an eligible employer which are paid or incurred in connection with—

"(i) the establishment or administration of an eligible employer plan, or

"(ii) the retirement-related education of employees with respect to such plan.

"(B) PLAN MUST HAVE AT LEAST 1 PARTICIPANT.—Such term shall not include any expense in connection with a plan that does not have at least 1 employee eligible to participate who is not a highly compensated employee.

"(2) ELIGIBLE EMPLOYER PLAN.—The term 'eligible employer plan' means a qualified employer plan within the meaning of section 4972(d).

"(3) FIRST CREDIT YEAR.—The term 'first credit year' means—

"(A) the taxable year which includes the date that the eligible employer plan to which such costs relate becomes effective, or

"(B) at the election of the eligible employer, the taxable year preceding the taxable year referred to in subparagraph (A).

"(e) SPECIAL RULES.—For purposes of this section—

"(1) AGGREGATION RULES.—All persons treated as a single employer under subsection (a) or (b) of section 52, or subsection (n) or (o) of section 414, shall be treated as one person. All eligible employer plans shall be treated as 1 eligible employer plan.

"(2) DISALLOWANCE OF DEDUCTION.—No deduction shall be allowed for that portion of the qualified startup costs paid or incurred for the taxable year which is equal to the credit determined under subsection (a).

"(3) ELECTION NOT TO CLAIM CREDIT.—This section shall not apply to a taxpayer for any taxable year if such taxpayer elects to have this section not apply for such taxable year.".

(b) CREDIT ALLOWED AS PART OF GENERAL BUSINESS CREDIT.—Section 38(b) (defining current year business credit) is amended by striking "plus" at the end of paragraph (12), by striking the period at the end of paragraph (13) and inserting ", plus", and by adding at the end the following new paragraph:

"(14) in the case of an eligible employer (as defined in section 45E(c)), the small employer pension plan startup cost credit determined under section 45E(a).".

(c) CONFORMING AMENDMENTS.—Section 39(d) is amended by adding at the end the following new paragraph:

"(10) NO CARRYBACK OF SMALL EMPLOYER PENSION PLAN STARTUP COST CREDIT BEFORE JANUARY 1, 2002.—No portion of the unused business credit for any taxable year which is attributable to the small employer pension plan startup cost credit determined under section 45E may be carried back to a taxable year beginning before January 1, 2002.".

(2) Subsection (c) of section 196 is amended by striking "and" at the end of paragraph (8), by striking the period at the end of paragraph (9) and inserting ", and", and by adding at the end the following new paragraph:

"(10) the small employer pension plan startup cost credit determined under section 45E(a).".

The table of sections for subpart D of part IV of subchapter A of chapter 1 is amended by adding at the end the following new item:

"Sec. 45E. Small employer pension plan startup costs.".

(d) EFFECTIVE DATE.—The amendments made by this section shall apply to costs paid or incurred in taxable years beginning after December 31, 2001, with respect to qualified employer plans established after such date.

Sec. 620. Elimination of User Fee for Requests to Irs Regarding Pension Plans

(a) ELIMINATION OF CERTAIN USER FEES.—The Secretary of the Treasury or the Secretary's delegate shall not require payment of user fees under the program established under section 10511 of the Revenue Act of 1987 for requests to the Internal Revenue Service for determination letters with respect to the qualified status of a pension benefit plan maintained solely by one or more eligible employers or any trust which is part of the plan. The preceding sentence shall not apply to any request—

(1) made after the later of—

(A) the fifth plan year the pension benefit plan is in existence; or

(B) the end of any remedial amendment period with respect to the plan beginning within the first 5 plan years; or

(2) made by the sponsor of any prototype or similar plan which the sponsor intends to market to participating employers

(b) PENSION BENEFIT PLAN.—For purposes of this section, the term "pension benefit plan" means a pension, profit-sharing, stock bonus, annuity, or employee stock ownership plan.

(c) ELIGIBLE EMPLOYER.—For purposes of this section, the term "eligible employer" means an eligible employer (as defined in section 408(p)(2)(C)(i)(I) of the Internal Revenue Code of 1986) which has at least one employee who is not a highly compensated employee (as defined in section 4 14(q)) and is participating in the plan. The determination of whether an employer is an eligible employer under this section shall be made as of the date of the request described in subsection (a).

(d) DETERMINATION OF AVERAGE FEES CHARGED.—For purposes of any determination of average fees charged, any request to which subsection (a) applies shall not be taken into account.

(e) EFFECTIVE DATE.—The provisions of this section shall apply Applicability. with respect to requests made after December 31, 2001.

Sec. 621. Treatment of Nonresident Aliens Engaged in International Transportation Services

(a) EXCLUSION FROM INCOME SOURCING RULES.—The second sentence of section 861(a)(3) (relating to gross income from sources within the United States) is amended by striking "except for purposes of sections 79 and 105 and subchapter D,".

(b) EFFECTIVE DATE.—The amendment made by subsection (a) shall apply to remuneration for services performed in plan years beginning after December 31, 2001.

Subtitle C—Enhancing Fairness for Women

Sec. 631. Catch-Up Contributions for Individuals Age 50 or Over

(a) IN GENERAL.—Section 414 (relating to definitions and special rules) is amended by adding at the end the following new subsection:

"(v) CATCH-UP CONTRIBUTIONS FOR INDIVIDUALS AGE 50 OR OVER.—

"(1) IN GENERAL.—An applicable employer plan shall not be treated as failing to meet any requirement of this title solely because the plan permits an eligible participant to make additional elective deferrals in any plan year.

"(2) LIMITATION ON AMOUNT OF ADDITIONAL DEFERRALS.—

"(A) IN GENERAL.—A plan shall not permit additional elective deferrals under paragraph (1) for any year in an amount greater than the lesser of—

"(i) the applicable dollar amount, or

"(ii) the excess (if any) of—

"(I) the participant's compensation (as defined in section 415(c)(3)) for the year, over

"(II) any other elective deferrals of the participant for such year which are made without regard to this subsection.

"(B) APPLICABLE DOLLAR AMOUNT.—For purposes of this paragraph—

"(i) In the case of an applicable employer plan other than a plan described in section 401(k)(11) or 408(p), the applicable dollar amount shall be determined in accordance with the following table:

"For taxable years beginning in:	The applicable dollar amount is:
2002	$1,000
2003	$2,000
2004	$3,000
2005	$4,000
2006 and thereafter	$5,000.

"(ii) In the case of an applicable employer plan described in section 401(k)(11) or 408(p), the applicable dollar amount shall be determined in accordance with the following table:

"For taxable years beginning in:	The applicable dollar amount is:
2002	$500
2003	$1,000
2004	$1,500
2005	$2,000
2006 and thereafter	$2,500.

"(C) COST-OF-LIVING ADJUSTMENT.—In the case of a year beginning after December 31, 2006, the Secretary shall adjust annually the $5,000 amount in subparagraph (B)(i) and the $2,500 amount in subparagraph (B)(ii) for increases in the cost-of-living at the same time and in the same manner as adjustments under section 415(d); except that the base period taken into account shall be the calendar quarter beginning July 1, 2005, and any increase under this subparagraph which is not a multiple of $500 shall be rounded to the next lower multiple of $500.".

"(3) TREATMENT OF CONTRIBUTIONS.—In the case of any contribution to a plan under paragraph (1)—

"(A) such contribution shall not, with respect to the year in which the contribution is made—

"(i) be subject to any otherwise applicable limitation contained in section 402(g), 402(h), 403(b), 404(a), 404(h), 408(k), 408(p), 415, or 457, or

"(ii) be taken into account in applying such limitations to other contributions or benefits under such plan or any other such plan, and

"(B) except as provided in paragraph (4), such plan shall not be treated as failing to meet the requirements of section 401(a)(4), 401(a)(26), 401(k)(3), 401(k)(11), 401(k)(12), 403(b)(12), 408(k), 408(p), 408B, 410(b), or 416 by reason of the making of (or the right to make) such contribution.

"(4) APPLICATION OF NONDISCRIMINATION RULES.—

"(A) IN GENERAL.—An applicable employer plan shall be treated as failing to meet the nondiscrimination requirements under section 401(a)(4) with respect to benefits, rights, and features unless the plan allows all eligible participants to make the same election with respect to the additional elective deferrals under this subsection

"(B) AGGREGATION.—For purposes of subparagraph (A), all plans maintained by employers who are treated as a single employer under subsection (b), (c), (m), or (o) of section 414 shall be treated as 1 plan.

"(5) ELIGIBLE PARTICIPANT.—For purposes of this subsection, the term 'eligible participant' means, with respect to any plan year, a participant in a plan—

"(A) who has attained the age of 50 before the close of the plan year, and

"(B) with respect to whom no other elective deferrals may (without regard to this subsection) be made to the plan for the plan year by reason of the application of any limitation or other restriction described in paragraph (3) or comparable limitation or restriction contained in the terms of the plan.

"(6) OTHER DEFINITIONS AND RULES.—For purposes of this subsection—

"(A) APPLICABLE EMPLOYER PLAN.—The term 'applicable employer plan' means—

"(i) an employees' trust described in section 40 1(a) which is exempt from tax under section 501(a),

"(ii) a plan under which amounts are contributed by an individual's employer for an annuity contract described in section 403(b),

"(iii) an eligible deferred compensation plan under section 457 of an eligible employer described in section 457(e)(1)(A), and

"(iv) an arrangement meeting the requirements of section 408 (k) or (p).

"(B) ELECTIVE DEFERRAL.—The term 'elective deferral' has the meaning given such term by subsection (u)(2)(C).

"(C) EXCEPTION FOR SECTION 457 PLANS.—This subsection shall not apply to an applicable employer plan described in subparagraph (A)(iii) for any year to which section 457(b)(3) applies.".

(b) EFFECTIVE DATE.—The amendment made by this section shall apply to contributions in taxable years beginning after December 31, 2001.

Sec. 632. Equitable Treatment for Contributions of Employees to Defined Contribution Plans

(a) EQUITABLE TREATMENT.—

(1) IN GENERAL.—Subparagraph (B) of section 415(c)(1) 26 USC 415. (relating to limitation for defined contribution plans) is amended by striking "25 percent" and inserting "100 percent".

(2) APPLICATION TO SECTION 403(b).—Section 403(b) is amended—

(A) by striking "the exclusion allowance for such taxable year" in paragraph (1) and inserting "the applicable limit under section 415",

(B) by striking paragraph (2), and

(C) by inserting "or any amount received by a former employee after the fifth taxable year following the taxable year in which such employee was terminated" before the period at the end of the second sentence of paragraph (3).

(3) CONFORMING AMENDMENTS.—

(A) Subsection (f) of section 72 is amended by striking "section 403(b)(2)(D)(iii))" and inserting "section 403(b)(2)(D)(iii), as in effect before the enactment of the Economic Growth and Tax Relief Reconciliation Act of 2001".

(B) Section 404(a)(10)(B) is amended by striking ", the exclusion allowance under section 403(b)(2),".

(C) Section 415(a)(2) is amended by striking ", and the amount of the contribution for such portion shall reduce the exclusion allowance as provided in section 403(b)(2)".

(D) Section 415(c)(3) is amended by adding at the end the following new subparagraph:

"(E) ANNUITY CONTRACTS.—In the case of an annuity contract described in section 403(b), the term 'participant's compensation' means the participant's includible compensation determined under section 403(b)(3).".

(E) Section 415(c) is amended by striking paragraph (4).

(F) Section 415(c)(7) is amended to read as follows:

"(7) CERTAIN CONTRIBUTIONS BY CHURCH PLANS NOT TREATED AS EXCEEDING LIMIT.—

"(A) IN GENERAL.—Notwithstanding any other provision of this subsection, at the election of a participant who is an employee of a church or a convention or association of churches, including an organization described in section 414(e)(3)(B)(ii), contributions and other additions for an annuity contract or retirement income account described in section 403(b) with respect to such participant, when expressed as an annual addition to such participant's account, shall be treated as not exceeding the limitation of paragraph (1) if such annual addition is not in excess of $10,000.

"(B) $40,000 AGGREGATE LIMITATION.—The total amount of additions with respect to any participant which may be taken into account for purposes of this subparagraph for all years may not exceed $40,000.

"(C) ANNUAL ADDITION.—For purposes of this paragraph, the term 'annual addition' has the meaning given such term by paragraph (2)"

(G) Subparagraph (B) of section 402(g)(7) (as redesignated by section 611(c)(3)) is amended by inserting before the period at the end the following: "(as in effect before the enactment of the Economic Growth and Tax Relief Reconciliation Act of 2001".

(H) Section 664(g) is amended—

(i) in paragraph (3)(E) by striking "limitations under section 4 15(c)" and inserting "applicable limitation under paragraph (7)", and

(ii) by adding at the end the following new paragraph:

"(7) APPLICABLE LIMITATION.—

"(A) IN GENERAL.—For purposes of paragraph (3)(E), the applicable limitation under this paragraph with respect to a participant is an amount equal to the lesser of—

"(i) $30,000, or

"(ii) 25 percent of the participant's compensation (as defined in section 415(c)(3))

"(B) COST-OF-LIVING ADJUSTMENT.—The Secretary shall adjust annually the $30,000 amount under subparagraph (A)(i) at the same time and in the same manner as under section 4 15(d), except that the base period shall be the calendar quarter beginning October 1, 1993, and any increase under this subparagraph which is not a multiple of $5,000 shall be rounded to the next lowest multiple of $5,000.".

(4) EFFECTIVE DATE.—The amendments made by this subsection shall apply to years beginning after December 31, 2001.

(b) SPECIAL RULES FOR SECTIONS 403(b) AND 408.—

(1) IN GENERAL.—Subsection (k) of section 415 is amended by adding at the end the following new paragraph:

"(4) SPECIAL RULES FOR SECTIONS 403(b) AND 408.—For purposes of this section, any annuity contract described in section 403(b) for the benefit of a participant shall be treated as a defined contribution plan maintained by each employer with respect to which the participant has the control required under subsection (b) or (c) of section 414 (as modified by subsection (h)). For purposes of this section, any contribution by an employer to a simplified employee pension plan for an individual for a taxable year shall be treated as an employer contribution to a defined contribution plan for such individual for such year"

(2) EFFECTIVE DATE.—

(A) IN GENERAL.—The amendment made by paragraph (1) shall apply to limitation years beginning after December 31, 1999.

(B) EXCLUSION ALLOWANCE.—Effective for limitation years beginning in 2000, in the case of any annuity contract described in section 403(b) of the Internal Revenue Code of 1986, the amount of the contribution disqualified by reason of section 415(g) of such Code shall reduce the exclusion allowance as provided in section 403(b)(2) of such Code.

(3) ELECTION TO MODIFY SECTION 403(b) EXCLUSION ALLOWANCE TO CONFORM TO SECTION 415 MODIFICATION.—In the case of taxable years beginning after December 31, 1999, and before January 1, 2002, a plan may disregard the requirement in the regulations regarding the exclusion allowance under section 403(b)(2) of the Internal Revenue Code of 1986 that contributions to a defined benefit pension plan be treated as previously excluded amounts for purposes of the exclusion allowance.

(c) DEFERRED COMPENSATION PLANS OF STATE AND LOCAL GOVERNMENTS AND TAX-EXEMPT ORGANIZATIONS.—

(1) IN GENERAL.—Subparagraph (B) of section 457(b)(2) (relating to salary limitation on eligible deferred compensation plans) is amended by striking "331⁄3 percent" and inserting "100 percent".

(2) EFFECTIVE DATE.—The amendment made by this subsection shall apply to years beginning after December 31, 2001.

Sec. 633. Faster Vesting of Certain Employer Matching Contributions

(a) IN GENERAL.—Section 411(a) (relating to minimum vesting standards) is amended in paragraph (2), by striking "A plan" and inserting "Except as provided in paragraph (12), a plan"; and by adding at the end the following:

"(12) FASTER VESTING FOR MATCHING CONTRIBUTIONS.—In the case of matching contributions (as defined in section 401(m)(4)(A)), paragraph (2) shall be applied—

"(A) by substituting '3 years' for '5 years' in subparagraph (A), and

"(B) by substituting the following table for the table contained in subparagraph (B):

"Years of service:	The nonforfeitable percentage is:
2	20
3	40
4	60
5	80
6	100"

(b) AMENDMENT OF ERISA.—Section 203(a) of the Employee Retirement Income Security Act of 1974 (29 U.S.C. 1053(a)) is amended—

(1) in paragraph (2), by striking "A plan" and inserting "Except as provided in paragraph (4), a plan", and

(2) by adding at the end the following:

"(4) In the case of matching contributions (as defined in section 401(m)(4)(A) of the Internal Revenue Code of 1986), paragraph (2) shall be applied—

"(A) by substituting '3 years' for '5 years' in subparagraph (A), and

"(B) by substituting the following table for the table contained in subparagraph (B):

(c) EFFECTIVE DATES.—

(1) IN GENERAL.—Except as provided in paragraph (2), the amendments made by this section shall apply to contributions for plan years beginning after December 31, 2001.

(2) COLLECTIVE BARGAINING AGREEMENTS.—In the case of a plan maintained pursuant to one or more collective bargaining agreements between employee representatives and one or more employers ratified by the date of the enactment of this Act, the amendments made by this section shall not apply to contributions on behalf of employees covered by any such agreement for plan years beginning before the earlier of—

(A) the later of—

"(i) the date on which the last of such collective bargaining agreements terminates (determined without regard to any extension thereof on or after such date of the enactment); or

"(ii) January 1, 2002; or

(B) January 1, 2006.

(3) SERVICE REQUIRED.—With respect to any plan, the amendments made by this section shall not apply to any employee before the date that such employee has 1 hour of service under such plan in any plan year to which the amendments made by this section apply.

Sec. 634. Modification to Minimum Distribution Rules

The Secretary of the Treasury shall modify the life expectancy tables under the regulations relating to minimum distribution requirements under sections 401(a)(9), 408(a)(6) and (b)(3), 403(b)(10), and 457(d)(2) of the Internal Revenue Code to reflect current life expectancy.

Sec. 635. Clarification of Tax Treatment of Division of Section 457 Plan Benefits Upon Divorce

(a) IN GENERAL.—Section 414(p)(11) (relating to application of rules to governmental and church plans) is amended—

(1) by inserting "or an eligible deferred compensation plan (within the meaning of section 457(b))" after "subsection (e))"; and

(2) in the heading, by striking "GOVERNMENTAL AND CHURCH PLANS" and inserting "CERTAIN OTHER PLANS".

(b) WAIVER OF CERTAIN DISTRIBUTION REQUIREMENTS.—Paragraph (10) of section 414(p) is amended by striking "and section 409(d)" and inserting "section 409(d), and section 45 7(d)".

(c) TAX TREATMENT OF PAYMENTS FROM A SECTION 457 PLAN.—Subsection (p) of section 414 is amended by redesignating paragraph (12) as paragraph (13) and inserting after paragraph (11) the following new paragraph:

> "(12) TAX TREATMENT OF PAYMENTS FROM A SECTION 457 PLAN.—If a distribution or payment from an eligible deferred compensation plan described in section 457(b) is made pursuant to a qualified domestic relations order, rules similar to the rules of section 402(e)(1)(A) shall apply to such distribution or payment.".

(d) EFFECTIVE DATE.—The amendment made by this section shall apply to transfers, distributions, and payments made after December 31, 2001.

Sec. 636. Provisions Relating to Hardship Distributions

(a) SAFE HARBOR RELIEF.—

(1) IN GENERAL.—The Secretary of the Treasury shall revise the regulations relating to hardship distributions under section 401(k)(2)(B)(i)(IV) of the Internal Revenue Code of 1986 to provide that the period an employee is prohibited from making elective and employee contributions in order for a distribution to be deemed necessary to satisfy financial need shall be equal to 6 months.

(2) EFFECTIVE DATE.—The revised regulations under this subsection shall apply to years beginning after December 31, 2001.

(b) HARDSHIP DISTRIBUTIONS NOT TREATED AS ELIGIBLE ROLLOVER DISTRIBUTIONS.—

(1) MODIFICATION OF DEFINITION OF ELIGIBLE ROLLOVER.—

Subparagraph (C) of section 402(c)(4) (relating to eligible rollover distribution) is amended to read as follows:

"(C) any distribution which is made upon hardship of the employee."

(2) EFFECTIVE DATE.—The amendment made by this subsection shall apply to distributions made after December 31, 2001

Sec. 637. Waiver of Tax on Nondeductible Contributions for Domestic or Similar Workers

(a) IN GENERAL.—Section 4972(c)(6) (relating to exceptions to nondeductible contributions), as amended by section 616, is amended by striking "and" at the end of subparagraph (A), by striking the period and inserting ", or" at the end of subparagraph (B), and by inserting after subparagraph (B) the following new subparagraph:

"(C) so much of the contributions to a simple retirement account (within the meaning of section 408(p)) or a simple plan (within the meaning of section 401(k)(11)) which are not deductible when contributed solely because such contributions are not made in connection with a trade or business of the employer.".

(b) EXCLUSION OF CERTAIN CONTRIBUTIONS.—Section 4972(c)(6), as amended by subsection (a), is amended by adding at the end the following new sentence: "Subparagraph (C) shall not apply to contributions made on behalf of the employer or a member of the employer's family (as defined in section 447(e)(1))"

(c) NO INFERENCE.—Nothing in the amendments made by this section shall be construed to infer the proper treatment of nondeductible contributions under the laws in effect before such amendments.

(d) EFFECTIVE DATE.—The amendments made by this section shall apply to taxable years beginning after December 31, 2001.

Subtitle D—Increasing Portability for Participants

Sec. 641. Rollovers Allowed Among Various Types of Plans

(a) ROLLOVERS FROM AND TO SECTION 457 PLANS.—

(1) ROLLOVERS FROM SECTION 457 PLANS.—

(A) IN GENERAL.—Section 457(e) (relating to other definitions and special rules) is amended by adding at the end the following:

"(16) ROLLOVER AMOUNTS.—

"(A) GENERAL RULE.—In the case of an eligible deferred compensation plan established and maintained by an employer described in subsection (e)(1)(A), if—

"(i) any portion of the balance to the credit of an employee in such plan is paid to such employee in an eligible rollover distribution (within the meaning of section 402(c)(4)),

"(ii) the employee transfers any portion of the property such employee receives in such distribution to an eligible retirement plan described in section 402(c)(8)(B), and

"(iii) in the case of a distribution of property other than money, the amount so transferred consists of the property distributed, then such distribution (to the extent so transferred) shall not be includible in gross income for the taxable year in which paid.

"(B) CERTAIN RULES MADE APPLICABLE.—The rules of paragraphs (2) through (7) and (9) of section 402(c) and section 402(f) shall apply for purposes of subparagraph (A).

"(C) REPORTING.—Rollovers under this paragraph shall be reported to the Secretary in the same manner as rollovers from qualified retirement plans (as defined in section 4974(c)).".

(B) DEFERRAL LIMIT DETERMINED WITHOUT REGARD TO 26
ROLLOVER AMOUNTS.—Section 457(b)(2) (defining eligible deferred compensation plan) is amended by inserting "(other than rollover amounts)" after "taxable year".

(C) DIRECT ROLLOVER.—Paragraph (1) of section 457(d) is amended by striking "and" at the end of subparagraph (A), by striking the period at the end of subparagraph (B) and inserting ", and", and by inserting after subparagraph (B) the following:

"(C) in the case of a plan maintained by an employer described in subsection (e)(1)(A), the plan meets requirements similar to the requirements of section 401(a)(3 1). Any amount transferred in a direct trustee-to-trustee transfer in accordance with section 401(a)(31) shall not be includible in gross income for the taxable year of transfer.".

(D) WITHHOLDING.—

(i) Paragraph (12) of section 3401(a) is amended by adding at the end the following:

"(E) under or to an eligible deferred compensation plan which, at the time of such payment, is a plan described in section 457(b) which is maintained by an eligible employer described in section 457(e)(1)(A), or".

(ii) Paragraph (3) of section 3405(c) is amended to read as follows:

"(3) ELIGIBLE ROLLOVER DISTRIBUTION.—For purposes of this subsection, the term 'eligible rollover distribution' has the meaning given such term by section 402(f)(2)(A).".

(iii) LIABILITY FOR WITHHOLDING.—Subparagraph

(B) of section 3405(d)(2) is amended by striking "or"at the end of clause (ii), by striking the period at the end of clause (iii) and inserting ", or", and by adding at the end the following:

"(iv) section 457(b) and which is maintained by an eligible employer described in section 457(e)(1)(A).".

(2) ROLLOVERS TO SECTION 457 PLANS.—

(A) IN GENERAL.—Section 402(c)(8)(B) (defining eligible retirement plan) is amended by striking "and" at the end of clause (iii), by striking the period at the end of clause (iv) and inserting ", and", and by inserting after clause (iv) the following new clause:

"(v) an eligible deferred compensation plan described in section 457(b) which is maintained by an eligible employer described in section 457(e)(1)(A).".

(B) SEPARATE ACCOUNTING.—Section 402(c) is amended by adding at the end the following new paragraph:

"(10) SEPARATE ACCOUNTING.—Unless a plan described in clause (v) of paragraph (8)(B) agrees to separately account for amounts rolled into such plan from eligible retirement plans not described in such clause, the plan described in such clause may not accept transfers or rollovers from such retirement plans."

(C) 10 PERCENT ADDITIONAL TAX.—Subsection (t) of section 72 (relating to 10-percent additional tax on early distributions from qualified retirement plans) is amended by adding at the end the following new paragraph:

"(9) SPECIAL RULE FOR ROLLOVERS TO SECTION 457 PLANS.—

For purposes of this subsection, a distribution from an eligible deferred compensation plan (as defined in section 457(b)) of an eligible employer described in section 457(e)(1)(A) shall be treated as a distribution from a qualified retirement plan described in 4974(c)(1) to the extent that such distribution is attributable to an amount transferred to an eligible deferred compensation plan from a qualified retirement plan (as defined in section 4974(c)).".

(b) ALLOWANCE OF ROLLOVERS FROM AND TO 403(b) PLANS.—

(1) ROLLOVERS FROM SECTION 403(b) PLANS.—Section 403(b)(8)(A)(ii) (relating to rollover amounts) is amended by striking "such distribution" and all that follows and inserting "such distribution to an eligible retirement plan described in section 402(c)(8)(B), and".

(2) ROLLOVERS TO SECTION 403(b) PLANS.—Section 402(c)(8)(B) (defining eligible retirement plan), as amended by subsection (a), is amended by striking "and" at the end of clause (iv), by striking the period at the end of clause (v) and inserting ", and", and by inserting after clause (v) the following new clause:

"(vi) an annuity contract described in section 403(b).".

(c) EXPANDED EXPLANATION TO RECIPIENTS OF ROLLOVER DISTRIBUTIONS.—Paragraph (1) of section 402(f) (relating to written explanation to recipients of distributions eligible for rollover treatment) is amended by striking "and" at the end of subparagraph (C), by striking the period at the end of subparagraph (D) and inserting ", and", and by adding at the end the following new subparagraph:

"(E) of the provisions under which distributions from the eligible retirement plan receiving the distribution may be subject to restrictions and tax consequences which are different from those applicable to distributions from the plan making such distribution.".

(d) SPOUSAL ROLLOVERS.—Section 402(c)(9) (relating to rollover where spouse receives distribution after death of employee) is amended by striking "; except that" and all that follows up to the end period.

(e) CONFORMING AMENDMENTS.—

(1) Section 72(o)(4) is amended by striking "and 408(d)(3)" and inserting "403(b)(8), 408(d)(3), and 457(e)(16)".

(2) Section 219(d)(2) is amended by striking "or 408(d)(3)" and inserting "408(d)(3), or 457(e)(16)".

(3) Section 401(a)(31)(B) is amended by striking "and 403(a)(4)" and inserting ", 403(a)(4), 403(b)(8), and 457(e)(16)".

(4) Subparagraph (A) of section 402(f)(2) is amended by striking "or paragraph (4) of section 403(a)" and inserting ", paragraph (4) of section 403(a), subparagraph (A) of section 403(b)(8), or subparagraph (A) of section 457(e)(16)".

(5) Paragraph (1) of section 402(f) is amended by striking "from an eligible retirement plan

(6) Subparagraphs (A) and (B) of section 402(f)(1) are 26 USC 402. amended by striking "another eligible retirement plan" and inserting "an eligible retirement plan".

(7) Subparagraph (B) of section 403(b)(8) is amended to read as follows:

"(B) CERTAIN RULES MADE APPLICABLE.—The rules of paragraphs (2) through (7) and (9) of section 402(c) and section 402(f) shall apply for purposes of subparagraph (A), except that section 402(f) shall be applied to the payor in lieu of the plan administrator.".

(8) Section 408(a)(1) is amended by striking "or 403(b)(8)," and inserting "403(b)(8), or 457(e)(16)".

(9) Subparagraphs (A) and (B) of section 415(b)(2) are each amended by striking "and 408(d)(3)" and inserting "403(b)(8), 408(d)(3), and 457(e)(16)".

(10) Section 415(c)(2) is amended by striking "and 408(d)(3)" and inserting "408(d)(3), and 457(e)(16)".

(11) Section 4973(b)(1)(A) is amended by striking "or 408(d)(3)" and inserting "408(d)(3), or 457(e)(16)".

(f) EFFECTIVE DATE; SPECIAL RULE.— 26 USC 402 note.

(1) EFFECTIVE DATE.—The amendments made by this sec Applicability. tion shall apply to distributions after December 31, 2001.

(2) REASONABLE NOTICE.—No penalty shall be imposed on a plan for the failure to provide the information required by the amendment made by subsection (c) with respect to any distribution made before the date that is 90 days after the date on which the Secretary of the Treasury issues a safe harbor rollover notice after the date of the enactment of this Act, if the administrator of such plan makes a reasonable attempt to comply with such requirement.

(3) SPECIAL RULE.—Notwithstanding any other provision of law, subsections (h)(3) and (h)(5) of section 1122 of the Tax Reform Act of 1986 shall not apply to any distribution from an eligible retirement plan (as defined in clause (iii) or (iv) of section 402(c)(8)(B) of the Internal Revenue Code of 1986) on behalf of an individual if there was a rollover to such plan on behalf of such individual which is permitted solely by reason of any amendment made by this section.

Sec. 642. Rollovers of Iras Into Workplace Retirement Plans

(a) IN GENERAL.—Subparagraph (A) of section 408(d)(3) (relating to rollover amounts) is amended by adding "or" at the end of clause (i), by striking clauses (ii) and (iii), and by adding at the end the following:

"(ii) the entire amount received (including money and any other property) is paid into an eligible retirement plan for the benefit of such individual not later than the 60th day after the date on which the payment or distribution is received, except that the maximum amount which may be paid into such plan may not exceed the portion of the amount received which is includible in gross income (determined without regard to this paragraph).

For purposes of clause (ii), the term 'eligible retirement plan' means an eligible retirement plan described in clause (iii), (iv), (v), or (vi) of section 402(c)(8)(B).".

(b) CONFORMING AMENDMENTS.—

(1) Paragraph (1) of section 403(b) is amended by striking "section 408(d)(3)(A)(iii)" and inserting "section 408(d)(3)(A)(ii)".

(2) Clause (i) of section 408(d)(3)(D) is amended by striking "(i), (ii), or (iii)" and inserting "(i) or (ii)".

(3) Subparagraph (G) of section 408(d)(3) is amended to read as follows:

> "(G) SIMPLE RETIREMENT ACCOUNTS.—In the case of any payment or distribution out of a simple retirement account (as defined in subsection (p)) to which section 72(t)(6) applies, this paragraph shall not apply unless such payment or distribution is paid into another simple retirement account.".

(c) EFFECTIVE DATE; SPECIAL RULE.—

(1) EFFECTIVE DATE.—The amendments made by this section shall apply to distributions after December 31, 2001.

(2) SPECIAL RULE.—Notwithstanding any other provision of law, subsections (h)(3) and (h)(5) of section 1122 of the Tax Reform Act of 1986 shall not apply to any distribution from an eligible retirement plan (as defined in clause (iii) or (iv) of section 402(c)(8)(B) of the Internal Revenue Code of 1986) on behalf of an individual if there was a rollover to such plan on behalf of such individual which is permitted solely by reason of the amendments made by this section.

Sec. 643. Rollovers of after-Tax Contributions

(a) ROLLOVERS FROM EXEMPT TRUSTS.—Paragraph (2) of section 402(c) (relating to maximum amount which may be rolled over) is amended by adding at the end the following: "The preceding sentence shall not apply to such distribution to the extent—

"(A) such portion is transferred in a direct trusteeto-trustee transfer to a qualified trust which is part of a plan which is a defined contribution plan and which agrees to separately account for amounts so transferred, including separately accounting for the portion of such distribution which is includible in gross income and the portion of such distribution which is not so includible, or

"(B) such portion is transferred to an eligible retirement plan described in clause (i) or (ii) of paragraph (8)(B).".

(b) OPTIONAL DIRECT TRANSFER OF ELIGIBLE ROLLOVER DISTRIBUTIONS.—Subparagraph (B) of section 401(a)(31) (relating to limitation) is amended by adding at the end the following: "The preceding sentence shall not apply to such distribution if the plan to which such distribution is transferred—

"(i) agrees to separately account for amounts so transferred, including separately accounting for the portion of such distribution which is includible in gross income and the portion of such distribution which is not so includible, or

"(ii) is an eligible retirement plan described in clause (i) or (ii) of section 402(c)(8)(B).".

(c) RULES FOR APPLYING SECTION 72 TO IRAS.—Paragraph (3) of section 408(d) (relating to special rules for applying section 72) is amended by inserting at the end the following:

"(H) APPLICATION OF SECTION 72.—

"(i) IN GENERAL.—If—

"(I) a distribution is made from an individual retirement plan, and

"(II) a rollover contribution is made to an eligible retirement plan described in section 402(c)(8)(B)(iii), (iv), (v), or (vi) with respect to all or part of such distribution, then, notwithstanding paragraph (2), the rules of clause (ii) shall apply for purposes of applying section 72.

"(ii) APPLICABLE RULES.—In the case of a distribution described in clause (i)—

"(I) section 72 shall be applied separately to such distribution,

"(II) notwithstanding the pro rata allocation of income on, and investment in, the contract to distributions under section 72, the portion of such distribution rolled over to an eligible retirement plan described in clause (i) shall be treated as from income on the contract (to the extent of the aggregate income on the contract from all individual retirement plans of the distributee), and

"(III) appropriate adjustments shall be made in applying section 72 to other distributions in such taxable year and subsequent taxable years.".

(d) EFFECTIVE DATE.—The amendments made by this section shall apply to distributions made after December 31, 2001.

Sec. 644. Hardship Exception to 60-Day Rule

(a) EXEMPT TRUSTS.—Paragraph (3) of section 402(c) (relating to transfer must be made within 60 days of receipt) is amended to read as follows:

"(3) TRANSFER MUST BE MADE WITHIN 60 DAYS OF RECEIPT.—

"(A) IN GENERAL.—Except as provided in subparagraph (B), paragraph (1) shall not apply to any transfer of a distribution made after the 60th day following the day on which the distributee received the property distributed.

"(B) HARDSHIP EXCEPTION.—The Secretary may waive the 60-day requirement under subparagraph (A) where the failure to waive such requirement would be against equity or good conscience, including casualty, disaster, or other events beyond the reasonable control of the individual subject to such requirement.".

(b) IRAS.—Paragraph (3) of section 408(d) (relating to rollover 26 USC 408. contributions), as amended by section 643, is amended by adding after subparagraph (H) the following new subparagraph:

"(I) WAIVER OF 60-DAY REQUIREMENT.—The Secretary may waive the 60-day requirement under subparagraphs

(A) and (D) where the failure to waive such requirement would be against equity or good conscience, including casualty, disaster, or other events beyond the reasonable control of the individual subject to such requirement.".

(c) EFFECTIVE DATE.—The amendments made by this section 26 USC 402 note. shall apply to distributions after December 31, 2001.

Sec. 645. Treatment of Forms of Distribution

(a) PLAN TRANSFERS.—

(1) AMENDMENT OF INTERNAL REVENUE CODE.—Paragraph (6) of section 411(d) (relating to accrued benefit not to be decreased by amendment) is amended by adding at the end the following:

"(D) PLAN TRANSFERS.—

"(i) IN GENERAL.—A defined contribution plan (in this subparagraph referred to as the 'transferee plan') shall not be treated as failing to meet the requirements of this subsection merely because the transferee plan does not provide some or all of the forms of distribution previously available under another defined contribution plan (in this subparagraph referred to as the 'transferor plan') to the extent that—

"(I) the forms of distribution previously available under the transferor plan applied to the account of a participant or beneficiary under the transferor plan that was transferred from the transferor plan to the transferee plan pursuant to a direct transfer rather than pursuant to a distribution from the transferor plan,

"(II) the terms of both the transferor plan and the transferee plan authorize the transfer described in subclause (I),

"(III) the transfer described in subclause (I) was made pursuant to a voluntary election by the participant or beneficiary whose account was transferred to the transferee plan,

"(IV) the election described in subclause (III) was made after the participant or beneficiary received a notice describing the consequences of making the election, and

"(V) the transferee plan allows the participant or beneficiary described in subclause (III) to receive any distribution to which the participant or beneficiary is entitled under the transferee plan in the form of a single sum distribution.

"(ii) SPECIAL RULE FOR MERGERS, ETC.—Clause (i) shall apply to plan mergers and other transactions having the effect of a direct transfer, including consolidations of benefits attributable to different employers within a multiple employer plan.

"(E) ELIMINATION OF FORM OF DISTRIBUTION.—Except to the extent provided in regulations, a defined contribution plan shall not be treated as failing to meet the requirements of this section merely because of the elimination of a form of distribution previously available thereunder. This subparagraph shall not apply to the elimination of a form of distribution with respect to any participant unless—

"(i) a single sum payment is available to such participant at the same time or times as the form of distribution being eliminated, and

"(ii) such single sum payment is based on the same or greater portion of the participant's account as the form of distribution being eliminated.".

AMENDMENT OF ERISA.—Section 204(g) of the Employee Retirement Income Security Act of 1974 (29 U.S.C. 1054(g)) is amended by adding at the end the following:

"(4)(A) A defined contribution plan (in this subparagraph referred to as the 'transferee plan') shall not be treated as failing to meet the requirements of this subsection merely because the transferee plan does not provide some or all of the forms of distribution previously available under another defined contribution plan (in this subparagraph referred to as the 'transferor plan') to the extent that—

"(i) the forms of distribution previously available under the transferor plan applied to the account of a participant or beneficiary under the transferor plan that was transferred from the transferor plan to the transferee plan pursuant to a direct transfer rather than pursuant to a distribution from the transferor plan;

"(ii) the terms of both the transferor plan and the transferee plan authorize the transfer described in clause (i);

"(iii) the transfer described in clause (i) was made pursuant to a voluntary election by the participant or beneficiary whose account was transferred to the transferee plan;

"(iv) the election described in clause (iii) was made after the participant or beneficiary received a notice describing the consequences of making the election; and

"(v) the transferee plan allows the participant or beneficiary described in clause (iii) to receive any distribution to which the participant or beneficiary is entitled under the transferee plan in the form of a single sum distribution.

"(B) Subparagraph (A) shall apply to plan mergers and other transactions having the effect of a direct transfer, including consolidations of benefits attributable to different employers within a multiple employer plan.

"(5) Except to the extent provided in regulations promulgated by the Secretary of the Treasury, a defined contribution plan shall not be treated as failing to meet the requirements of this subsection merely because of the elimination of a form of distribution previously available thereunder. This paragraph shall not apply to the elimination of a form of distribution with respect to any participant unless—

"(A) a single sum payment is available to such participant at the same time or times as the form of distribution being eliminated; and

"(B) such single sum payment is based on the same or greater portion of the participant's account as the form of distribution being eliminated.".

(3) EFFECTIVE DATE.—The amendments made by this subsection shall apply to years beginning after December 31, 2001.

(b) REGULATIONS.—

(1) AMENDMENT OF INTERNAL REVENUE CODE.—Paragraph (6)(B) of section 411(d) (relating to accrued benefit not to be decreased by amendment) is amended by inserting after the second sentence the following: "The Secretary shall by regulations provide that this subparagraph shall not apply to any plan amendment which reduces or eliminates benefits or subsidies which create significant burdens or complexities for the plan and plan participants, unless such amendment adversely affects the rights of any participant in a more than de minimis manner.".

(2) AMENDMENT OF ERISA.—Section 204(g)(2) of the Employee Retirement Income Security Act of 1974 (29 U.S.C 1054(g)(2)) is amended by inserting after the second sentence the following: "The Secretary of the Treasury shall by regulations provide that this paragraph shall not apply to any plan amendment which reduces or eliminates benefits or subsidies which create

significant burdens or complexities for the plan and plan participants, unless such amendment adversely affects the rights of any participant in a more than de minimis manner.".

(3) SECRETARY DIRECTED.—Not later than December 31, 2003, the Secretary of the Treasury is directed to issue regulations under section 411(d)(6) of the Internal Revenue Code of 1986 and section 204(g) of the Employee Retirement Income Security Act of 1974, including the regulations required by the amendment made by this subsection. Such regulations shall apply to plan years beginning after December 31, 2003, or such earlier date as is specified by the Secretary of the Treasury.

Sec. 646. Rationalization of Restrictions on Distributions

(a) MODIFICATION OF SAME DESK EXCEPTION.—

(1) SECTION 401(k).—

(A) Section 401(k)(2)(B)(i)(I) (relating to qualified cash or deferred arrangements) is amended by striking "separation from service" and inserting "severance from employment".

(B) Subparagraph (A) of section 401(k)(10) (relating to distributions upon termination of plan or disposition of assets or subsidiary) is amended to read as follows:

"(A) IN GENERAL.—An event described in this subparagraph is the termination of the plan without establishment or maintenance of another defined contribution plan (other than an employee stock ownership plan as defined in section 4975(e)(7)).".

(C) Section 401(k)(10) is amended—

(i) in subparagraph (B)—

(I) by striking "An event" in clause (i) and inserting "A termination"; and

(II) by striking "the event" in clause (i) and inserting "the termination";

(ii) by striking subparagraph (C); and

(iii) by striking "OR DISPOSITION OF ASSETS OR SUBSIDIARY" in the heading.

(2) SECTION 403(b).—

(A) Paragraphs (7)(A)(ii) and (11)(A) of section 403(b) are each amended by striking "separates from service"and inserting "has a severance from employment".

(B) The heading for paragraph (11) of section 403(b) is amended by striking "SEPARATION FROM SERVICE" and inserting "SEVERANCE FROM EMPLOYMENT".

(3) SECTION 457.—Clause (ii) of section 457(d)(1)(A) is amended by striking "is separated from service" and inserting "has a severance from employment".

(b) EFFECTIVE DATE.—The amendments made by this section shall apply to distributions after December 31, 2001.

Sec. 647. Purchase of Service Credit in Governmental Defined Benefit Plans

(a) SECTION 403(b) PLANS.—Subsection (b) of section 403 is amended by adding at the end the following new paragraph:

"(13) TRUSTEE-TO-TRUSTEE TRANSFERS TO PURCHASE PERMISSIVE SERVICE CREDIT.—No amount shall be includible in gross income by reason of a direct trustee-to-trustee transfer to a defined benefit governmental plan (as defined in section 4 14(d)) if such transfer is—

"(A) for the purchase of permissive service credit (as defined in section 415(n)(3)(A)) under such plan, or

"(B) a repayment to which section 415 does not apply by reason of subsection (k)(3) thereof.".

(b) SECTION 457 PLANS.—Subsection (e) of section 457, as amended by section 641, is amended by adding after paragraph (16) the following new paragraph:

"(17) TRUSTEE-TO-TRUSTEE TRANSFERS TO PURCHASE PERMISSIVE SERVICE CREDIT.—No amount shall be includible in gross income by reason of a direct trustee-to-trustee transfer to a defined benefit governmental plan (as defined in section 4 14(d)) if such transfer is—

"(A) for the purchase of permissive service credit (as defined in section 415(n)(3)(A)) under such plan, or

"(B) a repayment to which section 415 does not apply by reason of subsection (k)(3) thereof.".

(c) EFFECTIVE DATE.—The amendments made by this section shall apply to trustee-to-trustee transfers after December 31, 2001.

Sec. 648. Employers May Disregard Rollovers for Purposes of Cash-Out Amounts

(a) QUALIFIED PLANS.—

(1) AMENDMENT OF INTERNAL REVENUE CODE.—Section 411(a)(11) (relating to restrictions on certain mandatory distributions) is amended by adding at the end the following:

"(D) SPECIAL RULE FOR ROLLOVER CONTRIBUTIONS.—

A plan shall not fail to meet the requirements of this paragraph if, under the terms of the plan, the present value of the nonforfeitable accrued benefit is determined without regard to that portion of such benefit which is attributable to rollover contributions (and earnings allocable thereto). For purposes of this subparagraph, the term 'rollover contributions' means any rollover contribution under sections 402(c), 403(a)(4), 403(b)(8), 408(d)(3)(A)(ii), and 457(e)(16).".

(2) AMENDMENT OF ERISA.—Section 203(e) of the Employee Retirement Income Security Act of 1974 (29 U.S.C. 1053(c)) is amended by adding at the end the following:

"(4) A plan shall not fail to meet the requirements of this subsection if, under the terms of the plan, the present value of the nonforfeitable accrued benefit is determined without regard to that portion of such benefit which is attributable to rollover contributions (and earnings allocable thereto). For purposes of this subparagraph, the term 'rollover contributions' means any rollover contribution under sections 402(c), 403(a)(4), 403(b)(8), 408(d)(3)(A)(ii), and 457(e)(16) of the Internal Revenue Code of 1986."

(b) ELIGIBLE DEFERRED COMPENSATION PLANS.—Clause (i) of section 457(e)(9)(A) is amended by striking "such amount" and inserting "the portion of such amount which is not attributable to rollover contributions (as defined in section 411(a)(11)(D))".

(c) EFFECTIVE DATE.—The amendments made by this section shall apply to distributions after December 31, 2001.

Sec. 649. Minimum Distribution and Inclusion Requirements for Section 457 Plans

(a) MINIMUM DISTRIBUTION REQUIREMENTS.—Paragraph (2) of section 457(d) (relating to distribution requirements) is amended to read as follows:

"(2) MINIMUM DISTRIBUTION REQUIREMENTS.—A plan meets the minimum distribution requirements of this paragraph if such plan meets the requirements of section 401(a)(9).".

(b) INCLUSION IN GROSS INCOME.—

(1) YEAR OF INCLUSION.—Subsection (a) of section 457 (relating to year of inclusion in gross income) is amended to read as follows:

"(a) YEAR OF INCLUSION IN GROSS INCOME.—

"(1) IN GENERAL.—Any amount of compensation deferred under an eligible deferred compensation plan, and any income attributable to the amounts so deferred, shall be includible in gross income only for the taxable year in which such compensation or other income—

"(A) is paid to the participant or other beneficiary, in the case of a plan of an eligible employer described in subsection (e)(1)(A), and

"(B) is paid or otherwise made available to the participant or other beneficiary, in the case of a plan of an eligible employer described in subsection (e)(1)(B).

"(2) SPECIAL RULE FOR ROLLOVER AMOUNTS.—To the extent provided in section 72(t)(9), section 72(t) shall apply to any amount includible in gross income under this subsection.".

(2) CONFORMING AMENDMENTS.—

So much of paragraph (9) of section 45 7(e) as precedes subparagraph (A) is amended to read as follows:

"(9) BENEFITS OF TAX EXEMPT ORGANIZATION PLANS NOT TREATED AS MADE AVAILABLE BY REASON OF CERTAIN ELECTIONS, ETC.—In the case of an eligible deferred compensation plan of an employer described in subsection (e)(1)(B)—".

(A) Section 457(d) is amended by adding at the end the following new paragraph:

"(3) SPECIAL RULE FOR GOVERNMENT PLAN.—An eligible deferred compensation plan of an employer described in subsection (e)(1)(A) shall not be treated as failing to meet the requirements of this subsection solely by reason of making a distribution described in subsection (e)(9)(A).".

(c) EFFECTIVE DATE.—The amendments made by subsections (a) and (b) shall apply to distributions after December 31, 2001

Subtitle E—Strengthening Pension Security and Enforcement

PART I—GENERAL PROVISIONS

Sec. 651. Repeal of 160 Percent of Current Liability Funding Limit

(a) AMENDMENTS TO INTERNAL REVENUE CODE.—Section 412(c)(7) (relating to full-funding limitation) is amended—

(1) by striking "the applicable percentage" in subparagraph (A)(i)(I) and inserting "in the case of plan years beginning before January 1, 2004, the applicable percentage"; and

(2) by amending subparagraph (F) to read as follows:

"(F) APPLICABLE PERCENTAGE.—For purposes of subparagraph (A)(i)(I), the applicable percentage shall be determined in accordance with the following table:

“In the case of any plan year beginning in—	The applicable percentage is—
2002	165
2003	170”

(b) AMENDMENT OF ERISA.—Section 302(c)(7) of the Employee Retirement Income Security Act of 1974 (29 U.S.C. 1082(c)(7)) is amended—

(1) by striking “the applicable percentage” in subparagraph (A)(i)(I) and inserting “in the case of plan years beginning before January 1, 2004, the applicable percentage”, and

(2) by amending subparagraph (F) to read as follows:

“(F) APPLICABLE PERCENTAGE.—For purposes of subparagraph (A)(i)(I), the applicable percentage shall be determined in accordance with the following table:

“In the case of any plan year beginning in calendar year—	The applicable percentage is—
2002	165
2003	170.”.

(c) EFFECTIVE DATE.—The amendments made by this section shall apply to plan years beginning after December 31, 2001.

Sec. 652. Maximum Contribution Deduction Rules Modified and Applied to All Defined Benefit Plans

(a) IN GENERAL.—Subparagraph (D) of section 404(a)(1) (relating to special rule in case of certain plans) is amended to read as follows:

“(D) SPECIAL RULE IN CASE OF CERTAIN PLANS.—

"(i) IN GENERAL.—In the case of any defined benefit plan, except as provided in regulations, the maximum amount deductible under the limitations of this paragraph shall not be less than the unfunded current liability determined under section 4 12(l).

"(ii) PLANS WITH 100 OR LESS PARTICIPANTS.—For purposes of this subparagraph, in the case of a plan which has 100 or less participants for the plan year, unfunded current liability shall not include the liability attributable to benefit increases for highly compensated employees (as defined in section 4 14(q)) resulting from a plan amendment which is made or becomes effective, whichever is later, within the last 2 years.

"(iii) RULE FOR DETERMININGNUMBER OF PARTICIPANTS.—For purposes of determining the number of plan participants, all defined benefit plans maintained by the same employer (or any member of such employer's controlled group (within the meaning of section 412(l)(8)(C))) shall be treated as one plan, but only employees of such member or employer shall be taken into account.

"(iv) PLANS MAINTAINED BY PROFESSIONAL SERVICE EMPLOYERS.—In the case of a plan which, subject to section 4041 of the Employee Retirement Income Security Act of 1974, terminates during the plan year, clause (i) shall be applied by substituting for unfunded current liability the amount required to make the plan sufficient for benefit liabilities (within the meaning of section 4041(d) of such Act).".

(b) CONFORMING AMENDMENT.—Paragraph (6) of section 4972(c), as amended by sections 616 and 637, is amended—

(1) by striking subparagraph (A) and redesignating subparagraphs (B) and (C) as subparagraphs (A) and (B), respectively,

(2) by striking the first sentence following subparagraph (B) (as so redesignated),

(3) by striking "subparagraph (B)" in the next to last sentence and inserting "subparagraph (A)", and

(4) by striking "Subparagraph (C)" in the last sentence and inserting "Subparagraph (B)".

(c) EFFECTIVE DATE.—The amendments made by this section shall apply to plan years beginning after December 31, 2001.

Sec. 653. Excise Tax Relief for Sound Pension Funding

(a) IN GENERAL.—Subsection (c) of section 4972 (relating to nondeductible contributions) is amended by adding at the end the following new paragraph:

"(7) DEFINED BENEFIT PLAN EXCEPTION.—In determining the amount of nondeductible contributions for any taxable year, an employer may elect for such year not to take into account any contributions to a defined benefit plan except to the extent that such contributions exceed the full-funding limitation (as defined in section 412(c)(7), determined without regard to subparagraph (A)(i)(I) thereof). For purposes of this paragraph, the deductible limits under section 404(a)(7) shall first be applied to amounts contributed to defined contribution plans and then to amounts described in this paragraph. If an employer makes an election under this paragraph for a taxable year, paragraph (6) shall not apply to such employer for such taxable year.".

(b) EFFECTIVE DATE.—The amendment made by this section shall apply to years beginning after December 31, 2001.

Sec. 654. Treatment of Multiemployer Plans Under Section 415

(a) COMPENSATION LIMIT.—

(1) IN GENERAL.—Paragraph (11) of section 415(b) (relating to limitation for defined benefit plans) is amended to read as follows "(11) SPECIAL LIMITATION RULE FOR GOVERNMENTAL AND MULTIEMPLOYER PLANS.—In the case of a governmental plan (as defined in section 414(d)) or a multiemployer plan (as defined in section 4 14(f)), subparagraph (B) of paragraph (1) shall not apply.".

(2) CONFORMING AMENDMENT.—Section 4 15(b)(7) (relating 26 USC 415. to benefits under certain collectively bargained plans) is amended by inserting "(other than a multiemployer plan)" after "defined benefit plan" in the matter preceding subparagraph (A).

(b) COMBINING AND AGGREGATION OF PLANS.—

(1) COMBINING OF PLANS.—Subsection (f) of section 415 (relating to combining of plans) is amended by adding at the end the following:

"(3) EXCEPTION FOR MULTIEMPLOYER PLANS.—Notwithstanding paragraph (1) and subsection (g), a multiemployer plan (as defined in section 414(f)) shall not be combined or aggregated—

"(A) with any other plan which is not a multiemployer plan for purposes of applying subsection (b)(1)(B) to such other plan, or

"(B) with any other multiemployer plan for purposes of applying the limitations established in this section.".

(2) CONFORMING AMENDMENT FOR AGGREGATION OF

PLANS.—Subsection (g) of section 415 (relating to aggregation of plans) is amended by striking "The Secretary" and inserting "Except as provided in subsection (f)(3), the Secretary".

(c) EFFECTIVE DATE.—The amendments made by this section Applicability. shall apply to years beginning after December 31, 2001.

Sec. 655. Protection of Investment of Employee Contributions to 401(K) Plans

(a) IN GENERAL.—Section 1524(b) of the Taxpayer Relief Acto f 1997 is amended to read as follows:

"(b) EFFECTIVE DATE.—

"(1) IN GENERAL.—Except as provided in paragraph (2), the amendments made by this section shall apply to elective deferrals for plan years beginning after December 31, 1998.

"(2) NONAPPLICATION TO PREVIOUSLY ACQUIRED PROPERTY.—The amendments made by this section shall not apply to any elective deferral which is invested in assets consisting of qualifying employer securities, qualifying employer real property, or both, if such assets were acquired before January 1, 1999.”.

(b) EFFECTIVE DATE.—The amendment made by this section 29 USC 1107 shall apply as if included in the provision of the Taxpayer Relief note. Act of 1997 to which it relates.

Sec. 656. Prohibited Allocations of Stock in S Corporation Esop

(a) IN GENERAL.—Section 409 (relating to qualifications for tax credit employee stock ownership plans) is amended by redesignating subsection (p) as subsection (q) and by inserting after subsection (o) the following new subsection:

“(p) PROHIBITED ALLOCATIONS OF SECURITIES IN AN S CORPORATION.—

“(1) IN GENERAL.—An employee stock ownership plan holding employer securities consisting of stock in an S corporation shall provide that no portion of the assets of the plan attributable to (or allocable in lieu of) such employer securities may, during a nonallocation year, accrue (or be allocated directly or indirectly under any plan of the employer meeting the requirements of section 401(a)) for the benefit of any disqualified person.

“(2) FAILURE TO MEET REQUIREMENTS.—

IN GENERAL.—If a plan fails to meet the requirements of paragraph (1), the plan shall be treated as having distributed to any disqualified person the amount allocated to the account of such person in violation of paragraph (1) at the time of such allocation.

CROSS REFERENCE.—

“For excise tax relating to violations of paragraph (1) and ownership of synthetic equity, see section 4979A

“(3) NONALLOCATION YEAR.—For purposes of this subsection—

“(A) IN GENERAL.—The term ‘nonallocation year’ means any plan year of an employee stock ownership plan if, at any time during such plan year—

"(i) such plan holds employer securities consisting of stock in an S corporation, and

"(ii) disqualified persons own at least 50 percent of the number of shares of stock in the S corporation.

“(B) ATTRIBUTION RULES.—For purposes of subparagraph (A)—

“(i) IN GENERAL.—The rules of section 318(a) shall apply for purposes of determining ownership, except that—

"(I) in applying paragraph (1) thereof, the members of an individual’s family shall include members of the family described in paragraph (4)(D), and

"(II) paragraph (4) thereof shall not apply.

"(ii) DEEMED-OWNED SHARES.—Notwithstanding the employee trust exception in section 318(a)(2)(B)(i), an individual shall be treated as owning deemed-owned shares of the individual.

Solely for purposes of applying paragraph (5), this subparagraph shall be applied after the attribution rules of paragraph (5) have been applied.

"(4) DISQUALIFIED PERSON.—For purposes of this subsection—

"(A) IN GENERAL.—The term 'disqualified person' means any person if—

"(i) the aggregate number of deemed-owned shares of such person and the members of such person's family is at least 20 percent of the number of deemed-owned shares of stock in the S corporation, or

"(ii) in the case of a person not described in clause (i), the number of deemed-owned shares of such person is at least 10 percent of the number of deemed-owned shares of stock in such corporation.

"(B) TREATMENT OF FAMILY MEMBERS.—In the case of a disqualified person described in subparagraph (A)(i), any member of such person's family with deemed-owned shares shall be treated as a disqualified person if not otherwise treated as a disqualified person under subparagraph (A).

"(C) DEEMED-OWNED SHARES.—

"(i) IN GENERAL.—The term 'deemed-owned shares' means, with respect to any person—

"(I) the stock in the S corporation constituting employer securities of an employee stock ownership plan which is allocated to such person under the plan, and

"(II) such person's share of the stock in such corporation which is held by such plan but which is not allocated under the plan to participants.

"(ii) PERSON'S SHARE OF UNALLOCATED STOCK.— For purposes of clause (i)(II), a person's share of unallocated S corporation stock held by such plan is the amount of the unallocated stock which would be allocated to such person if the unallocated stock were allocated to all participants in the same proportions as the most recent stock allocation under the plan.

"(D) MEMBER OF FAMILY.—For purposes of this paragraph, the term 'member of the family' means, with respect to any individual—

"(i) the spouse of the individual,

"(ii) an ancestor or lineal descendant of the individual or the individual's spouse,

"(iii) a brother or sister of the individual or the individual's spouse and any lineal descendant of the brother or sister, and

"(iv) the spouse of any individual described in clause (ii) or (iii).

A spouse of an individual who is legally separated from such individual under a decree of divorce or separate maintenance shall not be treated as such individual's spouse for purposes of this subparagraph.

"(5) TREATMENT OF SYNTHETIC EQUITY.—For purposes of paragraphs (3) and (4), in the case of a person who owns synthetic equity in the S corporation, except to the extent provided in regulations, the shares of stock in such corporation on which such synthetic equity is based shall be treated as outstanding stock in such corporation and deemed-owned shares of such person if such treatment of synthetic equity of 1 or more such persons results in—

"(A) the treatment of any person as a disqualified person, or

"(B) the treatment of any year as a nonallocation year. For purposes of this paragraph, synthetic equity shall be treated as owned by a person in the same manner as stock is treated as owned by a person under the rules of paragraphs (2) and (3) of section 318(a). If, without regard to this paragraph, a person is treated as a disqualified person or a year is treated as a nonallocation year, this paragraph shall not be construed to result in the person or year not being so treated.

"(6) DEFINITIONS.—For purposes of this subsection—

"(A) EMPLOYEE STOCK OWNERSHIP PLAN.—The term 'employee stock ownership plan' has the meaning given such term by section 4975(e)(7).

"(B) EMPLOYER SECURITIES.—The term 'employer security' has the meaning given such term by section 409(l).

"(C) SYNTHETIC EQUITY.—The term 'synthetic equity' means any stock option, warrant, restricted stock, deferred issuance stock right, or similar interest or right that gives the holder the right to acquire or receive stock of the S corporation in the future. Except to the extent provided in regulations, synthetic equity also includes a stock appreciation right, phantom stock unit, or similar right to a future cash payment based on the value of such stock or appreciation in such value.

"(7) REGULATIONS AND GUIDANCE.—

"(A) IN GENERAL.—The Secretary shall prescribe such regulations as may be necessary to carry out the purposes of this subsection.

"(B) AVOIDANCE OR EVASION.—The Secretary may, by regulation or other guidance of general applicability, provide that a nonallocation year occurs in any case in which the principal purpose of the ownership structure of an S corporation constitutes an avoidance or evasion of this subsection.".

(b) COORDINATION WITH SECTION 4975(e)(7).—The last sentence of section 4975(e)(7) (defining employee stock ownership plan) is amended by inserting ", section 409(p)," after "409(n)".

EXCISE TAX.—

(1) APPLICATION OF TAX.—Subsection (a) of section 4979A (relating to tax on certain prohibited allocations of employer securities) is amended—

"(A) by striking "or" at the end of paragraph (1), and

"(B) by striking all that follows paragraph (2) and inserting the following:

"(3) there is any allocation of employer securities which violates the provisions of section 409(p), or a nonallocation year described in subsection (e)(2)(C) with respect to an employee stock ownership plan, or

"(4) any synthetic equity is owned by a disqualified person in any nonallocation year, there is hereby imposed a tax on such allocation or ownership equal to 50 percent of the amount involved.".

(2) LIABILITY.—Section 4979A(c) (defining liability for tax) is amended to read as follows:

"(c) LIABILITY FOR TAX.—The tax imposed by this section shall be paid—

"(1) in the case of an allocation referred to in paragraph (1) or (2) of subsection (a), by—

"(A) the employer sponsoring such plan, or

"(B) the eligible worker-owned cooperative, which made the written statement described in section 664(g)(1)(E) or in section 1042(b)(3)(B) (as the case may be), and

"(2) in the case of an allocation or ownership referred to in paragraph (3) or (4) of subsection (a), by the S corporation the stock in which was so allocated or owned.".

(3) DEFINITIONS.—Section 4979A(e) (relating to definitions) is amended to read as follows:

"(e) DEFINITIONS AND SPECIAL RULES.—For purposes of this section—

"(3) DEFINITIONS.—Except as provided in paragraph (2), terms used in this section have the same respective meanings as when used in sections 409 and 4978.

"(4) SPECIAL RULES RELATING TO TAX IMPOSED BY REASON OF PARAGRAPH (3) OR (4) OF SUBSECTION (a).—

"(A) PROHIBITED ALLOCATIONS.—The amount involved with respect to any tax imposed by reason of subsection (a)(3) is the amount allocated to the account of any person in violation of section 409(p)(1).

"(B) SYNTHETIC EQUITY.—The amount involved with respect to any tax imposed by reason of subsection (a)(4) is the value of the shares on which the synthetic equity is based.

"(C) SPECIAL RULE DURING FIRST NONALLOCATION YEAR.—For purposes of subparagraph (A), the amount involved for the first nonallocation year of any employee stock ownership plan shall be determined by taking into account the total value of all the deemed-owned shares of all disqualified persons with respect to such plan.

"(D) STATUTE OF LIMITATIONS.—The statutory period for the assessment of any tax imposed by this section by reason of paragraph (3) or (4) of subsection (a) shall not expire before the date which is 3 years from the later of—

"(i) the allocation or ownership referred to in such paragraph giving rise to such tax, or

"(ii) the date on which the Secretary is notified of such allocation or ownership.".

(d) EFFECTIVE DATES.—

(1) IN GENERAL.—The amendments made by this section shall apply to plan years beginning after December 31, 2004.

(2) EXCEPTION FOR CERTAIN PLANS.—In the case of any—

(A) employee stock ownership plan established after March 14, 2001, or

(B) employee stock ownership plan established on or before such date if employer securities held by the plan consist of stock in a corporation with respect to which an election under section 1362(a) of the Internal Revenue Code of 1986 is not in effect on such date, the amendments made by this section shall apply to plan years ending after March 14, 2001.

Sec. 657. Automatic Rollovers of Certain Mandatory Distributions

(a) DIRECT TRANSFERS OF MANDATORY DISTRIBUTIONS.—

(1) IN GENERAL.—Section 401(a)(31) (relating to optional 26 USC 401. direct transfer of eligible rollover distributions), as amended by section 643, is amended by redesignating subparagraphs (B), (C), and (D) as subparagraphs (C), (D), and (E), respectively, and by inserting after subparagraph (A) the following new subparagraph:

"(B) CERTAIN MANDATORY DISTRIBUTIONS.—

"(i) IN GENERAL.—In case of a trust which is part of an eligible plan, such trust shall not constitute a qualified trust under this section unless the plan of which such trust is a part provides that if—

"(I) a distribution described in clause (ii) in excess of $1,000 is made, and

"(II) the distributee does not make an election under subparagraph (A) and does not elect to receive the distribution directly, the plan administrator shall make such transfer to an individual retirement plan of a designated trustee or issuer and shall notify the distributee in writing (either separately or as part of the notice under section 402(f)) that the distribution may be transferred to another individual retirement plan.

"(ii) ELIGIBLE PLAN.—For purposes of clause (i), the term 'eligible plan' means a plan which provides that any nonforfeitable accrued benefit for which the present value (as determined under section 411(a)(11)) does not exceed $5,000 shall be immediately distributed to the participant.".

(2) CONFORMING AMENDMENTS.—

(A) The heading of section 40 1(a)(3 1) is amended by striking "OPTIONAL DIRECT" and inserting "DIRECT".

(B) Section 401(a)(3 1)(C), as redesignated by paragraph (1), is amended by striking "Subparagraph (A)" and inserting "Subparagraphs (A) and (B)".

(b) NOTICE REQUIREMENT.—Subparagraph (A) of section 402(f)(1) is amended by inserting before the comma at the end the following: "and that the automatic distribution by direct transfer applies to certain distributions in accordance with section 401(a)(31)(B)".

(c) FIDUCIARY RULES.—

(1) IN GENERAL.—Section 404(c) of the Employee Retirement Income Security Act of 1974 (29 U.S.C. 1104(c)) is amended by adding at the end the following new paragraph:

"(3) In the case of a pension plan which makes a transfer to an individual retirement account or annuity of a designated trustee or issuer under section 401(a)(31)(B) of the Internal Revenue Code of 1986, the participant or beneficiary shall, for purposes of paragraph (1), be treated as exercising control over the assets in the account or annuity upon—

"(A) the earlier of the earlier of—

"(i) a rollover of all or a portion of the amount to another individual retirement account or annuity; or

"(ii) one year after the transfer is made; or

"(B) if the transfer is made in a manner consistent with guidance provided by the Secretary.".

(2) REGULATIONS.—

(A) AUTOMATIC ROLLOVER SAFE HARBOR.—Not later than 3 years after the date of enactment of this Act, the Secretary of Labor shall prescribe regulations providing for safe harbors under which the designation of an institution and investment of funds in accordance with section 401(a)(31)(B) of the Internal Revenue Code of 1986 is deemed to satisfy the fiduciary requirements of section 404(a) of the Employee Retirement Income Security Act of 1974 (29 U.S.C. 1104(a)).

(B) USE OF LOW-COST INDIVIDUAL RETIREMENT PLANS.—

The Secretary of the Treasury and the Secretary of Labor may provide, and shall give consideration to providing, special relief with respect to the use of low-cost individual retirement plans for purposes of transfers under section 401(a)(3 1)(B) of the Internal Revenue Code of 1986 and for other uses that promote the preservation of assets for retirement income purposes.

(d) EFFECTIVE DATE.—The amendments made by this section shall apply to distributions made after final regulations implementing subsection (c)(2)(A) are prescribed.

Sec. 658. Clarification of Treatment of Contributions to Multiemployer Plan

(a) NOT CONSIDERED METHOD OF ACCOUNTING.—For purposes of section 446 of the Internal Revenue Code of 1986, a determination under section 404(a)(6) of such Code regarding the taxable year with respect to which a contribution to a multiemployer pension plan is deemed made shall not be treated as a method of accounting of the taxpayer. No deduction shall be allowed for any taxable year for any contribution to a multiemployer pension plan with respect to which a deduction was previously allowed.

(b) REGULATIONS.—The Secretary of the Treasury shall promulgate such regulations as necessary to clarify that a taxpayer shall not be allowed an aggregate amount of deductions for contributions to a multiemployer pension plan which exceeds the amount of such contributions made or deemed made under section 404(a)(6) of the Internal Revenue Code of 1986 to such plan.

(c) EFFECTIVE DATE.—Subsection (a), and any regulations promulgated under subsection (b), shall be effective for years ending after the date of the enactment of this Act.

PART II—TREATMENT OF PLAN AMENDMENTS REDUCING FUTURE BENEFIT ACCRUALS

Sec. 659. Excise Tax on Failure to Provide Notice by Defined Benefit Plans Significantly Reducing Future Benefit Accruals

(a) AMENDMENT OF INTERNAL REVENUE CODE.—

(1) IN GENERAL.—Chapter 43 (relating to qualified pension, etc., plans) is amended by adding at the end the following new section:

"SEC. 4980F. Failure of Applicable Plans Reducing Benefit Accruals to Satisfy Notice Requirements

"(a) IMPOSITION OF TAX.—There is hereby imposed a tax on the failure of any applicable pension plan to meet the requirements of subsection (e) with respect to any applicable individual.

"(b) AMOUNT OF TAX.—

"(A) IN GENERAL.—The amount of the tax imposed by subsection (a) on any failure with respect to any applicable individual shall be $100 for each day in the noncompliance period with respect to such failure.

"(B) NONCOMPLIANCE PERIOD.—For purposes of this section, the term 'noncompliance period' means, with respect to any failure, the period beginning on the date the failure first occurs and ending on the date the notice to which the failure relates is provided or the failure is otherwise corrected.

"(c) LIMITATIONS ON AMOUNT OF TAX.— "(1) TAX NOT TO APPLY WHERE FAILURE NOT DISCOVERED AND REASONABLE DILIGENCE EXERCISED.—No tax shall be imposed by subsection (a) on any failure during any period for which it is established to the satisfaction of the Secretary that any person subject to liability for the tax under subsection (d) did not know that the failure existed and exercised reasonable diligence to meet the requirements of subsection (e).

"(2) TAX NOT TO APPLY TO FAILURES CORRECTED WITHIN 30 DAYS.—No tax shall be imposed by subsection (a) on any failure if—

"(A) any person subject to liability for the tax under subsection (d) exercised reasonable diligence to meet the requirements of subsection (e), and

"(B) such person provides the notice described in subsection (e) during the 30-day period beginning on the first date such person knew, or exercising reasonable diligence would have known, that such failure existed.

"(3) OVERALL LIMITATION FOR UNINTENTIONAL FAILURES.—

"(A) IN GENERAL.—If the person subject to liability for tax under subsection (d) exercised reasonable diligence to meet the requirements of subsection (e), the tax imposed by subsection (a) for failures during the taxable year of the employer (or, in the case of a multiemployer plan, the taxable year of the trust forming part of the plan) shall not exceed $500,000. For purposes of the preceding sentence, all multiemployer plans of which the same trust forms a part shall be treated as 1 plan.

"(B) TAXABLE YEARS IN THE CASE OF CERTAIN CONTROLLED GROUPS.—For purposes of this paragraph, if all persons who are treated as a single employer for purposes of this section do not have the same taxable year, the taxable years taken into account shall be determined under principles similar to the principles of section 1561.

"(4) WAIVER BY SECRETARY.—In the case of a failure which is due to reasonable cause and not to willful neglect, the Secretary may waive part or all of the tax imposed by subsection (a) to the extent that the payment of such tax would be excessive or otherwise inequitable relative to the failure involved.

"(d) LIABILITY FOR TAX.—The following shall be liable for the tax imposed by subsection (a):

"(1) In the case of a plan other than a multiemployer plan, the employer.

"(2) In the case of a multiemployer plan, the plan.

"(e) NOTICE REQUIREMENTS FOR PLANS SIGNIFICANTLY REDUCING BENEFIT ACCRUALS.—

"(1) IN GENERAL.—If an applicable pension plan is amended to provide for a significant reduction in the rate of future benefit accrual, the plan administrator shall provide written notice to each applicable individual (and to each employee organization representing applicable individuals).

"(2) NOTICE.—The notice required by paragraph (1) shall be written in a manner calculated to be understood by the average plan participant and shall provide sufficient information (as determined in accordance with regulations prescribed by the Secretary) to allow applicable individuals to understand the effect of the plan amendment. The Secretary may provide a simplified form of notice for, or exempt from any notice requirement, a plan—

"(A) which has fewer than 100 participants who have accrued a benefit under the plan, or

"(B) which offers participants the option to choose between the new benefit formula and the old benefit formula.

"(3) TIMING OF NOTICE.—Except as provided in regulations, the notice required by paragraph (1) shall be provided within a reasonable time before the effective date of the plan amendment.

"(4) DESIGNEES.—Any notice under paragraph (1) may be provided to a person designated, in writing, by the person to which it would otherwise be provided.

"(5) NOTICE BEFORE ADOPTION OF AMENDMENT.—A plan shall not be treated as failing to meet the requirements of paragraph (1) merely because notice is provided before the adoption of the plan amendment if no material modification of the amendment occurs before the amendment is adopted.

"(f) DEFINITIONS AND SPECIAL RULES.—For purposes of this section—

"(1) APPLICABLE INDIVIDUAL.—The term 'applicable individual' means, with respect to any plan amendment—

"(A) each participant in the plan, and

"(B) any beneficiary who is an alternate payee (within the meaning of section 414(p)(8)) under an applicable qualified domestic relations order (within the meaning of section 414(p)(1)(A)),

whose rate of future benefit accrual under the plan may reasonably be expected to be significantly reduced by such plan amendment.

"(2) APPLICABLE PENSION PLAN.—The term 'applicable pension plan' means—

"(A) any defined benefit plan, or

"(B) an individual account plan which is subject to the funding standards of section 412.

Such term shall not include a governmental plan (within the meaning of section 414(d)) or a church plan (within the meaning of section 4 14(e)) with respect to which the election provided by section 4 10(d) has not been made.

"(3) EARLY RETIREMENT.—A plan amendment which eliminates or significantly reduces any early retirement benefit or retirement-type subsidy (within the meaning of section 411(d)(6)(B)(i)) shall be treated as having the effect of significantly reducing the rate of future benefit accrual.

"(g) NEW TECHNOLOGIES.—The Secretary may by regulations allow any notice under subsection (e) to be provided by using new technologies.".

(2) CLERICAL AMENDMENT.—The table of sections for chapter 43 is amended by adding at the end the following new item:

"Sec. 4980F. Failure of applicable plans reducing benefit accruals to satisfy notice requirements"

(b) AMENDMENT OF ERISA.—Subsection (h) of section 204 of the Employee Retirement Income Security Act of 1974 (29 U.S.C. 1054) is amended to read as follows:

"(h)(1) An applicable pension plan may not be amended so as to provide for a significant reduction in the rate of future benefit accrual unless the plan administrator provides the notice described in paragraph (2) to each applicable individual (and to each employee organization representing applicable individuals).

"(2) The notice required by paragraph (1) shall be written in a manner calculated to be understood by the average plan participant and shall provide sufficient information (as determined in accordance with regulations prescribed by the Secretary of the Treasury) to allow applicable individuals to understand the effect of the plan amendment. The Secretary of the Treasury may provide a simplified form of notice for, or exempt from any notice requirement, a plan—

"(A) which has fewer than 100 participants who have accrued a benefit under the plan, or

"(B) which offers participants the option to choose between the new benefit formula and the old benefit formula.

"(3) Except as provided in regulations prescribed by the Secretary of the Treasury, the notice required by paragraph (1) shall be provided within a reasonable time before the effective date of the plan amendment.

"(4) Any notice under paragraph (1) may be provided to a person designated, in writing, by the person to which it would otherwise be provided.

"(5) A plan shall not be treated as failing to meet the requirements of paragraph (1) merely because notice is provided before the adoption of the plan amendment if no material modification of the amendment occurs before the amendment is adopted.

"(6)(A) In the case of any egregious failure to meet any requirement of this subsection with respect to any plan amendment, the provisions of the applicable pension plan shall be applied as if such plan amendment entitled all applicable individuals to the greater of—

"(i) the benefits to which they would have been entitled without regard to such amendment, or

"(ii) the benefits under the plan with regard to such amendment.

"(B) For purposes of subparagraph (A), there is an egregious failure to meet the requirements of this subsection if such failure is within the control of the plan sponsor and is—

"(i) an intentional failure (including any failure to promptly provide the required notice or information after the plan administrator discovers an unintentional failure to meet the requirements of this subsection),

"(ii) a failure to provide most of the individuals with most of the information they are entitled to receive under this subsection, or

"(iii) a failure which is determined to be egregious under regulations prescribed by the Secretary of the Treasury.

"(7) The Secretary of the Treasury may by regulations allow any notice under this subsection to be provided by using new technologies.

"(8) For purposes of this subsection—

"(A) The term 'applicable individual' means, with respect to any plan amendment—

"(i) each participant in the plan; and

"(ii) any beneficiary who is an alternate payee (within the meaning of section 206(d)(3)(K)) under an applicable qualified domestic relations order (within the meaning of section 206(d)(3)(B)(i)),

whose rate of future benefit accrual under the plan may reasonably be expected to be significantly reduced by such plan amendment.

"(B) The term 'applicable pension plan' means—

"(i) any defined benefit plan; or

"(ii) an individual account plan which is subject to the funding standards of section 412 of the Internal Revenue Code of 1986.

"(9) For purposes of this subsection, a plan amendment which eliminates or significantly reduces any early retirement benefit or retirement-type subsidy (within the meaning of subsection (g)(2)(A)) shall be treated as having the effect of significantly reducing the rate of future benefit accrual.".

(c) EFFECTIVE DATES.—

(1) IN GENERAL.—The amendments made by this section shall apply to plan amendments taking effect on or after the date of the enactment of this Act.

(2) TRANSITION.—Until such time as the Secretary of the Treasury issues regulations under sections 4980F(e)(2) and (3) of the Internal Revenue Code of 1986, and section 204(h) of the Employee Retirement Income Security Act of 1974, as added by the amendments made by this section, a plan shall be treated as meeting the requirements of such sections if it makes a good faith effort to comply with such requirements.

(3) SPECIAL NOTICE RULE.—

(1) IN GENERAL.—The period for providing any notice required by the amendments made by this section shall not end before the date which is 3 months after the date of the enactment of this Act.

(2) REASONABLE NOTICE.—The amendments made by this section shall not apply to any plan amendment taking effect on or after the date of the enactment of this Act if, before April 25, 2001, notice was provided to participants and beneficiaries adversely affected by the plan amendment (or their representatives) which was reasonably expected to notify them of the nature and effective date of the plan amendment.

Subtitle F—Reducing Regulatory Burdens

Sec. 661. Modification of Timing of Plan Valuations

(a) IN GENERAL.—Paragraph (9) of section 4 12(c) (relating to 26 USC 412. annual valuation) is amended to read as follows:

"(9) ANNUAL VALUATION.—

"(A) IN GENERAL.—For purposes of this section, a determination of experience gains and losses and a valuation of the plan's liability shall be made not less frequently than once every year, except that such determination shall be made more frequently to the extent required in particular cases under regulations prescribed by the Secretary.

"(B) VALUATION DATE.—

a) IN GENERAL.—Paragraph (4) of section 1114(c) of the Tax Reform Act of 1986 is hereby repealed.

"(i) CURRENT YEAR.—Except as provided in clause (ii), the valuation referred to in subparagraph (A) shall be made as of a date within the plan year to which the valuation refers or within one month prior to the beginning of such year.

"(ii) USE OF PRIOR YEAR VALUATION.—The valuation referred to in subparagraph (A) may be made as of a date within the plan year prior to the year to which the valuation refers if, as of such date, the value of the assets of the plan are not less than 125 percent of the plan's current liability (as defined in paragraph (7)(B)).

"(iii) ADJUSTMENTS. Information under clause (ii) shall, in accordance with regulations, be actuarially adjusted to reflect significant differences in participants.".

(b) AMENDMENT OF ERISA.—Paragraph (9) of section 302(c) of the Employee Retirement Income Security Act of 1974 (29 U.S.C. 1053(c)) is amended—

(1) by inserting "(A)" after "(9)", and

(2) by adding at the end the following:

"(B)(i) Except as provided in clause (ii), the valuation referred to in subparagraph (A) shall be made as of a date within the plan year to which the valuation refers or within one month prior to the beginning of such year.

(ii) The valuation referred to in subparagraph (A) may be made as of a date within the plan year prior to the year to which the valuation refers if, as of such date, the value of the assets of the plan are not less than 125 percent of the plan's current liability (as defined in paragraph (7)(B)).

(iii) Information under clause (ii) shall, in accordance with regulations, be actuarially adjusted to reflect significant differences in participants.".

(c) EFFECTIVE DATE.—The amendments made by this section shall apply to plan years beginning after December 31, 2001.

Sec. 662. Esop Dividends May Be Reinvested without Loss of Dividend Deduction

(a) IN GENERAL.—Section 404(k)(2)(A) (defining applicable dividends) is amended by striking "or" at the end of clause (ii), by redesignating clause (iii) as clause (iv), and by inserting after clause (ii) the following new clause:

"(iii) is, at the election of such participants or their beneficiaries—

"(I) payable as provided in clause (i) or (ii), or

"(II) paid to the plan and reinvested in qualifying employer securities, or".

(b) STANDARDS FOR DISALLOWANCE.—Section 404(k)(5)(A) (relating to disallowance of deduction) is amended by inserting "avoidance or" before "evasion".

(c) EFFECTIVE DATE.—The amendments made by this section shall apply to taxable years beginning after December 31, 2001.

Sec. 663. Repeal of Transition Rule Relating to Certain Highly Compensated Employees

(b) EFFECTIVE DATE.—The repeal made by subsection (a) shall apply to plan years beginning after December 31, 2001.

Sec. 664. Employees of Tax-Exempt Entities

(a) IN GENERAL.—The Secretary of the Treasury shall modify Treasury Regulations section 1.410(b)–6(g) to provide that employees of an organization described in section 403(b)(1)(A)(i) of the Internal Revenue Code of 1986 who are eligible to make contributions under section 403(b) of such Code pursuant to a salary reduction agreement may be treated as excludable with respect to a plan under section 40 1(k) or (m) of such Code that is provided under the same general arrangement as a plan under such section 401(k), if—

(1) no employee of an organization described in section 403(b)(1)(A)(i) of such Code is eligible to participate in such section 401(k) plan or section 401(m) plan; and

(2) 95 percent of the employees who are not employees of an organization described in section 403(b)(1)(A)(i) of such Code are eligible to participate in such plan under such section 401(k) or (m).

(b) EFFECTIVE DATE.—The modification required by subsection (a) shall apply as of the same date set forth in section 1426(b) of the Small Business Job Protection Act of 1996.

Sec. 665. Clarification of Treatment of Employer-Provided Retirement Advice

(a) IN GENERAL.—Subsection (a) of section 132 (relating to exclusion from gross income) is amended by striking “or” at the end of paragraph (5), by striking the period at the end of paragraph (6) and inserting “, or”, and by adding at the end the following new paragraph:

“(7) qualified retirement planning services.”.

(b) QUALIFIED RETIREMENT PLANNING SERVICES DEFINED.—Section 132 is amended by redesignating subsection (m) as subsection (n) and by inserting after subsection (l) the following:

“(m) QUALIFIED RETIREMENT PLANNING SERVICES.—

"(1) IN GENERAL.—For purposes of this section, the term ‘qualified retirement planning services’ means any retirement planning advice or information provided to an employee and his spouse by an employer maintaining a qualified employer plan.

"(2) NONDISCRIMINATION RULE.—Subsection (a)(7) shall apply in the case of highly compensated employees only if such services are available on substantially the same terms to each member of the group of employees normally provided education and information regarding the employer’s qualified employer plan.

"(3) QUALIFIED EMPLOYER PLAN.—For purposes of this subsection, the term ‘qualified employer plan’ means a plan, contract, pension, or account described in section 219(g)(5).”.

(c) EFFECTIVE DATE.—The amendments made by this section shall apply to years beginning after December 31, 2001.

Sec. 666. Repeal of the Multiple Use Test

(a) IN GENERAL.—Paragraph (9) of section 401(m) is amended to read as follows:

"(9) REGULATIONS.—The Secretary shall prescribe such regulations as may be necessary to carry out the purposes of this subsection and subsection (k), including regulations permitting appropriate aggregation of plans and contributions.".

(b) EFFECTIVE DATE.—The amendment made by this section shall apply to years beginning after December 31, 2001.

Subtitle G—Miscellaneous Provisions

Sec. 671. Tax Treatment and Information Requirements of Alaska Native Settlement Trusts

(a) TREATMENT OF ALASKA NATIVE SETTLEMENT TRUSTS.—Subpart A of part I of subchapter J of chapter 1 (relating to general rules for taxation of trusts and estates) is amended by adding at the end the following new section:

"Sec. 646. Tax Treatment of Electing Alaska Native Settlement Trusts

"(a) IN GENERAL.—If an election under this section is in effect with respect to any Settlement Trust, the provisions of this section shall apply in determining the income tax treatment of the Settlement Trust and its beneficiaries with respect to the Settlement Trust.

"(b) TAXATION OF INCOME OF TRUST.—Except as provided in subsection (f)(1)(B)(ii)—

"(a) IN GENERAL.—There is hereby imposed on the taxable income of an electing Settlement Trust, other than its net capital gain, a tax at the lowest rate specified in section 1(c).

"(b) CAPITAL GAIN.—In the case of an electing Settlement Trust with a net capital gain for the taxable year, a tax is hereby imposed on such gain at the rate of tax which would apply to such gain if the taxpayer were subject to a tax on its other taxable income at only the lowest rate specified in section 1(c).

Any such tax shall be in lieu of the income tax otherwise imposed by this chapter on such income or gain.

"(c) ONE-TIME ELECTION.—

"(1) IN GENERAL.—A Settlement Trust may elect to have the provisions of this section apply to the trust and its beneficiaries.

"(2) TIME AND METHOD OF ELECTION.—An election under paragraph (1) shall be made by the trustee of such trust—

"(A) on or before the due date (including extensions) for filing the Settlement Trust's return of tax for the first taxable year of such trust ending after the date of the enactment of this section, and

"(B) by attaching to such return of tax a statement specifically providing for such election.

"(3) PERIOD ELECTION IN EFFECT.—Except as provided in subsection (f), an election under this subsection—

"(A) shall apply to the first taxable year described in paragraph (2)(A) and all subsequent taxable years, and

"(B) may not be revoked once it is made.

"(d) CONTRIBUTIONS TO TRUST.—

"(1) BENEFICIARIES OF ELECTING TRUST NOT TAXED ON CONTRIBUTIONS.—In the case of an electing Settlement Trust, no amount shall be includible in the gross income of a beneficiary of such trust by reason of a contribution to such trust "(2) EARNINGS AND PROFITS.—The earnings and profits of the sponsoring Native Corporation shall not be reduced on account of any contribution to such Settlement Trust.

"(e) TAX TREATMENT OF DISTRIBUTIONS TO BENEFICIARIES.—

Amounts distributed by an electing Settlement Trust during any taxable year shall be considered as having the following characteristics in the hands of the recipient beneficiary:

"(1) First, as amounts excludable from gross income for the taxable year to the extent of the taxable income of such trust for such taxable year (decreased by any income tax paid by the trust with respect to the income) plus any amount excluded from gross income of the trust under section 103.

"(2) Second, as amounts excludable from gross income to the extent of the amount described in paragraph (1) for all taxable years for which an election is in effect under subsection (c) with respect to the trust, and not previously taken into account under paragraph (1).

"(3) Third, as amounts distributed by the sponsoring Native Corporation with respect to its stock (within the meaning of section 30 1(a)) during such taxable year and taxable to the recipient beneficiary as amounts described in section 301(c)(1), to the extent of current or accumulated earnings and profits of the sponsoring Native Corporation as of the close of such taxable year after proper adjustment is made for all distributions made by the sponsoring Native Corporation during such taxable year.

"(4) Fourth, as amounts distributed by the trust in excess of the distributable net income of such trust for such taxable year.

Amounts distributed to which paragraph (3) applies shall not be treated as a corporate distribution subject to section 3 11(b), and for purposes of determining the amount of a distribution for purposes of paragraph (3) and the basis to the recipients, section 643(e) and not section 301 (b) or (d) shall apply.

"(f) SPECIAL RULES WHERE TRANSFER RESTRICTIONS MODIFIED.—

"(1) TRANSFER OF BENEFICIAL INTERESTS.—If, at any time, a beneficial interest in an electing Settlement Trust may be disposed of to a person in a manner which would not be permitted by section 7(h) of the Alaska Native Claims Settlement Act (43 U.S.C. 1606(h)) if such interest were Settlement Common Stock—

"(A) no election may be made under subsection (c) with respect to such trust, and

"(B) if such an election is in effect as of such time—

"(i) such election shall cease to apply as of the first day of the taxable year in which such disposition is first permitted,

"(ii) the provisions of this section shall not apply to such trust for such taxable year and all taxable years thereafter, and

"(iii) the distributable net income of such trust shall be increased by the current or accumulated earnings and profits of the sponsoring Native Corporation as of the close of such taxable year after proper adjustment is made for all distributions made by the sponsoring Native Corporation during such taxable year.

In no event shall the increase under clause (iii) exceed the fair market value of the trust's assets as of the date the beneficial interest of the trust first becomes so disposable. The earnings and profits of the sponsoring Native Corporation shall be adjusted as of the last day of such taxable year by the amount of earnings and profits so included in the distributable net income of the trust.

"(2) STOCK IN CORPORATION.—If—

"(A) stock in the sponsoring Native Corporation may be disposed of to a person in a manner which would not be permitted by section 7(h) of the Alaska Native Claims Settlement Act (43 U.S.C. 1606(h)) if such stock were Settlement Common Stock, and

"(B) at any time after such disposition of stock is first permitted, such corporation transfers assets to a Settlement Trust,

paragraph (1)(B) shall be applied to such trust on and after the date of the transfer in the same manner as if the trust permitted dispositions of beneficial interests in the trust in a manner not permitted by such section 7(h).

"(3) CERTAIN DISTRIBUTIONS.—For purposes of this section, the surrender of an interest in a Native Corporation or an electing Settlement Trust in order to accomplish the whole or partial redemption of the interest of a shareholder or beneficiary in such corporation or trust, or to accomplish the whole or partial liquidation of such corporation or trust, shall be deemed to be a transfer permitted by section 7(h) of the Alaska Native Claims Settlement Act.

"(g) TAXABLE INCOME.—For purposes of this title, the taxable income of an electing Settlement Trust shall be determined under section 641(b) without regard to any deduction under section 651 or 661.

"(h) DEFINITIONS.—For purposes of this section—

"(1) ELECTING SETTLEMENT TRUST.—The term 'electing Settlement Trust' means a Settlement Trust which has made the election, effective for a taxable year, described in subsection (c).

"(2) NATIVE CORPORATION.—The term 'Native Corporation' has the meaning given such term by section 3(m) of the Alaska Native Claims Settlement Act (43 U.S.C. 1602(m)).

"(3) SETTLEMENT COMMON STOCK.—The term 'Settlement Common Stock' has the meaning given such term by section 3(p) of the Alaska Native Claims Settlement Act (43 U.S.C. 1602(p)).

"(4) SETTLEMENT TRUST.—The term 'Settlement Trust' means a trust that constitutes a settlement trust under section 3(t) of the Alaska Native Claims Settlement Act (43 U.S.C. 1602(t)).

"(5) SPONSORING NATIVE CORPORATION.—The term 'sponsoring Native Corporation' means the Native Corporation which transfers assets to an electing Settlement Trust.

"(i) SPECIAL LOSS DISALLOWANCE RULE.—Any loss that would otherwise be recognized by a shareholder upon a disposition of a share of stock of a sponsoring Native Corporation shall be reduced (but not below zero) by the per share loss adjustment factor. The per share loss adjustment factor shall be the aggregate of all contributions to all electing Settlement Trusts sponsored by such Native Corporation made on or after the first day each trust is treated as an electing Settlement Trust expressed on a per share basis and determined as of the day of each such contribution.

"(j) CROSS REFERENCE.—

"For information required with respect to electing Settlement Trusts and sponsoring Native Corporations, see section 6039H.".

(b) REPORTING.—Subpart A of part III of subchapter A of chapter 61 of subtitle F (relating to information concerning persons subject to special provisions) is amended by inserting after section 6039G the following new section:

"Sec. 6039h. Information with Respect to Alaska Native Settlement Trusts and Sponsoring Native Corporations

"(a) REQUIREMENT.—The fiduciary of an electing Settlement Trust (as defined in section 646(h)(1)) shall include with the return of income of the trust a statement containing the information required under subsection (c).

"(b) APPLICATION WITH OTHER REQUIREMENTS.—The filing of any statement under this section shall be in lieu of the reporting requirements under section 6034A to furnish any statement to a beneficiary regarding amounts distributed to such beneficiary (and such other reporting rules as the Secretary deems appropriate).

"(c) REQUIRED INFORMATION.—The information required under this subsection shall include—

"(1) the amount of distributions made during the taxable year to each beneficiary,

"(2) the treatment of such distribution under the applicable provision of section 646, including the amount that is excludable from the recipient beneficiary's gross income under section 646, and

"(3) the amount (if any) of any distribution during such year that is deemed to have been made by the sponsoring Native Corporation (as defined in section 646(h)(5)).

"(d) SPONSORING NATIVE CORPORATION.—

"(1) IN GENERAL.—The electing Settlement Trust shall, on or before the date on which the statement under subsection (a) is required to be filed, furnish such statement to the sponsoring Native Corporation (as so defined).

"(2) DISTRIBUTEES.—The sponsoring Native Corporation shall furnish each recipient of a distribution described in section 646(e)(3) a statement containing the amount deemed to have been distributed to such recipient by such corporation for the taxable year.".

(c) CLERICAL AMENDMENT.—

(1) The table of sections for subpart A of part I of subchapter J of chapter 1 of such Code is amended by adding at the end the following new item:

"Sec. 646. Tax treatment of electing Alaska Native Settlement Trusts"

(2) The table of sections for subpart A of part III of subchapter A of chapter 61 of subtitle F of such Code is amended by inserting after the item relating to section 6039G the following new item:

"Sec. 6039H. Information with respect to Alaska Native Settlement Trusts and sponsoring Native Corporations"

(d) EFFECTIVE DATE.—The amendments made by this section shall apply to taxable years ending after the date of the enactment of this Act and to contributions made to electing Settlement Trusts for such year or any subsequent year.

TITLE VII-ALTERNATIVE MINIMUM TAX

Sec. 701. Increase in Alternative Minimum Tax Exemption

(a) IN GENERAL.—

(1) Subparagraph (A) of section 55(d)(1) (relating to exemption amount for taxpayers other than corporations) is amended by striking "$45,000" and inserting "$45,000 ($49,000 in the case of taxable years beginning in 2001, 2002, 2003, and 2004)".

(2) Subparagraph (B) of section 55(d)(1) (relating to exemption amount for taxpayers other than corporations) is amended by striking "$33,750" and inserting "$33,750 ($35,750 in the case of taxable years beginning in 2001, 2002, 2003, and 2004)".

(b) CONFORMING AMENDMENTS.—

(1) Paragraph (1) of section 55(d) is amended by striking "and" at the end of subparagraph (B), by striking subparagraph (C), and by inserting after subparagraph (B) the following new subparagraphs:

"(C) 50 percent of the dollar amount applicable under paragraph (1)(A) in the case of a married individual who files a separate return, and

"(D) $22,500 in the case of an estate or trust.".

(2) Subparagraph (C) of section 55(d)(3) is amended by striking "paragraph (1)(C)" and inserting "subparagraph (C) or (D) of paragraph (1)".

(3) The last sentence of section 55(d)(3) is amended—

(A) by striking "paragraph (1)(C)(i)" and inserting "paragraph (1)(C)"; and

(B) by striking "$165,000 or (ii) $22,500" and inserting "the minimum amount of such income (as so determined) for which the exemption amount under paragraph (1)(C) is zero, or (ii) such exemption amount (determined without regard to this paragraph)".

©EFFECTIVE DATE.—The amendments made by this section shall apply to taxable years beginning after December 31, 2000

TITLE VIII-OTHER PROVISIONS

Sec. 801. Time for Payment of Corporate Estimated Taxes

Notwithstanding section 6655 of the Internal Revenue Code of 1986—

(1) 100 percent of the amount of any required installment of corporate estimated tax which is otherwise due in September 2001 shall not be due until October 1, 2001; and

(2) 20 percent of the amount of any required installment of corporate estimated tax which is otherwise due in September 2004 shall not be due until October 1, 2004.

Sec. 802. Expansion of Authority to Postpone Certain Tax- Related Deadlines by Reason of Presidentially Declared Disaster

(a) IN GENERAL.—Section 7508A(a) (relating to authority to postpone certain tax-related deadlines by reason of presidentially declared disaster) is amended by striking "90 days" and inserting "120 days".

(b) EFFECTIVE DATE.—The amendment made by this section shall take effect on the date of enactment of this Act.

Sec. 803. No Federal Income Tax on Restitution Received by Victims of the Nazi Regime or Their Heirs or Estates

(a) IN GENERAL.—For purposes of the Internal Revenue Code of 1986, any excludable restitution payments received by an eligible individual (or the individual's heirs or estate) and any excludable interest—

(1) shall not be included in gross income; and

(2) shall not be taken into account for purposes of applying any provision of such Code which takes into account excludable income in computing adjusted gross income, including section 86 of such Code (relating to taxation of Social Security benefits).

For purposes of such Code, the basis of any property received by an eligible individual (or the individual's heirs or estate) as part of an excludable restitution payment shall be the fair market value of such property as of the time of the receipt.

(b) ELIGIBLE INDIVIDUAL.—For purposes of this section, the term "eligible individual" means a person who was persecuted on the basis of race, religion, physical or mental disability, or sexual orientation by Nazi Germany, any other Axis regime, or any other Nazi-controlled or Nazi-allied country.

(c) EXCLUDABLE RESTITUTION PAYMENT.—For purposes of this section, the term "excludable restitution payment" means any payment or distribution to an individual (or the individual's heirs or estate) which—

(1) is payable by reason of the individual's status as an eligible individual, including any amount payable by any foreign country, the United States of America, or any other foreign or domestic entity, or a fund established by any such country or entity, any amount payable as a result of a final resolution of a legal action, and any amount payable under a law providing for payments or restitution of property;

(2) constitutes the direct or indirect return of, or compensation or reparation for, assets stolen or hidden from, or otherwise lost to, the individual before, during, or immediately after World War II by reason of the individual's status as an eligible individual, including any proceeds of insurance under policies issued on eligible individuals by European insurance companies immediately before and during World War II; or

(3) consists of interest which is payable as part of any payment or distribution described in paragraph (1) or (2).

(d) EXCLUDABLE INTEREST.—For purposes of this section, the term "excludable interest" means any interest earned by-

(1) escrow accounts or settlement funds established pursuant to the settlement of the action entitled "In re: Holocaust Victim Assets Litigation," (E.D.N.Y.) C.A. No. 96–4849,

(2) funds to benefit eligible individuals or their heirs created by the International Commission on Holocaust Insurance Claims as a result of the Agreement between the Government of the United States of America and the Government of the Federal Republic of Germany concerning the Foundation "Remembrance, Responsibility, and Future," dated July 17, 2000, or

(3) similar funds subject to the administration of the United States courts created to provide excludable restitution payments to eligible individuals (or eligible individuals' heirs or estates).

(e) EFFECTIVE DATE.—

(1) IN GENERAL.—This section shall apply to any amount received on or after January 1, 2000.

(2) NO INFERENCE.—Nothing in this Act shall be construed to create any inference with respect to the proper tax treatment of any amount received before January 1, 2000.

TITLE IX—COMPLIANCE WITH CONGRESSIONAL BUDGET ACT

Sec. 901. Sunset of Provisions of Act

(a) IN GENERAL.—All provisions of, and amendments made by, this Act shall not apply—

(1) to taxable, plan, or limitation years beginning after December 31, 2010, or

(2) in the case of title V, to estates of decedents dying, gifts made, or generation skipping transfers, after December 31, 2010.

(b) APPLICATION OF CERTAIN LAWS.—The Internal Revenue Code of 1986 and the Employee Retirement Income Security Act of 1974 shall be applied and administered to years, estates, gifts, and transfers described in subsection (a) as if the provisions and amendments described in subsection (a) had never been enacted.

Approved June 7, 2001.

In: Estate and Gift Taxes
Editor: Clay B. Apperton

ISBN 978-1-60692-129-6

Chapter 6

THE ESTATE TAX: MYTHS AND REALITIES*

The estate tax has been an important source of federal revenue for nearly a century. It also encourages billions of dollars in charitable donations each year (http://www.cbpp.org/6-7- 06tax.htm), since donations substantially reduce the tax on large estates. Despite these benefits, a number of misconceptions continue to surround the tax.

Myth 1. Repealing the Estate Tax Wouldn't Significantly Worsen the Deficit Because the Tax Doesn't Raise Much Revenue

- Reality: Repealing the estate tax would add trillions of dollars to future deficits.

  Permanent repeal of the estate tax would cost more than $1 trillion over the first ten years in which its cost would be fully felt, 2012-2021. This cost includes $859 billion in lost revenue and $251 billion in increased interest payments on the national debt. (The official ten-year cost estimate is much lower: $499 billion. But that estimate is misleading because it covers an earlier ten-year period, 2008-2017, that captures the full cost of only six years of extending repeal.) (http://www.cbpp.org/6-5-06tax.htm)

* Excerpted from Center of Budget and Policy Priorities Report, dated October 11, 2007.

Given the current fiscal situation — and, more importantly, the looming budgetary challenges posed by the baby boomers' retirement — it would be extremely unwise for the federal government to forgo such large revenues.

Myth 2. The Estate Tax Forces Estates to Turn Over Half of Their Assets to the Government

- Reality: The few estates that pay any estate tax at all generally pay less than 20 percent of the value of their estate in taxes.

  Today, more than 99 percent of estates pay no estate tax at all. Among the few estates that do owe taxes, the "effective" tax rate — that is, the percentage of the estate that is paid in taxes — averaged about 20 percent in 2005 (the latest year for which IRS data are available), far below the top estate tax rate of 48 percent that these estates faced.

  Why is the effective tax rate so much lower than the top tax rate? Estate taxes are due only on the portion of an estate's value that exceeds the exemption level, not on the entire estate. For example, at today's $2.0 million exemption level, a $2.5 million estate would owe estate taxes on $500,000 at most. In addition, a large portion of the estate's remaining value can be shielded from taxation through available deductions (for charitable bequests and state estate taxes paid, for instance). (http: / /www.cbpp.org/6-1 4-06tax.htm)

  It's also worth noting that the effective estate tax rate will fall below 20 percent over the next few years, as the exemption level rises and the top estate tax rate declines.

Myth 3. Many Small, Family-Owned Farms and Businesses Must Be Liquidated to Pay Estate Taxes

- Reality: The number of small, family-owned farms and businesses that owe any estate tax is small — and shrinking rapidly.

  Despite oft-repeated claims that the estate tax has dire consequences for family farms and small businesses, there is in fact very little evidence that it has an outsize impact on these groups. Indeed, the American Farm Bureau Federation acknowledged to the New York Times that it could not cite a single example of a farm having to be sold to pay estate taxes.

Most recently, an analysis by the Congressional Budget Office confirmed that exceedingly few family farms and small businesses face the estate tax (http://www.cbpp.org/7-11-05tax.htmandhttp://www.cbo.gov/ftpdocs/65xx/doc6512/07-06-EstateTax.pdf). The CBO report found that if the current exemption level of $2.0 million had been in place in 2000, only 123 farm estates and only 135 family-owned businesses nationwide would have owed any estate tax. The number of taxable farm estates would have dropped to 65 nationwide at a $3.5 million exemption level, the level that takes effect in 2009. The number of taxable family-owned business estates would have fallen to just 94 under the $3.5 million exemption.

The CBO report also found that of the few farm and family business estates that would owe any estate tax, the vast majority would have sufficient liquid assets (such as bank accounts, stocks, bonds, and insurance) in the estate to pay the tax without having to touch the farm or business. For instance, of the 65 farm estates that would have owed tax under a $3.5 million exemption, just 13 would have faced liquidity constraints

Myth 4: The Estate Tax is Best Characterized as the "Death Tax."

- Reality: The estate tax would more appropriately be called an "inheritance tax," as it ultimately affects only the heirs of large estates.

  Today, the estates of only 1 out of every 200 people who die owe any estate tax whatsoever, because the first $2.0 million of the value of any estate ($4.0 million for a couple) is totally exempt from the tax. (http://www.cbpp.org/5-31-06tax2.htm)

  Further, the exemption level is scheduled to rise to $3.5 million ($7 million for a couple) in 2009 under current law. At this level, only 3 of every 1,000 people who die will have an estate large enough to owe any tax.

That is why repealing the estate tax, which some people describe as "killing the death tax," has been described more aptly by others as the "Paris Hilton tax cut" after Paris Hilton, the heir to the Hilton hotel fortune.

Myth 5. The Estate Tax Unfairly Punishes Success

- Reality: The estate tax affects only those most able to pay, and the funds it raises are used to support a range of programs that benefit the nation.

  The estate tax is the most progressive component of a tax code that overall is only modestly progressive (particularly when regressive state and local taxes are taken into account). The money it raises funds essential programs, from health care to education to defending the nation. If the estate tax were repealed, then other taxpayers — presumably a more numerous and less well-off group than the taxpayers paying the estate tax — would have to foot the bill for these programs, face cuts in the benefits and services provided, or bear the burden of a higher national debt.

  Like other Americans, the very wealthy benefit from public investments in areas such as defense, education, health care, scientific research, environmental protection, and infrastructure, and they rely even more than others on the government's protection of individual property rights (since they have so much more to protect). Bill Gates, Sr., a prominent advocate of the estate tax, explains, "The reason the estate tax makes so much sense is that there is a direct relationship between the net worth people have when they pass on and where they live. The government that protects their business activities, the traditions that enable them to rely on certain things happening, that's what creates capital and enables net worth to increase." (http://www.cbpp.org/6-1- 06tax-transcript.pdf)

  It seems fair that people who have prospered the most in this society help to preserve it for future generations through tax revenues that derive from their estates. Indeed, as President Theodore Roosevelt stated in 1906 that "the man of great wealth owes a particular obligation to the State because he derives special advantages from the mere existence of government."

Myth 6. Eliminating the Estate Tax Would Encourage People to Save and Thereby Make More Capital Available for Investment

- Reality: Eliminating the estate tax wouldn't dramatically affect private saving, and it would greatly increase government dissaving (i.e., deficits).

A recent Congressional Research Service report found that the estate tax's net impact on private saving is unclear — it causes some people to save more and others to save less — and that its overall impact on national saving is likely negative. "[I] f the only objective [of eliminating the estate tax] were increased savings," the report concluded, "it would probably be more effective to simply keep the estate and gift tax and use the proceeds to reduce the national debt."

The reason is simple: while repealing the estate tax might lead some people to save more, it also would lead the government to borrow more to offset the lost revenue.

Government borrowing "soaks up" capital that would otherwise be available for investment in the economy. In the case of estate-tax repeal, the added government borrowing would more than outweigh any added private saving, leaving the economy no better off, and quite possibly worse off. (http://www.cbpp.org/6-8-06tax.htm)

Myth 7. The Estate Tax Constitutes "Double Taxation" Because It Applies to Assets That Already Have Been Taxed Once as Income

- Reality: Large estates are comprised mostly of "unrealized" capital gains that have never been taxed; the estate tax is the only means of taxing this income.

Income taxes on the appreciation of assets, such as real estate or artwork, are only paid when the asset is sold. Therefore, the increase in the value of an asset is never subject to income tax if the asset is held until a person dies. These "unrealized" capital gains can make up a significant share of an estate's total value (http: / /www.cbpp.org/6-1 7- 05tax.htm), especially among large estates — the ones likely to owe estate tax.

One reason the estate tax was created was to serve as a backstop to the income tax, taxing income that was never taxed under the income tax. That is, the taxation of this income is essentially deferred and ultimately taxed for the first time through the estate tax

Myth 8: If The Estate Tax is Reformed and Retained, the Logical Top Tax Rate Would Be 15 Percent, the Same as the Capital Gains Rate

- Reality: To match the effective tax rate on capital gains, the top estate tax rate would have to be 35-40 percent, not 15 percent.

  Since the estate tax serves in part to tax capital gains that have not been taxed, some people have proposed taxing estates at the capital gains rate of 15 percent. But the capital gains rate is typically applied to all capital gains income, whereas the estate tax is applied only to part of the estate (see Myth 2 above).

  As a result, a 15 percent top estate tax rate would result in an effective tax rate on taxable estates of only 5 or 6 percent — about one-third of the capital gains rate. A top estate tax rate of 35-40 percent would be needed to generate an effective rate of 15 percent.

  Moreover, from the standpoint of the effect on the deficit and the national debt, cutting the top estate tax rate to 15 percent rate would differ little from repealing the tax entirely. Joint Committee on Taxation estimates indicate that with a 15 percent top rate and an exemption level of $3.5 million, the tax would lose 78 percent of the revenue that would be lost under repeal. With a 15 percent rate and a $5 million exemption, the loss would grow to 84 percent. (http://www.cbpp.org/5-31-06tax.htm)

Myth 9. The Cost of Complying with the Estate Tax Is Nearly Equal to the Total Amount of Revenue the Tax Raises

- Reality: The cost of estate tax compliance is modest, and is not much different than the cost of complying with other taxes.

Studies find that all of the various public and private costs associated with estate tax compliance (http://www.cbpp.org/6-14-05tax.htm) — including the IRS's costs of administering the tax and the cost taxpayers bear in terms of estate planning and administering an estate when a person dies — are about 7 percent of estate tax revenues. These costs are consistent with the compliance costs for other taxes. For instance, administrative and compliance costs represent about 14.5 percent of revenue for the individual and corporate income taxes, 3-5 percent for value added taxes, and 2-5 percent for the sales tax.

Furthermore, the estate tax compliance burden will disappear for a growing number of families each year under current law, as the exemption level rises and fewer estates are subject to the estate tax.

Part of the confusion around the cost of estate tax compliance is that some estimates incorrectly include the cost of activities that would be necessary even in the absence of an estate tax — hiring estate executors and trustees, drafting provisions and documents for the disposition of property, and allocating bequests among family, for example. These activities account for about half of all costs sometimes associated with estate planning.

In: Estate and Gift Taxes
Editor: Clay B. Apperton

ISBN 978-1-60692-129-6

Chapter 7

TESTIMONY OF JOSEPH M. DODGE

STEARNS WEAVER MILLER WEISSLER ALHADEFF AND SITTERSON PROFESSOR OF LAW
FLORIDA STATE UNIVERSITY COLLEGE OF LAW

BEFORE

COMMITTEE ON FINANCE
U. S. SENATE
MARCH 12, 2008

Thank you for inviting me to appear before this distinguished body to testify concerning possible alternatives to the current federal transfer taxes. I am testifying on my own behalf and do not speak for any other person, organization, or entity. My extensive writings in this area are noted in an Appendix at the end. A somewhat more formal comparison of (1) the accessions tax, (2) the income-inclusion approach, and (3) the deemed-realization-at-gift-or-bequest approach is found in Appendix A to the Task Force Report on Federal Transfer Taxes (item 2 of the Articles listed in the Appendix), of which I am a co-author. (However, my comments today differ in a few respects from the analysis in the Task Force Report.) More detailed discussions of the topics covered by this testimony are found in items 4, 5, and 16 of the Articles listed in the Appendix. (For some of my views on reforming the current system, see items 9 and 13 of the Articles listed in the Appendix.)

A. Possible Alternatives to the Current Transfer Taxes

There are five possible alternatives to the current estate, gift, and generation-skipping system:

(6) classic inheritance tax
(7) accessions tax
(8) income-inclusion approach
(9) deemed-realization-at-gift-or-bequest approach, and
(10)carryover-basis approach.

What these approaches have in common is the imposition of tax (sooner or later) by reason of a gratuitous transfer. The first two (inheritance tax and accessions tax) are transfer taxes. A transfer tax is a separate tax from the income tax, and a transfer tax can operate as a "second" tax on previously-taxed income of the transferor. The last two (deemed-realization and carryover-basis approaches) are designed to overturn the current rule, found in § 1014, that eliminates unrealized gains of a decedent permanently from the income tax. The motivation of either proposal is to eliminate an existing hole in the income tax. Since transfer taxes can exist simultaneously with an income tax, it is possible to combine either (1) or (2) above (or an estate tax) with either of (4) or (5).

Alternative (3) is more of a "fusion" approach: it imposes a tax on the gratuitous transfer itself (like a transfer tax) but "within" the income tax. Alternative (3) entails taxing a (non-charitable) gratuitous transfer to the transferee by including the transfer in the annual income tax base, without deduction by the transferor. Since the value of the transfer is taxed in full to the transferee, the transferor's basis is irrelevant, and becomes an obsolete datum of tax history. Hence alternative (3) could not be comprehensively combined with alternatives (4) and (5), both of which play off of the transferor's income tax basis.

A general theme of my testimony is that each "system" has an internal logic of its own, and caution should be used in transplanting features of one system into another system.

B. Inheritance Taxes and Carryover Basis Should Be Taken off the Table

Alternatives (1) and (5) should be rejected. An inheritance tax is basically like an estate and gift tax, but with a more complicated rate and exemption structure. An inheritance tax distorts bequest choices by creating tax incentives in favor of certain classes of legatees. An inheritance tax also creates an incentive for the dispersion of wealth among legatees, but such an incentive isn't especially needed in contemporary American legal practice and culture, which has generally abandoned primogeniture. Finally, it is hard to integrate a gift tax with an inheritance tax.

A carryover-basis rule under the income tax suffers from the following defects: (1) it attributes gain that accrued to one party to another party, (2) it creates inequities among legatees receiving equal-value bequests, (3) it requires keeping basis data for excessively long periods of time, (4) it is procedurally awkward in positing a basis-

determination date that is different from the taxable event (realization by the legatee), and (5) it has, in its 1976 and 2010 incarnations, already proven to be so complex as to be unworkable.

C. Mitigating Valuation Problems

Alternatives (2), (3), and (4) share a common advantage over the current transfer tax system, which requires all relevant facts (including values) to be determined as of the date of transfer (usually, the decedent's death). Valuation is a costly and fact-specific exercise that is best avoided where feasible. All of alternatives (2), (3), and (4) would involve valuation at the time of gratuitous transfer as a general rule, but allow for deferral of the taxable event (or even exclusion) in appropriate circumstances. For example, under the deemed-realization approach, the general rule would be that a gratuitous transfer of property would produce realized gain to the decedent (or donor) in an amount equal to the difference between the asset's basis and its fair market value at the time of transfer. However, a transfer to one's spouse would not be a realization event, and the transferor spouse's basis would carry over to the transferee spouse, which is an extension of current § 1041 of the income tax. Similarly, gain with respect to a principal personal residence could be covered by the exclusionary rule of current § 121.

In all three systems, difficult valuation problems (as with closely-held business interests) could be postponed, though "tailored" deferred-realization rules, as are common under the income tax.

D. Transfer Tax Features Do Not Necessarily "Transfer" to the Income Tax

None of alternatives (3), (4), and (5), which are all located within the income tax, should incorporate transfer tax features unless there is a compelling reason to do so. These approaches all have internal-to-income-tax rationales. In contrast, the transfer taxes, with high rates and large exemptions, serve the external-to-tax purpose of curbing undue accumulations of wealth. Hence, there should be no "minimum" stepped-up basis within the income tax designed to serve as an income-tax proxy for a lifetime transfer tax exemption. Similarly, it should not be simply assumed that an unlimited marital exemption is warranted. In terms of system design, each alternative should be approached with a view to internal consistency with the aims, norms, and principles that govern that system.

E. Comparing the Accessions Tax with the Income-Inclusion Approach

I wish now to focus on the income-inclusion approach, with particular attention to comparing it with an accessions tax. These two approaches might appear to be virtually identical, except for the rate and exemption structure, but it turns out that there could be significant differences.

1. The Value of a Transferee-Oriented Approach

Instead of the current transfer taxes, which can be perceived as a penalty on a decedent's success in the market economy, a transferee-oriented tax is can be sold as a tax on "unearned windfalls" of transferees. Furthermore, a tax that bears explicitly on transferees can be perceived as compatible with the goal of equality of opportunity.

Although carry-over basis is a transferee-oriented approach, it operates erratically and capriciously in terms of trying to achieve any non-tax goals, because the built-in gain bears no systematic correlation with the value of what is received. The deemed- realization approach is not transferee-oriented at all. The inheritance tax only considers the mostly-irrelevant factor of closeness of relationship. That leaves the income- inclusion and accessions-tax approaches, which both explicitly impose taxes on transferees.

Under a transferee approach, the amount subject to tax is net of transaction costs, such as debts, funeral costs, administration expenses, and costs of obtaining gratuitous receipts. Since the tax is imposed on the transferee with respect to the net amount received, the transferee tax is not itself subtracted from the tax base. In this respect, all gratuitous receipts are treated equally, whether in the form of gifts or otherwise.

2. Rate and Exemption Structure

The main difference between the accessions tax and the income-inclusion approach is the rate and exemption structure. An accessions tax would look like the present system because there would be a cumulative lifetime tax base consisting only of gratuitous receipts, a substantial lifetime exemption, and a potentially high rate on accessions above the exemption. These features are appropriate to carry out the principal purpose of such a tax, namely, to curb undue accumulations of unearned wealth by a given individual. The accessions tax is conceived of separately from the income tax, which is a tax on the acquisition of wealth by whatever means, with an aim to generate substantial revenue without undue economic distortion. The income tax is an annual tax that, ideally, does not discriminate according to source or use. The annual "exclusion" under an income tax is basically a set of allowances that eliminate subsistence income from the tax base. Under the income-inclusion approach, gratuitous receipts of low- income persons would be shielded from tax by these subsistence allowances.

3. The Exclusion for Support and Its Penumbra

Under both the accessions tax and the income tax, support received in kind is inherently excluded on the ground that it is not a true wealth transfer. Support in-kind basically involves one person spending money in a way that benefits another. Even support in cash can be excluded on the theory that its purpose is consumption spending of the donee, rather than one aimed to effectuate a true wealth transfer.

If support is excluded, both the accessions tax and the income-inclusion approach would be required to draw the line between support (which is not taxed) and gratuitous receipts (which would be taxed). This problem already exists under the existing gift tax, and it is probably fair to say that the annual gift tax exclusion is best rationalized as a mechanism for managing this difficult borderline area. The fact that the exclusion is an annual one (and on a per-donee basis) has the effect of expanding the category of support. This same general approach could be adopted for both the accessions tax and the income tax.

The annual exclusion concept should nevertheless be re-designed to conform to the transferee orientation of the accessions tax and the income-inclusion approach. For starters, there should be a single fixed-amount annual exclusion of a transferee for all includible gratuitous receipts during the year from all living transferors. Perhaps only transfers from persons who plausibly owe a support obligation to the transferee should be eligible. The exclusion should be designed to exclude donor-financed donee consumption (within reason) from being a taxable gratuitous receipt.

4. Gratuitous Accessions Are Income under a Personal Income Tax

The rationale of the income inclusion approach is that gratuitous receipts really are "income" under a personal income tax. The exclusion of current law is an historical anachronism based on trust accounting rules and the concept that income is distinct from "original endowment." But there are different concepts of income that serves different purposes, both tax and non-tax. For example, there's "national income" (GDP). A VAT of a certain type would be a tax on national income. Transfers are ignored under a tax on national income. In contrast, a tax on personal income is a tax on an individual's net accessions to wealth "from whatever source derived." (If that phrase sounds familiar, it is because it is found both in the 16th Amendment to the Constitution and the § 61(a) definition of catch-all income.) If § 102(a) were repealed, gratuitous receipts would then become non-excluded gross income.

A personal income tax is founded on the concept of the ability to pay of an individual taxpayer relative to that of others. Gratuitous receipts constitute an increase in the recipient's ability-to-pay tax base to the same extent as wages, lottery winnings, or any other accession to wealth. There is no reason why a gratuitous transfer should bear a lighter tax than wages paid for a personal service (such as a home repair): in both cases, the transferee has income and the transferor has a non-deductible expense.

Including gratuitous receipts in income, which is an annual tax, implies that there are no lifetime exclusions or special rates. However, as with the existing income tax, there could be special rates (as with net capital gains) or an income-averaging rule (or maximum rate) to mitigate the "bunching effect." Similarly, some kind of lifetime exclusion could be incorporated into the system, although such a feature would be inconsistent with the nature of an income tax. A lifetime exemption would require the keeping of records over time, and this would be the only feature of an income-inclusion approach that would create a new record-keeping obligation. (In contrast, an annual exclusion – conceived as a way of defining "support" – is not inconsistent with an income tax.)

An accessions tax, being keyed to a cumulative lifetime tax base (and lifetime exemption) mandates the long-term record-keeping obligations.

An income-inclusion approach without a large cumulative lifetime exclusion has the potential (even with an annual exclusion) to raise a lot more tax revenue than the existing system, even though the highest income tax rates are lower than the highest estate tax rates. The incremental revenue yield could be used to lower rates generally, or for any other purpose.

5. Deferred-Realization Rules

As mentioned earlier, deferred realization rules are common in the income tax, and can be deployed specially in the income-inclusion scheme for gratuitous-receipts. Likely candidates for deferred realization are non-liquid assets, hard-to-value assets, and tax-favored assets. Assets that are likely to depreciate in value should not be eligible for any deferred-realization rule.

Deferred realization allows avoidance of valuation until the asset is disposed of in a market transaction or ceases to meet any applicable "qualified use" requirement.

An asset that has not yet been included in income would have a zero basis. An asset that has been included in income takes a basis equal to the amount included.

Even where deferred realization is not allowed, modest valuation errors would be tolerable, because the erroneous amount included, memorialized as the asset's new basis, is automatically "corrected" upon subsequent realization. This correction does not occur under an accessions tax, where the value at the time of the accession is fixed.

The income-inclusion system has the big advantage of wiping out the "historical" basis of the asset in the hands of the transferor.

An accessions tax could also have deferral rules, but they would presumably not be modeled on the realization principle of the income tax, but would instead be confined to tax-favored assets and transactions, such as bequests of interests in closely-held business. Since an accessions tax is a transfer tax, valuation thereunder (whenever it occurs) is "final," as under the current estate tax.

The operation of an accessions tax produces no necessary consequences under an income tax, which is a separate tax. For example, it would be hard to justify a step-up in basis of an asset that is "subject to" the accessions tax but avoids tax on account of the lifetime exemption. Indeed, a basis step-up for a taxed accession would undermine the very purpose of the accessions tax: the accessions tax would be partially offset by a reduction in the future income tax of the same person.

6. Hybrid Transfers

A problem under the current system is the necessary reliance on actuarial tables to value future interests. A related problem is created by the need to design timing rules for "hybrid" (retained-interest-or-power) inter vivos transfers. Actuarial tables are not only inaccurate in individual cases, but can be "gamed" by such devices as GRATs and private annuities.

Hindsight is better than estimates and guesses. Under both the accessions tax and income-inclusion system, the taxable event is generally the receiving of an outright transfer or (as will be explained below) of a trust distribution. The gratuitous receipt of a present or future interest in property (or the vesting of any such interest) would generally not be considered to be an accession or income-realization event. There is no norm that commands that tax law must slavishly follow property law all of the time. The income tax has never been burdened by property-law concepts.

7. Life insurance

The receipt of life insurance proceeds would be taxable as a gratuitous receipt regardless of who held the incidents of ownership and regardless of the owner's income tax basis in the policy. If the beneficiary was also the owner, the receipt of the proceeds would result in investment gain or loss, as opposed to being gratuitous-receipt income.

The same analysis would apply under the accessions tax.

8. Spousal Transfers

A major design issue is that of inter-spousal transfers. Inter-spousal gifts would be ignored (exempted) under both approaches, but death-triggered transfers might be viewed differently. Since inter vivos inter-spousal transfers would be ignored, transfers to either spouse from any third party should be attributed 50-50 to each spouse.

Under an accessions tax, each spouse would be considered a separate taxpayer, because the purpose of the accessions tax is to curb undue concentrations of unearned wealth. Thus, a person should not be allowed to accumulate twice as much unearned wealth simply by reason of having been married, or three times as much unearned wealth by reason of having been married twice. Likewise, a widow or widower should not be favored relative, say, to a person who receives accessions from two ancestors. It follows that there should not, in principle, be an unlimited inter-spousal exclusion over and above the lifetime exemption, because it is the lifetime exemption that is supposed to operate as the baseline for ascertaining what is an "undue" accumulation of unearned wealth by a given individual.

Wealth acquired by earnings avoids the accessions tax. Stated differently, asserting control over one's own wealth is not an accession. A common legal and cultural norm is to view marriage as a kind of economic partnership. Accordingly, it is not unreasonable to stipulate that accessions from the deceased spouse, not to exceed half of the value of the deceased spouse's estate (or half of the combined estates), are really "earned" wealth that is already equitably owned by the surviving spouse (and not really an accession at all). Most current estate plans involving the wealthy do not give the surviving spouse fee ownership of the entire marital estate, but rather create interests in individuals other than the surviving spouse. If this pattern continues under an accessions tax, it is unlikely that the limitation on the marital exclusion will be exceeded. Moreover, the surviving spouse still has her own lifetime exclusion. Thus, it is quite unlikely that the surviving spouse will receive accessions from the decedent that exceed both the marital exclusion and the surviving spouse's own exclusion. Accessions by third parties from the deceased spouse will be scattered among such persons' separate accessions tax bases and lifetime exclusions. Even if the surviving spouse actually pays accessions tax, there is no necessary estate planning disaster, because the surviving spouse can control both the timing and the existence of accessions tax at the next generation, because the surviving spouse would be able to control the disposition of virtually everything that appears in her accessions tax base.

Under the accessions tax, there would be no terminable interest rule to impede qualification for the spousal exclusion, since the accession occurs upon the actual receipt of money or property, not upon the acquisition of a future interest.

Under the income tax, a married couple is treated as a single taxable unit for many purposes, one of which is that inter vivos inter-spousal transfers are ignored, and another of which is that there is a common basis in spousal assets, regardless of the form of ownership or the mode of disposition. This income tax taxable unit can be treated as continuing beyond the death of the first spouse to the extent that the surviving spouse ends up with the marital estate. It follows that amounts that were previously subject to income tax prior to, or during, marriage would not be taxed again to the surviving spouse simply by reason of the death of the deceased spouse, and unrealized gains and losses would continue in their unrealized state. Thus, the survivor should, in principle, (1) obtain an exemption for all cash received from the deceased spouse, (2) obtain sole ownership of marital assets in kind without a deemed-realization event, and (3) inherit the couple's common basis (without adjustments). These results are wholly consistent with current § 1041. Again, there would be no qualification rules.

9. Treatment of Trusts and Beneficiaries

The accessions tax and income-inclusion approaches differ slightly in the case of trusts. The accessions tax is potentially simpler: the trust is not a taxpayer under the accessions tax, and distributions (whether out of income or corpus) are accessions of the distributees in full. This approach allows for deferral, but deferral is revenue neutral (assuming a flat rate with no exemptions) if the tax base increases at a rate no less than the discount rate. If anything, the tax-avoidance concern would be with attempts to accelerate accessions (say, by a sale of a remainder interest) at a time when the value of such interest is low relative to its likely future yield.

If deferral is deemed to be a problem, a more complicated approach – that might be suitable for large trusts - would be to impose a withholding tax on the trust when receiving the funding gift or bequest. Thereafter, a distribution of income or corpus would be a taxable accession to the distributee, but the distributee would receive a (refundable) credit, without interest, against accessions tax for her appropriate share of the earlier withholding tax.

Under the income tax, a trust is currently treated as a taxpayer. Therefore, the receipt by the trust of funding gifts and bequests would be treated as current income of the trust. Otherwise, a gratuitous transfer to a trust would be treated more favorably than an equivalent transfer to an individual. Whatever deferred-realization rules that are available to individuals would be available to trusts as well. Thereafter the rules of Subchapter J would operate as they do at present to allocate post-transfer income and gains of the trust to the beneficiaries or the trust. (The trust would not itself be viewed as if it were a donor. That is, distributions would be deductible by the trust to the extent included by distributees. In the absence of a distribution deduction, trust transfers would be treated worse than transfers to individuals.)

10. The Effect of Powers

Under the current system, possession of a general power of appointment results in a person being treated as the owner of property and the income therefrom. If this concept were carried over to the accessions tax and an income-inclusion system, it would result in taxing the same gratuitous receipt to two taxpayers: the holder of the power would be deemed to have received the distribution, and then the actual distributee would be deemed to receive a gift from the holder of the general power. This result seems unnecessarily harsh. At the same time, general powers should not be allowed to be used as artificial devices to attribute gratuitous receipts from a high bracket distributee to a low bracket power holder. Accordingly, general powers of appointment should be ignored under both the accessions tax and the income-inclusion system, and the receipt should be attributed only to the person who actually receives it.

A related issue is that of grantor trusts. Under the accessions tax, the grantor trust rules would attribute income to the grantor, but any distribution to a person other than the grantor would be an includible accession. This result would somewhat inhibit the use of "defective grantor trusts."

Under the income-inclusion approach, the grantor-trust rules, unless modified, would result in double taxation of distributions to third parties: the income would be taxed to the donor, and the distributee would include the distribution as a gift from the donor. One option is to allow this result to occur in all cases in which the trust or its income is deemed to be owned by the grantor under current law, in which case the distributee might (or might not) avoid tax (in whole or in part) under the annual exclusion. Apart from the annual exclusion, it cannot be the case under an income- inclusion system that a distribution is wholly excluded by a distributee simply because the income represented by the distribution is taxed to the grantor. To avoid such a backhanded generic (as opposed to annual) gift exclusion, the remaining option would be to limit the double taxation result only to revocable trusts, provided that the creation of any irrevocable trust would result in an income inclusion by the trust, followed by application of the Subchapter J rules (rather than grantor-trust rules).

F. Conclusion

The foregoing is an overview of the obvious issues. Other issues would need to be worked out.

The general conclusion is that income-inclusion system and the accessions tax are superior to the other alternatives as possible replacements for the current transfer taxes. (If Congress decides that no "replacement" is desirable, it should at least eliminate the hole in the income tax created by § 1014.) Both the accessions tax and the income- inclusion system offer numerous advantages relative to the existing system. The income tax alternative seems better than the accessions tax by being able to raise the most revenue with the least administrative effort and minimal changes in existing law.

In any event, any replacement system should be constructed from the ground up, as opposed to being a grafting of existing transfer tax features onto some new, but barely visible, root stock.

APPENDIX: WRITINGS OF JOSEPH M. DODGE ON THE FEDERAL TRANSFER TAXES AND ALTERNATIVES THERETO

I. Articles (in reverse chronological order)

1. *Debunking the Basis Myth under the Income Tax* (with Jay Soled, Rutgers University), 81 Ind. L. J. 539 (2006) (61 pp.)
2. *Alternatives to the Current Federal Wealth Transfer Tax System* (with Joseph Kartiganer and Sherwin Kamin), *published as* Appendix A to Task Force on Federal Wealth Transfer Taxes, Report on Reform of Federal Wealth Transfer Taxes, 58 The Tax Lawyer 93, 279-3 12 (2004).
3. *Inflated Tax Basis and the Quarter-Trillion Dollar Revenue Question*, 106 Tax Notes 453 (Jan. 24, 2005) (with Jay Soled), reported in (*inter alia*) David Cay Johnson, "Overstating of Assets Is Seen To Cost U.S. Billions

of Dollars," New York Times (Jan. 24, 2005), p. C-2, and Albert B. Crenshaw, "First, Go After The Tax Cheats," The Washington Post (Sunday, Jan. 30, 2005), p. F-1.

4. *Comparing a Reformed Estate Tax with an Accessions Tax and an Income-Inclusion System, and Abandoning the Generation-Skipping Tax*, 56 S.M.U. Law Rev. 551 (2003) (49pp)
5. *Why a Deemed-Realization Rule for Gratuitous Transfers Is Superior to Carryover Basis and Avoids Most of the Problems of the Present Estate and Gift Tax*, 54 Tax L. Rev. 421 (2001) (132pp)
6. *What's Wrong with Carryover Basis, Especially the Carryover Basis Provisions of H.R. 8*, 91 Tax Notes 961 (May 7, 2001)
7. *Simplifying Models for the Income Taxation of Trusts and Estates*, 14 Am. J. Tax Policy 127 (1997) (127pp), and *A Pass-Through Replacement to Subchapter J - Putting It in Perspective*, 14 Am. J. Tax Policy 267 (1997) (14 pp)
8. *Lifting the Shroud over Estate of Hubert: The Logic of the Income and Estate Tax Treatment of Estate Administration Expenses*, 3 Fla. Tax Rev. 647 (1998) (30pp), and *How the Treasury Should Solve the Estate of Hubert Problem*, 78 Tax Notes 1715 (March 30, 1998)
9. *A Feminist Perspective on the QTIP Trust and the Unlimited Marital Deduction*, 76 N. Car. L. Rev. 1729 (1998) (30pp).
10. *Taxation of Gratuitous Transfers under a Consumption Tax*, 51 Tax Law Rev. 529 (1996) (70pp)
11. *Further Thoughts on Realizing Gains and Losses at Death*, 47 Vand. L. Rev. 1827 (1994) (34pp), *excerpts reprinted in* P. Caron et al., Federal Wealth Transfer Tax Anthology 373-80 (1997).
12. *Rethinking Section 2036(c)*, 49 Tax Notes 199 (Oct. 8, 1990) (12pp)
13. *Redoing the Federal Estate and Gift Taxes Along Easy-to-Value Lines*, 43 Tax Law Review 241 (1988) (151pp), *excerpts reprinted in* P. Caron et al., Federal Wealth Transfer Tax Anthology 192-96, 246-47, 284-88, and 373-80 (1997).
14. *The Taxation of Wealth and Wealth Transfers: Where Do We Go After ERTA?*, 34 Rutgers L. Rev. 738 (1982) (38pp)
15. *Retentions, Receipts, Transfers, and Accumulations of Income and Income Rights: Thoughts on the Post-Byrum Role of Federal Estate Tax Sections 2036, 2037, 2039, and 2043*, 58 Texas L. Rev. 1 (1979) (89pp)
16. *Beyond Estate and Gift Tax Reform: Including Gifts and Bequests in Income*, 91 Harv. L. Rev. 1177 (1978) (34pp), excerpts reprinted in P. Oliver and F. Peel, Jr., Tax Policy Readings and Materials 428-435 (1976)

17. *Generation-Skipping Transfers After the Tax Reform Act of 1976*, 125 U. Pa. L. Rev. 1265 (1977) (43pp), *reprinted in* April, 1978, Monthly Digest of Tax Arts., p. 16
18. *Substantial Ownership and Substance vs. Form: Proposals for Unification of Federal Estate and Gift Taxes and for Taxation of Generation-Skipping Transfers*, 1976 U. Ill. L. F. 657 (1976) (60pp)

II. Monographs and Casebooks

1. Transfers with Retained Interests and Powers, 50-5th T.M. (1986) (revised edition 1992) (Tax Management Portfolio), and Transfers Taking Effect at Death, 256 T.M. (1972) (predecessor Tax Management Portfolio)
2. Wills, Trusts, And Estate Planning (1988) (West)
3. Federal Taxation Of Estates, Trusts, And Gifts (1981) (West), with Teacher's Manual (1981), and Supplement (1982)

INDEX

A

B

C

D

G

H

I

J

K

L

M

N

O

P

Q

R

S

T

U

V

W

Y